# ANCIENT
# GREECE
# AND
# ROME

## AN ENCYCLOPEDIA
## FOR STUDENTS

# ANCIENT GREECE AND ROME

## AN ENCYCLOPEDIA FOR STUDENTS

Carroll Moulton, *Editor in Chief*

## VOLUME 3

CHARLES SCRIBNER'S SONS

Simon & Schuster Macmillan
New York

Developed for Charles Scribner's Sons by Visual Education Corporation, Princeton, N.J.

**Library of Congress Cataloging-in-Publication Data**

Ancient Greece and Rome : an encyclopedia for students / Carroll Moulton, editor in chief.
   p.   cm.
   Includes bibliographical references and index.
   Summary: Presents a history of Ancient Greece and Rome as well as information about the literature and daily life of these early civilizations.
   ISBN 0-684-80507-3 (4 vol. set : alk. paper). — ISBN 0-684-80503-0 (vol. 1 : alk. paper). — ISBN 0-684-80504-9 (vol. 2 : alk. paper) — ISBN 0-684-80505-7 (vol. 3 : alk. paper) — ISBN 0-684-80506-5 (vol. 4 : alk. paper)
   1. Civilization, Classical—Encyclopedias—Juvenile literature.   [1. Civilization, Classical—Encyclopedias.]   I. Moulton, Carroll.
DE5.A57 1998
938—dc21                                            98-13728
                                                   CIP
                                                       AC

# A TIME LINE OF ANCIENT GREECE AND ROME

**ca. 2000–ca. 1400 B.C.** *Minoan civilization flourishes in Crete*

**ca. 1400–ca. 1200 B.C.** *Mycenaean civilization flourishes on mainland Greece*

**ca. 1200 B.C.** *Dorians migrate to southern Greece; Greek Dark Age begins (to ca. 750 B.C.)*

**1183 B.C.** *Fall of Troy*

**776 B.C.** *First Olympic Games*

**753 B.C.** *Legendary founding of Rome by Romulus and Remus; monarchy begins in Rome (to 510 B.C.)*

**ca. 750 B.C.** *Archaic period begins in Greece (to 500 B.C.); Greeks found colonies in other regions of the Mediterranean region*

Homer *(700s B.C.)*

Hesiod *(ca. 700 B.C.)*

**736 B.C.** *Messenian revolt against Sparta (to 716 B.C.)*

Solon *(ca. 630–ca. 560 B.C.)*

Thales of Miletus *(ca. 625–547 B.C.)*

**ca. 620 B.C.** *Draco formulates his law code in Athens*

Sappho *(born ca. 612 B.C.)*

**ca. 592 B.C.** *Solon alters Athenian law code and reforms political system*

Pythagoras *(born ca. 580 B.C.)*

**ca. 560 B.C.** *Pisistratid dynasty of tyrants begins in Athens (to 510 B.C.)*

Croesus *(reigned ca. 560–546 B.C.)*

Aeschylus *(525–456 B.C.)*

**550 B.C.** *Persian Empire is founded*

Themistocles *(ca. 524–459 B.C.)*

Pindar *(ca. 518–ca. 438 B.C.)*

**510 B.C.** *Tarquin the Proud, the last king of Rome, is exiled*

**509 B.C.** *Roman Republic is founded (to 31 B.C.)*

**508/507 B.C.** *Cleisthenes reforms government of Athens*

**ca. 500 B.C.** *Classical period in Greece begins (to 323 B.C.)* Heraclitus *(ca. 500s B.C.)*

**499 B.C.** *Ionian Revolt by Greek cities in Asia Minor against the Persian Empire (to 493 B.C.); Persian Wars begin (to 479 B.C.)*

Sophocles *(ca. 496–406 B.C.)*

Pericles *(ca. 495–429 B.C.)*

| | |
|---|---|
| **490 B.C.** | *Battle of Marathon* |
| | Phidias *(ca. 490–ca. 430 B.C.)* |
| **480 B.C.** | *Battle of Thermopylae and Battle of Salamis; Persian king Xerxes withdraws from Greece* |
| | Xerxes *(reigned 486–465 B.C.)* |
| | Herodotus *(ca. 484–ca. 420 B.C.)* |
| | Leonidas *(died 480 B.C.)* |
| | Euripides *(ca. 480–406 B.C.)* |
| **479 B.C.** | *Greeks defeat Persians at Battle of Plataea* |
| **478 B.C.** | *Delian League, alliance of Greek cities led by Athens, is founded* |
| | Pausanias *(died 470 B.C.)* |
| | Socrates *(469–399 B.C.)* |
| **460 B.C.** | *Pericles dominates Athenian politics (to 429 B.C.)* |
| | Democritus *(460–370 B.C.)* |
| | Hippocrates *(ca. 460–ca. 380 B.C.)* |
| | Thucydides *(ca. 459–399 B.C.)* |
| **450 B.C.** | *The Twelve Tables, first written Roman law code, is established* |
| | Alcibiades *(ca. 450–404 B.C.)* |
| **449 B.C.** | *Peace is established between Persian Empire and Delian League* |
| **447 B.C.** | *Construction of Parthenon begins on Athenian Acropolis (finished 438 B.C.)* |
| | Aristophanes *(ca. 445–385 B.C.)* |
| **431 B.C.** | *Peloponnesian War begins (to 404 B.C.)* |
| | Isocrates *(ca. 435–338 B.C.)* |
| | Xenophon *(ca. 428–ca. 355 B.C.)* |
| | Plato *(428–348 B.C.)* |
| **421 B.C.** | *Peace of Nicias temporarily halts Peloponnesian War* |
| **415 B.C.** | *Athens sends expedition against Sicily (to 413 B.C.)* |
| **405 B.C.** | *Sparta defeats Athens at Aegospotami in last sea battle of the Peloponnesian War* |
| **404 B.C.** | *The "Thirty Tyrants" rule Athens (to 403 B.C.)* |
| **399 B.C.** | *Socrates is sentenced to death for "corrupting the young"* |
| | Aristotle *(384–322 B.C.)* |
| | Demosthenes *(ca. 384–322 B.C.)* |
| | Philip II *(382–336 B.C.)* |
| **387 B.C.** | *Gauls invade Rome* |
| | Praxiteles *(300s B.C.)* |
| | Theophrastus *(ca. 371–287 B.C.)* |
| **358 B.C.** | *Philip II becomes king of Macedonia* |
| | Alexander the Great *(356–323 B.C.)* |
| | Menander *(ca. 342–ca. 291 B.C.)* |
| **338 B.C.** | *Philip defeats Athenians and Thebans at Battle of Chaeronea* |
| | Epicurus *(341–270 B.C.)* |
| **336 B.C.** | *Philip is assassinated; Alexander the Great becomes king of Macedonia* |

**334 B.C.** *Alexander invades Asia*

**331 B.C.** *Alexander founds the city of Alexandria in Egypt and defeats King Darius of Persia at Battle of Gaugamela*

**330 B.C.** *Darius assassinated; Alexander expands Macedonian empire*

**323 B.C.** *Alexander dies; Hellenistic period begins (to 31 B.C.)*

**312 B.C.** *Construction of Appian Way begins (finishes 244 B.C.)*

**305 B.C.** *Ptolemaic dynasty of rulers of Egypt begins (to 30 B.C.)*

**Callimachus** *(ca. 305–ca. 240 B.C.)*
**Euclid** *(active ca. 300 B.C.)*
**Theocritus** *(ca. 300–ca. 260 B.C.)*

**ca. 295 B.C.** *Library of Alexandria is founded*

**Archimedes** *(ca. 287–212 B.C.)*
**Eratosthenes** *(ca. 285–ca. 195 B.C.)*

**280 B.C.** *Pyrrhic War between Rome and Pyrrhus, king of Epirus, begins (to 275 B.C.)*

**264 B.C.** *First Punic War between Rome and Carthage begins (to 241 B.C.)*

**Plautus** *(254–184 B.C.)*
**Hannibal** *(ca. 246–182 B.C.)*
**Scipio Africanus** *(236–183 B.C.)*

**227 B.C.** *Sicily becomes the first Roman province*

**Cato the Elder** *(234–149 B.C.)*

**218 B.C.** *Hannibal marches the Carthaginian army across the Alps to Italy; Second Punic War begins (to 201 B.C.)*

**Polybius** *(ca. 205–125 B.C.)*
**Terence** *(ca. 185–159 B.C.)*

**149 B.C.** *Third Punic War begins (to 146 B.C.)*

**Tiberius Gracchus** *(163–133 B.C.)*
**Marius** *(ca. 157–86 B.C.)*

**146 B.C.** *Rome destroys Carthage and Corinth*

**Gaius Gracchus** *(154–121 B.C.)*
**Sulla** *(ca. 138–78 B.C.)*

**133 B.C.** *Last king of Pergamum wills his kingdom to Rome; Tiberius Gracchus attempts reform of Roman government and is assassinated*

**Crassus** *(112–53 B.C.)*
**Pompey** *(106–48 B.C.)*
**Cicero** *(106–43 B.C.)*
**Julius Caesar** *(100–44 B.C.)*

**123 B.C.** *Gaius Gracchus extends the reforms of his brother*

**Cato the Younger** *(95–46 B.C.)*
**Lucretius** *(ca. 94–ca. 50 B.C.)*
**Sallust** *(86–35 B.C.)*

**121 B.C.** *Gaius Gracchus is assassinated*

**Brutus** *(85–42 B.C.)*
**Catullus** *(84–54 B.C.)*

**82 B.C.** *Sulla is named dictator (to 79 B.C.)*

**Mark Antony** *(ca. 82–30 B.C.)*

| | | |
|---|---|---|
| **73** B.C. | *Spartacus leads slave revolt (to 71 B.C.)* | **Vitruvius Pollio** (*first century B.C.*) |
| | | **Herod the Great** (*ca. 73–4 B.C.*) |
| **63** B.C. | *Catiline leads conspiracy against Rome, is exposed by Cicero* | **Vergil** (*70–19 B.C.*) |
| | | **Cleopatra** (*69–30 B.C.*) |
| | | **Horace** (*65–8 B.C.*) |
| **60** B.C. | *First Triumvirate is formed by Pompey, Julius Caesar, and Crassus* | **Strabo** (*ca. 64 B.C.–after A.D. 21*) |
| | | **Augustus, Caesar Octavianus** (*63 B.C.–A.D. 14*) |
| **58** B.C. | *Caesar's conquests of Gauls (to 50 B.C.)* | **Livy** (*ca. 59 B.C.–ca. A.D. 17*) |
| **53** B.C. | *Crassus is defeated and killed by Parthians* | **Tibullus** (*ca. 54 B.C.–A.D. 18*) |
| | | **Propertius** (*ca. 50 B.C.–ca. A.D. 16*) |
| **49** B.C. | *Caesar enters Italy with his army, beginning a civil war with Pompey and his followers (to 45 B.C.)* | |
| **44** B.C. | *Caesar becomes dictator for life; senators led by Brutus and Cassius assassinate Caesar* | |
| **43** B.C. | *Second Triumvirate is formed by Mark Antony, Octavian (later Augustus), and Marcus Lepidus* | **Ovid** (*43 B.C.–A.D. 18*) |
| **42** B.C. | *Antony and Octavian defeat Brutus and Cassius* | **Tiberius** (*42 B.C.–A.D. 37*) |
| **31** B.C. | *Octavian defeats Antony and Cleopatra; Roman Republic ends and Roman Empire begins* | **Claudius** (*10 B.C.–A.D. 54*) |
| | | **Seneca the Younger** (*ca. 4 B.C.–A.D. 65*) |
| | | **Vespasian** (*A.D. 9–79*) |
| **27** B.C. | *Octavian receives title of Augustus; Augustus becomes first Roman emperor (to A.D. 14)* | **Caligula** (*A.D. 12–41*) |
| | | **Pliny the Elder** (*ca. A.D. 23–79*) |
| | | **Persius** (*A.D. 34–62*) |
| | | **Nero** (*A.D. 37–68*) |
| **A.D. 6** | *Judaea becomes Roman province* | **Josephus** (*ca. A.D. 37–100*) |
| | | **Lucan** (*A.D. 39–65*) |
| **A.D. 14** | *Tiberius becomes emperor (to A.D. 37)* | **Titus** (*A.D. 39–81*) |
| | | **Quintilian** (*ca. A.D. 40–ca. 96*) |
| **A.D. 37** | *Caligula becomes emperor (to A.D. 41)* | **Martial** (*ca. A.D. 40–ca. 104*) |
| | | **Plutarch** (*ca. A.D. 40–ca. 120*) |
| **A.D. 41** | *Caligula is assassinated; Claudius becomes emperor (to A.D. 54)* | **Statius** (*ca. A.D. 45–ca. 96*) |
| | | **Epictetus** (*ca. A.D. 50–ca. 120*) |
| | | **Domitian** (*A.D. 51–96*) |
| **A.D. 43** | *Claudius invades Britain and makes it a Roman province (to A.D. 47)* | **Tacitus** (*ca. A.D. 55–ca. 120*) |
| | | **Trajan** (*A.D. 57–117*) |
| | | **Juvenal** (*ca. A.D. 60–130*) |
| **A.D. 54** | *Nero becomes emperor (to A.D. 68)* | **Pliny the Younger** (*ca. A.D. 61–ca. 112*) |

| | |
|---|---|
| **A.D. 66** *Jewish Revolt begins (to A.D. 70)* | Petronius Arbiter *(dies A.D. 66)* |
| **A.D. 68** *Nero commits suicide* | |
| **A.D. 69** *Vespasian becomes emperor (to A.D. 79)* | **Suetonius** *(ca. A.D. 69–after 122)* |
| | **Longinus** *(first century A.D.)* |
| **A.D. 79** *Titus becomes emperor (to A.D. 81)* | **Hadrian** *(A.D. 76–138)* |
| **A.D. 79** *Mt. Vesuvius erupts and destroys the cities of Pompeii and Herculaneum* | |
| **A.D. 80** *Colosseum opens for public entertainments* | |
| **A.D. 81** *Domitian becomes emperor (to A.D. 96)* | |
| **A.D. 98** *Trajan becomes emperor (to A.D. 117)* | |
| **A.D. 101** *Trajan wages war against Dacia (to A.D. 106)* | Ptolemy *(ca. A.D. 100–ca. 170)* |
| **A.D. 117** *Hadrian becomes emperor following the death of Trajan (to A.D. 138)* | **Lucian** *(born ca. A.D. 120)* |
| | **Apuleius** *(born ca. A.D. 120)* |
| | **Marcus Aurelius** *(A.D. 121–180)* |
| **A.D. 122** *Construction of Hadrian's Wall begins* | **Galen** *(A.D. 129–ca. 200)* |
| | **Septimius Severus** *(ca. A.D. 145–211)* |
| **A.D. 161** *Marcus Aurelius becomes emperor (to A.D. 180)* | **Tertullian** *(ca. A.D. 160–ca. 240)* |
| **A.D. 193** *Septimius Severus becomes emperor (to A.D. 211)* | |
| **A.D. 200s** *Germans raid Roman Empire* | Plotinus *(A.D. 205–269/270)* |
| **A.D. 212** *Emperor Caracalla grants citizenship to all free persons of the Roman Empire* | Diocletian *(ca. A.D. 240–313)* |
| | Constantine I *(A.D. 272–337)* |
| **A.D. 284** *Diocletian becomes emperor (to A.D. 305)* | |
| **A.D. 303** *Persecution of Christians begins (to A.D. 311)* | |
| **A.D. 312** *Constantine I becomes emperor (to A.D. 337)* | |
| **A.D. 313** *Constantine issues edict granting tolerance to Christianity* | |
| **A.D. 330** *Constantinople is founded* | **Ammianus Marcellinus** *(ca. A.D. 330–ca. 395)* |

**A.D. 361**  *Julian the Apostate becomes emperor (to A.D. 363) and attempts to reinstate pagan religion*

Julian the Apostate *(ca. A.D. 331–363)*
Theodosius *(ca. A.D. 346–395)*
St. Augustine *(A.D. 354–430)*

**A.D. 376**  *Visigoths settle within Roman Empire*

**A.D. 379**  *Theodosius becomes emperor (to A.D. 395)*

**A.D. 410**  *Visigoths sack Rome*

**ca. A.D. 450**  *Huns reach the height of their power in Europe*

**A.D. 476**  *Romulus Augustulus, last emperor of Western Roman Empire, is overthrown*

Boethius *(ca. A.D. 480–524)*
Justinian I *(ca. A.D. 482–565)*

**A.D. 493**  *Theodoric forms kingdom of Ostrogoths in Italy*

**A.D. 527**  *Justinian becomes Eastern Roman emperor (to A.D. 565)*

**A.D. 529**  *Justinian closes pagan philosophical schools*

## LEGION

See *Armies, Roman.*

## LEONIDAS

DIED 480 B.C.
KING OF SPARTA

* **city-state** independent state consisting of a city and its surrounding territory

See map in Sparta (vol. 4).

**L**eonidas was the king of the Greek city-state* of SPARTA from about 490 to 480 B.C. He succeeded his half-brother, Cleomenes I, who had no son to succeed him, and he married Cleomenes' daughter, Gorgo. Leonidas is best remembered for his heroic leadership of Greek forces at THERMOPYLAE against the invading Persian army led by XERXES.

In 480 B.C., while the rest of Sparta was celebrating an annual festival, Leonidas marched to the mountain pass of Thermopylae with a select Spartan force of only 300 troops, his personal bodyguard. His goal was to secure the pass as part of a combined naval and land operation. Other troops joined Leonidas on the way, and the pass was successfully secured. However, Leonidas and his troops could hold off the Persian assault for only two days. At that point, Leonidas dismissed the main body of soldiers, who managed to escape, while he and his elite troops fiercely counterattacked the Persians. According to legend, there were so many Persian fighters that their arrows hid the sun. Despite the valor of the Spartans, Leonidas and all of his troops were killed.

The death of Leonidas was said to fulfill a Delphic ORACLE, which had predicted that unless a Spartan king was killed, Sparta would be captured and looted. Leonidas's bravery at Thermopylae demonstrated that Sparta was committed to the defense of Greece, and it was commemorated in a famous poem by the Greek poet Simonides: "Leonidas the Spartan, in whose story/A wreath of famous virtue ever lives." Many years after Leonidas's death, his remains were brought back to Sparta for ceremonial reburial, and a shrine was established in his honor.

## LETTER WRITING

* **papyrus** writing material made by pressing together thin strips of the inner stem of the papyrus plant

**L**etter writing in ancient Greece and Rome was more than just a way to keep in touch with friends and relatives or to carry on business. Letter writing was also used to tell stories in prose or poetry, to express philosophical or political views, or to convey official or scholarly information. Letters were written most often with a reed pen and ink on papyrus*, which was then rolled up and tied with thread. Other materials were sometimes used instead of papyrus, including metal, wood, wax, pottery, or animal skin.

**LETTER WRITING IN GREECE.** The earliest known letter from ancient Greece dates to the 500s B.C., although it was not until about 300 B.C. that letter writing became widespread. Starting from about the middle of the 200s B.C., several different types of letters have survived. Many of these were letters written by unknown private individuals and government officials, ranging from business reports to students' letters home. These letters reveal a great deal about the language as well as the social and economic conditions of the times.

Other letters that have survived include official letters between government leaders, which were preserved mainly in inscriptions on monuments, and private letters written by famous people, including the philosopher ARISTOTLE. Many of Aristotle's letters were collected and published, usually by someone other than the author himself. There were also public letters that were written to apologize, persuade, advise, or instruct, including letters written by the Greek philosophers PLATO and EPICURUS. Finally, there were fictitious letters, in which a story was told through a series of letters.

LETTER WRITING IN ROME.   Letters of all types played an even more important role in ancient Rome because of the vastness of the empire. Although there are fewer surviving examples of Roman letters, the importance of letter writing in ancient Rome is evident from the establishment of a system of postal carriers for official correspondence by the first Roman emperor, AUGUSTUS. In addition, private individuals sometimes used slaves to carry letters, and companies of farmers had their own postal service.

The best-known Roman letters are the nearly 800 letters that were written in the last century B.C. by the Roman statesman CICERO. They consist of many different types of letters, and they provide important insights into Cicero the man. They also paint a clear picture of the turbulent political conditions of his time. Similarly, letters of the Roman author PLINY THE YOUNGER, which were collected in ten books, reveal a great deal about Roman society and politics under the emperor TRAJAN, around A.D. 100.

As in Greece, letters were written by Roman philosophers to convey their views. Letters on morality written by SENECA THE YOUNGER are the best-known examples. Unique to Roman letter writing was the use of poetry. Roman poets HORACE and OVID, among others, wrote many letters in verse.

Letter writing of all types was especially common among Christians in Rome, perhaps because the New Testament and other early Christian texts used this form of expression. The collected letters of St. AUGUSTINE and of St. Jerome are notable examples of letter writing during the last years of the empire. (*See also* **Alphabets and Writing; Books and Manuscripts; Literacy; Postal Service.**)

## LIBRARIES

* **papyrus** writing material made by pressing together thin strips of the inner stem of the papyrus plant

With widespread literacy, books were important in ancient Greece and Rome. However, books had to be painstakingly written by hand, usually on fragile, hard-to-care-for papyrus*, which was the preferred writing material in the Mediterranean area from about 500 B.C. to A.D. 300. Libraries arose as places to store and protect fragile manuscripts, as well as places where works of literature could be collected and used for scholarly purposes. Libraries were often built in association with schools, cities, or rulers, and they came to rank among the grandest of civic monuments.

GREEK LIBRARIES.   By 400 B.C. books were in wide circulation in Greece. Athens had booksellers, and books were exported as far away as the Black Sea. Some individuals had large private collections of books, typically the works of the best-known poets and philosophers. The philosopher ARISTOTLE had a very famous collection, which he made accessible to students at the Lyceum, his school in Athens. This library—and those that were established later in association with other Greek schools of philosophy—served the same purpose as university libraries of today.

The first truly public libraries in the Greek world were established by the Hellenistic* kings who followed ALEXANDER THE GREAT. The most famous library of ancient times was the Library in ALEXANDRIA in EGYPT, which was said to be modeled after Aristotle's library. The Library of Alexandria was established by the kings of the Ptolemaic dynasty*, and it contained the greatest collection of books in the ancient world. The Ptolemies obtained copies of all books carried on ships that docked at Alexandria, and they borrowed books from libraries in Athens and other cities and had them copied. According to legend, Ptolemy II confined 72 scholars on an island until they produced the first known Greek translation of the Hebrew Old Testament. This translation became known as the Septuagint.

The Library at Alexandria eventually came to hold a copy of every existing scroll known to Greek scholars. It housed as many as half a million papyrus rolls, the equivalent of about 100,000 modern books. Its librarians were leading scholars, and its director, a writer named CALLIMACHUS, developed a 120-volume catalog, which made the contents of the library more accessible to scholars. The Library became famous for the scholarly studies it supported as well as for its huge collection of books.

* **Hellenistic** referring to the Greek-influenced culture of the Mediterranean world during the three centuries after Alexander the Great, who died in 323 B.C.

* **dynasty** succession of rulers from the same family or group

The earliest Roman libraries were private collections owned by wealthy citizens. In 39 B.C. Gaius Asinious Pollio founded the first public library in Rome. Eventually, many more libraries were erected throughout the empire, including the famous library at Ephesus, which housed 12,000 papyrus rolls.

However, no trace remains of the Alexandrian Library, which was destroyed by fire.

Large libraries were built in other major cities as well. For example, a well-known library was founded in the 100s B.C. at Pergamum in what is now Turkey. It was said to house at least 200,000 papyrus rolls. Smaller cities also had their own libraries, sometimes attached to gymnasia. In addition, special libraries grew up around medical schools, synagogues*, and churches.

**ROMAN LIBRARIES.** The ancient Romans continued the library-founding tradition of the Greeks, and as in Greece, the earliest Roman libraries were private collections. By 100 B.C. large private collections of books existed in Rome, of which the best-known collection belonged to the Roman statesman CICERO. In fact, the possession of a personal library became a status symbol for wealthy Romans. The bulk of these private collections consisted of Greek literature, which the Romans admired, and at least some of the books came directly from libraries in Greece. For example, the Roman general SULLA was said to have obtained Aristotle's books when he conquered ATHENS in 84 B.C.

In the tradition of the earlier Hellenistic monarchs, the Roman soldier-statesman CAESAR planned the first public library in Rome. The library was actually built in 39 B.C. by his close friend and patron of literature, Asinius Pollio. Caesar's example was followed by the first Roman emperor, AUGUSTUS, who built two libraries, and by the emperor TRAJAN, who built another. Trajan's library had separate buildings for Greek and Latin books. By the A.D. 300s, Rome had 28 libraries, with a head librarian to oversee the entire system.

The Romans also encouraged the establishment of libraries throughout their huge empire. For example, the emperor HADRIAN built a library at the foot of the ACROPOLIS in Athens about A.D. 125. When the new Roman capital was built at CONSTANTINOPLE in the A.D. 300s, a library was one of the first institutions to be provided. It eventually contained 120,000 books.

The great libraries of the Roman Empire disappeared like those of ancient Greece. However, one private collection, which belonged to a Roman nobleman, has survived. The nobleman lived in the town of Herculaneum, which was at the foot of Mt. Vesuvius. When Vesuvius erupted in A.D. 79, the town was buried under lava, which partially preserved the library and its contents. In the 1750s, excavators uncovered the library and the remains of about 1,800 papyrus scrolls. (*See also* **Alphabets and Writing; Books and Manuscripts; Literacy; Ptolemaic Dynasty.**)

* **synagogue** building of worship for Jews

## VISITING A LIBRARY IN ANCIENT ROME

If you visited a public library in ancient Rome you would not need a library card because books could not be borrowed. Instead, you would have to read the books in the library's reading room. If you had a lot to read, you would want to arrive at the library early. (The library was likely to open at dawn and close at midday.) You would not be allowed to browse through the library's collection because books were stored in cupboards to protect them. Instead, you would select books from the library's catalog, which listed authors under broad subject headings, and then ask an attendant to fetch them for you.

## LIBYA

Libya was the ancient Greek name for the land of the Libyans, the original people of the north coast of AFRICA. By the 400s B.C., the term *Libya* was used to refer not just to this coastal region but to the entire continent of Africa, an area that was then thought to be about as large as Europe. The Romans used the term *Libya* in much the same way as the Greeks. Today, Libya is the name of a country on the Mediterranean coast of Africa, lying between Egypt to the east and Tunisia to the west.

This part of the north coast of Africa was first explored by the Greeks and by the PHOENICIANS, who went on to explore the west coast of Africa as well. The Phoenicians were also the first to establish trade in the northern coastal region, where they eventually founded the city-state* of CARTHAGE. In the 200s B.C., the region became part of the kingdom of the Greek-influenced PTOLEMAIC DYNASTY*, which was centered in Egypt. Then, during the 100s B.C., the region was taken over by the Romans.

Historians learned about the Libyans from both ancient literary sources and archaeological evidence. In the 800s B.C., the Greek poet HOMER described Libya as a fertile land populated by shepherds. About four centuries later, the Greek historian HERODOTUS gave a detailed account of the many different tribes in the region. Although these and other historical sources tended to stress the wandering, herding lifestyle of the people, archaeological evidence suggests that there were also large agricultural settlements. However, Carthaginian, Greek, and Roman influences may have contributed to the tendency of Libyans to settle and become farmers. Libyans also intermarried with the colonists, resulting in a blend of populations and cultures in the region.

* **city-state** independent state consisting of a city and its surrounding territory

* **dynasty** succession of rulers from the same family or group

# LITERACY

It is difficult to know how widespread the ability to read or write was in the ancient world. Neither the Greeks nor the Romans kept statistics on literacy rates as modern countries do. Scholars have estimated that at the high point of Greek civilization, fewer than one-third of the adult population could read or write. Even so, literacy was more widespread in the Greco-Roman world than it was in many other ancient civilizations, where the ability to read or write was limited to a small number of priests or scribes*.

The level of literacy in any society is related to the need for reading and writing skills. During their early development, both Greece and Rome were largely agricultural societies in which such skills were of little importance. As the two cultures became more urban and complex, literacy spread to meet the changing needs of each.

* **scribe** person who copies manuscripts by hand

**LITERACY IN GREECE.** The Greeks had a long tradition of oral poetry and oratory*. In both speaking and writing, the Greeks placed great value on the skill of rhetoric*. Most public functions, including politics, law, and education, were conducted orally. Although speeches, poetry, and scholarly works were composed in written form, they were generally communicated aloud. As they wrote, Greek writers usually quoted the works of others from memory, sometimes inaccurately.

While Greeks were attuned to hearing and not reading, literacy became more important with the development of democracy. For example, the Athenians inscribed lists of honors, new laws, and dedications to the gods on tablets for public display. Their existence does not mean that

* **oratory** art of public speaking

* **rhetoric** art of using words effectively in speaking or writing

## NOT HOOKED ON BOOKS

The level of literacy in most developed nations today is such that one can expect to find books in most homes. In the Greek world, by contrast, private ownership of manuscripts was rare, even among citizens in a cultural center such as Athens. The fact that the poet Euripides had a private library was unusual enough that it is noted by Greek historians. Written texts were costly to reproduce, so very few people had access to complete books.

* **Hellenistic** referring to the Greek-influenced culture of the Mediterranean world during the three centuries after Alexander the Great, who died in 323 B.C.

* **artisan** skilled craftsperson

everyone could read them—and the majority of people could not—but it suggests that access to the written word was valuable in a society in which the citizens actively participated in government. Athenian citizens did not need literacy in order to participate in their democracy, except to vote for an OSTRACISM—the expulsion of a citizen from the city. Ostracism required citizens to be able to write the name of the person they wished to expel. This may have been possible even for illiterate citizens, since it involved writing only a name, and the Greek alphabet is relatively simple. Literate bystanders might also have written names at the request of citizen voters who could not read or write.

LITERACY IN ROME.    Little writing has survived from the earliest period of Roman culture except for some laws and religious inscriptions. During the early republic, the Romans inscribed documents on tablets for public view, as the Greeks had done. These include the famous Twelve Tables, the first Roman law code, which was displayed in the Roman Forum. However, the Romans during this period wrote no literature that has survived to the present.

Although the early Romans had songs, hymns, prayers, and other spoken verse, the Roman oral tradition was nowhere near as rich as that of the Greek. When Roman literature finally emerged, it developed not from native roots but out of the Greek literary tradition. Greek literature spread to Rome during the Hellenistic* period. The first appearance of literature in the Latin language is a translation from the 200s B.C. of HOMER's Greek epic the *Odyssey*. The first Roman writers translated, adapted, and imitated the works of Homer and other Greek masters. Having absorbed Greek literary forms, Roman literature suddenly flourished, and writing became a fundamental part of Roman culture.

Literacy was probably more common in Rome than it was in Greece, especially among artisans* in the cities. However, it was not so deeply rooted that it could survive the collapse of the Roman Empire. Latin as a written language continued among educated persons, including priests and monks in the Christian church. However, spoken Latin gradually evolved into various modern languages, such as Italian, French, Spanish, and Romanian. Exactly when this occurred for each language is not known for certain. (*See also* **Alphabets and Writing; Books and Manuscripts; Education and Rhetoric, Greek; Education and Rhetoric, Roman; Inscriptions, Monumental; Languages and Dialects; Oratory.**)

# LITERATURE, GREEK

Ancient Greek literature spanned more than a thousand years, from prehistoric times to the A.D. 300s. To most people today, Greek literature means epic* poems and tragic dramas, but the ancient Greeks also expressed themselves in many other literary forms, including lyric* poems, comedies, essays, and novels. Historians turn to Greek literature for insights into the beliefs, customs, and ways of life of

* **epic** long poem about legendary or historical heroes, written in a grand style

* **lyric** poem expressing personal feelings, often similar in form to a song

See color plate 12, vol. 3.

* **didactic** intended to instruct

* **prose** writing without meter or rhyme, as distinguished from poetry

* **dialogue** text presenting an exchange of ideas between people

* **philosopher** scholar or thinker concerned with the study of ideas, including science

## SEEING THE WORLD AS OPPOSITES

Greek thinking, especially in myth, tended to be organized around opposites. The Pythagorean table of opposites associated men with the right side of the body, with light, and with good, and women with the left side, with darkness, and with disaster. Ancient Greek writers frequently represented or associated women with the opposite of the cultural ideal: irrational as opposed to reasoning; deceitful as opposed to honorable. Playwrights sometimes challenged these cultural stereotypes in their works, but at other times maintained them. Of all Greek literature, Aeschylus, in his triology *Oresteia,* perhaps most often depicted women as possessing qualities that were the opposite of the Greek ideal.

the ancient Greeks, but its importance goes far beyond its historical value. Some of the works of the Greek writers rank among the finest contributions to the world's literary heritage. The influence of ancient Greek literature was one of the strongest forces in European culture for centuries, long after the decline of the civilization that had produced it.

The Greeks acquired the alphabet and the art of writing in the 700s B.C. Long before that time, however, they had folklore and EPIC as part of their oral literature, which was communicated by word of mouth rather than in writing. Poems were passed from generation to generation and from place to place by poets who were also storytellers. The performances of each poet were not word-for-word reproductions of an "original" poem. Instead, each performance was a new variation on a familiar tale.

Examples of this ancient oral literature survive in the *Iliad* and the *Odyssey,* two epic poems believed to be the work of the poet HOMER. Although these lengthy poems were probably first written down in the 700s B.C., they are about events that occurred hundreds of years earlier, and some modern scholars believe that the poems existed for a long time—perhaps for several centuries—before they first appeared in written form. The two epics display many features of oral literature. They are rhythmic, and they repeat certain descriptive phrases, called epithets, which made it easier for poets to remember them. All storytellers knew certain standard phrases, such as "the rosy-fingered dawn" and "the wine-dark sea," that could be inserted into the poem wherever it was metrically convenient.

Another of the earliest Greek authors was HESIOD, who was active around 700 B.C. His two surviving works, the *Theogony* and *Works and Days,* are examples of didactic* poetry. Like the epic poems, Hesiod's works were passed on orally before they were written down in about 600 B.C. By that time, writing was becoming widespread in Greece. Literature shifted from works that were recited or sung to works that were written and read. The tragedies of AESCHYLUS, SOPHOCLES, and EURIPIDES—the chief playwrights of the "golden age" of Greek drama in the 400s B.C.—were staged at the great musical festivals of Athens, and copies were made of their texts.

The shift from the spoken to the written word introduced two important new elements to Greek literature. One was the notion of an author, a person who created a specific literary work. Unlike Homer and the anonymous storyteller-poets, authors of written poems had definite identities. They wrote lyric poetry, which included autobiographical details and expressed personal feelings. The great lyric poet SAPPHO made herself the subject of her own poems.

The second change brought about by writing was the development of prose*, which was a new literary style. Earlier literary works, based on the oral tradition that relied on memorization, had all been poems. Prose, a purely written use of language, enabled people to keep records and to organize their ideas in a logical way. Prose made possible new forms of literature, such as the histories of HERODOTUS and THUCYDIDES, the dialogues* of the philosopher* PLATO, and the scientific works of ARISTOTLE.

The writers of Greek literature lived not only in Greece but also in Greek colonies in ASIA MINOR, the islands of the AEGEAN SEA, and southern

One of the greatest of all Greek writers was immortalized in the *Apotheosis of Homer*. This stone monument commemorates Homer's work and depicts him in an almost godly fashion.

Italy. In the 300s B.C., the conquests of ALEXANDER THE GREAT introduced the Hellenistic* age, during which Greeks ruled EGYPT and other lands of the eastern Mediterranean. Greek became the literary language of the entire region. Many authors who did not speak Greek as their native language wrote in Greek to attract a wider audience for their works. ALEXANDRIA, a Greek city at the mouth of the Nile River in Egypt, was the site of the great Library and an important center of Hellenistic literary activity. After Greece came under Roman rule in 146 B.C., a new culture that combined Greek and Roman elements developed. Although Greek literature from this period contained few outstanding poems or plays, many scholarly writings—such as histories and works of philosophy and science—were produced.

Much of ancient Greek literature did not survive. Many lost works are known only from fragments or from passing references to them in surviving texts. Most surviving Greek literature is known from copies made long after the author composed the original—in some cases, hundreds of years later. Over the centuries, as works were copied and recopied by hand, changes and mistakes were introduced into the text. Indeed, some surviving works exist in several different versions. Often, it is impossible to know exactly what an ancient author wrote, what an audience heard, or what a reader read.

The Greek literature that survived had an enormous influence on European culture in general. The myths and stories of Greek literature became part of the shared heritage of educated people in the Western world. Until the late A.D. 1800s, most Western authors were familiar with Greek literature and expected their readers to be knowledgeable about it as well. When an author wrote that a character was "between Scylla and Charybdis," for example, educated readers recognized the reference to an episode in the *Odyssey*. They knew that the character was in a dangerous position between two deadly perils or between two difficult choices. (*See also* **Alphabets and Writing; Drama, Greek; Hellenistic Culture;** *Iliad*; **Letter Writing; Literature, Roman; Novel, Greek and Roman;** *Odyssey;* **Poetry, Greek and Hellenistic.**)

# LITERATURE, ROMAN

* **Roman Republic** Rome during the period 509 B.C. to 31 B.C., when popular assemblies annually elected their governmental officials

* **prose** writing without meter or rhyme, as distinguished from poetry

* **oratory** art of public speaking

* **epic** long poem about legendary or historical heroes, written in a grand style

* **lyric** poem expressing personal feelings, often similar in form to a song

* **satire** literary technique that uses wit and sarcasm to expose or ridicule vice and folly

Roman literature is the work of the authors of the Roman Republic* and the Roman Empire, most of whom wrote in Latin. The literature of the Romans included poetry, plays, and prose* works, such as novels, essays, oratory*, histories, and collections of letters. Although Roman literature began with translations and imitations of Greek works, it developed an identity of its own. VERGIL, HORACE, OVID, and CICERO are among the Roman writers who contributed to the world's literary heritage.

The Romans acquired the alphabet of the Greeks, probably through the ETRUSCANS, in the 600s B.C. and adapted it to their own language. Although for the next four centuries they wrote law codes and inscriptions on tombstones, there is no surviving evidence of literary writing in this period. When the Romans did begin writing literature in the 200s B.C., they mainly translated Greek works. Greek literature became the model of excellence. The Romans took over the major genres of literature from the Greeks, such as the epic*, lyric* poetry, comedy and tragedy, history, and oratory. Comedy particularly appealed to Roman audiences, especially the works of the early Roman comic playwrights PLAUTUS and TERENCE. The Romans also perfected the art of satire*, and verse satire is considered original to Rome.

One important development in Roman literature was a gradual division of the Latin language into two different styles. The first was used in higher forms of poetry and prose, such as epic and lyric poetry, history, and oratory. The second style was more natural and more closely related to the everyday speech of ordinary people. The authors of handbooks used this second style, as did the writers of satire and comedy. Some

Aeneas was one of the great heroes of Roman literature. This fresco from Pompeii illustrates a scene from Vergil's acclaimed epic the *Aeneid,* in which the wounded Aeneas is cared for after battle.

authors, such as Cicero, moved back and forth between styles, depending on the subject and the intended audience for his work.

Literary historians refer to the years from 70 B.C. to A.D. 18 as the Golden Age of Roman literature. During this period, Cicero developed his brilliant oratorical style, combining the clear organization of complex thoughts with elegant prose. All later Roman writers of prose either modeled their writing style on Cicero's or rebelled against it. The many significant poets of the Golden Age include Horace, CATULLUS, and Ovid. Vergil wrote the *Aeneid,* the national epic of Rome, during the Golden Age, and LIVY produced a monumental history of Rome. Outstanding historical writers of the time also included Julius CAESAR and SALLUST.

The Golden Age of literature was followed by the Silver Age, which lasted until A.D. 133. The literature of this period shines less brilliantly than that of the preceding hundred years. Rome was controlled by an emperor, and the imperial* state restricted many freedoms, including the freedom of writers to express themselves without fear of censorship. Ovid was just one of many Roman writers whom the state exiled or prevented from

* imperial  pertaining to an emperor or empire

* **mysticism** belief that divine truths or direct knowledge of God can be experienced through faith, spiritual insight, and intuition

* **pagan** referring to a belief in more than one god; non-Christian

## A LITERARY CONQUEST

Roman literature started with an act of war. In 272 B.C., the Romans captured Tarentum, a southern Italian city that was a colony of the Greek city-state Sparta. The Romans enslaved the captured Greeks, some of whom became tutors to young Roman noblemen. One of these learned slaves—later freed—was Livius Andronicus, who wrote a play in the style of a Greek tragedy for the Roman games in 240 B.C. Livius also translated Homer's *Odyssey* into Latin, and two centuries later, Roman schools still used Livius's version of the Greek epic. Livius Andronicus awakened the Romans' interest in literature and established Greek works as the model for Roman writers who followed.

publishing their views. Yet the Silver Age produced important works of literature—angry satires by JUVENAL; history by TACITUS; the philosophy of SENECA; and PETRONIUS's *Satyricon,* a racy and satirical novel of which only fragments remain. Some years later, APULEIUS wrote a novel called *The Golden Ass,* which survived in its entirety. Like many other Greek and Roman prose fictions of the time, it combined comic incidents with an interest in mysticism* and magic.

One of the best-known works of Roman literature in the years immediately following the Silver Age is the *Meditations* of Marcus AURELIUS, who was emperor from A.D. 161 to A.D. 180. Possibly never intended to be read by anyone other than himself, this work shows the emperor applying the philosophy of STOICISM to the task of governing the empire. Although Marcus Aurelius was the Roman emperor, he wrote in Greek, which shows how closely connected were the cultures of Greece and Rome.

As the people of the Roman Empire converted to Christianity, Christian literature overshadowed the works of pagan* writers. The towering literary figures of this era were TERTULLIAN and St. AUGUSTINE. BOETHIUS, a Christian philosopher of the early A.D. 500s, was a bridge between the Roman era and the Middle Ages. Christianity kept Roman culture at least partly alive in western Europe. The influence of the Roman Catholic Church made Latin the language not only of religion but of instruction, and monks and scholars pursuing religious studies saved many manuscripts of Roman literature from destruction. (*See also* **Alphabets and Writing; Drama, Roman; Epic, Roman; Letter Writing; Literature, Greek; Novel, Greek and Roman; Poetry, Roman.**)

## LIVY

ca. 59 B.C.–ca. A.D. 17
ROMAN HISTORIAN

Titus Livius, known as Livy, wrote a history of Rome that he called *Ab urbe condita libri (Books from the Foundation of the City).* This monumental work consisted of 142 volumes and covered 745 years of Roman history, from the legendary founding of the city in 753 B.C. to 9 B.C. Fewer than one-third of the volumes of Livy's history survive today, but they illustrate the lively, colorful writing style that made him the most widely read Roman historian in the ancient world. The surviving volumes also exhibit Livy's deep concern for the central drama of Roman history as he saw it: the rise and fall of Rome's morals and national character.

LIVY'S LIFE. Livy was born in Patavium, a coastal town in northern Italy that is now called Padua. The people of Patavium were known for clinging to traditional virtues, such as respect for the gods, self-control, and patriotism—virtues that in Livy's day seemed rather old-fashioned to many Romans.

Scholars know little about Livy's life. He probably did not serve in the army, for his writings indicate no knowledge of military life. He was not a senator, and he did not participate in politics. Evidence suggests that he married and had two sons and a daughter. Livy spent much of his adult life

* **Roman Republic** Rome during the period from 509 B.C. to 31 B.C., when popular assemblies annually elected their governmental officials

* **hero** in mythology, a person of great strength or ability, often descended from a god

* **patrician** member of the upper class who traced his ancestry to a senatorial family in the earliest days of the Roman Republic

* **plebeian** member of the general body of Roman citizens, as distinct from the upper class

in Rome, but the dates and place of his residence there are unknown. Later, he moved back to Patavium, where he died. A tombstone found in Patavium marked a grave of someone called Titus Livius. Many historians believe that it was Livy's.

The period in which Livy lived clearly shaped his life's work. He grew up during the years of Rome's violent civil wars, in which factions fought in the streets of Rome, dictators seized power, and the Roman Republic* fell apart—forever, as it turned out. Shocked and saddened by these events, Livy began his history of Rome with a dim view of its present and future prospects. All around him he saw signs that Rome and the Roman people no longer had the pride, dignity, and virtue that had been so much a part of Rome's beginnings. This theme of the decline of Roman virtues was part of his strategy to encourage his readers to return to the greatness of the past. Under Augustus and his worthiest successors, Rome actually did so.

Over the course of his 40-year writing career, Livy produced about four books a year. He was famous throughout the Roman Empire. According to one story, a man from a remote part of SPAIN, impressed by Livy's history, traveled all the way to Rome simply to look at the author. Having done so, he turned around and went back to Spain. Whether or not that story is true, Livy was a well-known literary figure whose work won him the friendship of the emperor AUGUSTUS. However, he did not mingle with other leading Roman literary figures of his time, such as VERGIL, HORACE, and OVID. He dedicated his entire life to researching and writing his huge history, and he once wrote, "I have attained enough personal fame and could lay my pen aside—but my very soul, restless within me, draws sustenance from work."

LIVY'S HISTORY OF ROME.   The 35 surviving volumes of Livy's great work are books 1 through 10, which cover the years 753 B.C. to 293 B.C., and books 21 through 45, which cover the much shorter period of 218 B.C. to 167 B.C. Some information about Livy's lost volumes comes from other writers who quoted or referred to passages from Livy's work, and from summaries of Livy's history that date from the A.D. 300s. These summaries are probably not completely reliable as guides to the missing volumes.

Books 1 through 5 cover the period from the founding of Rome to the burning of the city in 390 B.C. Livy recognized the difficulty of writing about that period. The fire had destroyed many old documents and records that might have cast light on Rome's early history. Furthermore, accounts of the city's founding were a mix of history, legend, and myth in which the deeds of gods, goddesses, and heroes* were mingled with the activities of people who had actually existed. Despite these difficulties, Livy focused these volumes on the birth of the republic and the struggles between two classes of Roman citizens, the patricians* and the plebeians*. He made it clear that this internal conflict, which continued throughout the history of the republic, threatened to tear Rome apart.

Books 6 through 10 cover Rome's rise to greatness through the conquest of the Italian peninsula and victories in foreign wars. Rome's power expanded, Livy wrote, because the people of Rome were disciplined and faithful to the gods and to one another. In these volumes, Livy emphasized one of the major themes of his history—the importance of public morals. He wanted his readers to think about the conduct and character of the Roman men who created and extended the empire. Livy struck a depressing note that is repeated again and again in his work—the people of Rome are less noble and virtuous than they used to be. The message contained a warning. If Rome rose to power because its people were morally strong, as Livy believed, then the decline in virtue must bring about a decline in power.

Books 21 through 30 cover the Second Punic War with CARTHAGE. Modern historians still follow Livy's outline of the causes and events of this conflict. Books 31 through 45 examine many events, including the wars through which Rome became the principal power in Asia. During this period, according to Livy, Rome's national character began to show traces of decline. He wrote, "In his mind let the reader follow the way morals at first subsided, as it were, as discipline slipped little by little." Livy believed that Asian luxury had a bad effect on the Roman people, especially on soldiers, who grew more interested in loot than in battle. Asian religions, foods, languages, and customs crept into Roman culture and, in Livy's opinion, gradually corrupted and weakened it.

For Livy, history was far more than a collection of facts. His account of Rome's past had a higher purpose. By pointing out the things that had made Rome and Romans great, Livy hoped to encourage a return to earlier ideals. He brought much imagination and skill to this great task, creating a history that is an outstanding work of literature. He created stirring speeches for the heroes and generals of many nations, he recreated dramatic scenes with all the tension and excitement of a storyteller, and he captured the emotions that people feel when they are in the midst of stirring historic events. Above all, he urged his readers to learn from the lessons of history. The Romans of Livy's time were shaken by a century of civil wars. They wondered when and how Rome had lost its glory and if it could be recovered. Livy tried to provide the answers. (*See also* **Civil Wars, Roman; Punic Wars; Rome, History of.**)

## LIVY'S MISTAKES

Dante Alighieri, the famous Italian poet of the late Middle Ages, called Livy *"Livio che non erra"* (Livy who makes no mistakes). By this, he meant that Livy's moral judgment and good sense never faltered. Livy did make factual errors. He recorded dates incorrectly and made blunders in geography. When his sources contained different versions of a historic event, Livy sometimes used the wrong one. For these reasons, some modern scholars consider Livy a poor historian. Today's experts, however, owe their knowledge of the past to archaeology and other methods of inquiry that did not exist in Livy's time. Livy knew that some of his sources were unreliable, but he felt his job was to convey the grand sweep of history, not to check its details.

# LONGINUS

FIRST CENTURY A.D.
LITERARY CRITIC

\* **rhetoric** art of using words effectively in speaking or writing

The name *Longinus* refers to the unknown author of *On the Sublime,* an important essay of literary criticism. For a long time, the work was mistakenly attributed to Cassius Longinus, a Greek teacher of rhetoric\* who lived in the A.D. 400s. It is now generally believed that the work was written during the first century A.D., perhaps during Nero's reign (A.D. 54–68). It was rediscovered by European scholars in the A.D. 1500s and had a major influence on literary theory and criticism in the 1700s and 1800s.

*On the Sublime* is an examination of the elements that make for great literature. In the essay, which is written in the form of a letter from a teacher to a student, Longinus challenges the idea that writing is simply a technical skill that can be mastered by understanding and applying a set of rules. This was the traditional view of classical rhetoricians. Rather, Longinus insists, there is something more to writing than that which can be taught or learned. That "something more" is the power of inspiration or genius. While the rules of rhetoric and composition are important, writing is an art that balances technical skill and talent. The mark of a great poem or other literary work is that it reaches the sublime. In other words, important ideas and elegant language come together to form perfect expression. Sublime art transports the listener or reader beyond the ordinary and the merely good. It does more than simply persuade or please an audience. The idea of the sublime became popular among poets and philosophers* of the A.D. 1700s and especially influenced the Romantic movement in literature, music, and the visual arts.

* **philosopher** scholar or thinker concerned with the study of ideas, including science

In his essay, Longinus analyzes numerous passages from classical Greek literature, particularly from HOMER, as examples of sublime expression. His remarks show him to be an insightful and original literary critic, as well as a persuasive theorist. (*See also* **Education and Rhetoric, Greek; Literature, Greek; Literature, Roman.**)

## LONGUS

See *Novel, Greek and Roman.*

## LOVE, THE IDEA OF

The modern Western idea of love usually involves the notion of two people "falling in love"—seeing each another, recognizing an attraction, and coming together. The ideal outcome is marriage, followed by a family and living "happily ever after." This modern idea of love usually includes the following assumptions: that the feeling between the two people is mutual; that the man and woman share similar ideals, beliefs, and tastes; that the relationship is one between equal partners; and that the course of the relationship is determined by the individuals themselves. As surprising as it may seem, the ancient concept of love shared very few of these assumptions.

See color plate 3, vol. 3.

ROMANTIC LOVE AND MARRIAGE.    The Greeks and Romans often acknowledged the physical and sexual side of love. In Homer's epic poem the *Iliad,* it is the kidnapping of the beautiful Helen by the Trojan prince Paris that leads to the war between Greece and TROY. Poets and storytellers throughout the Greek and Roman world wrote of love and passion and about their effects on human behavior. To the ancients, intense passion was a sort of sickness or madness which, while fascinating and often irresistible, was certainly neither healthy nor natural. And passion was, by no means, the basis for marriage. The idea that emotions or romantic feelings should determine the choice of a marriage partner was flatly rejected.

The purpose of marriage in the ancient world was primarily to produce legitimate children. Marriages were often made with an eye toward political or social advantage as well, but continuing the husband's family line was the main consideration. The vast majority of marriages were arranged, usually at an early age, with little thought given to the wishes or objections of the man and woman involved. The parents were concerned

The ancient world did not place the same value on love as the modern Western world. Marriages were often based on practical rather than emotional needs. This tender depiction of a loving couple on a funerary stela, however, shows the affection that often existed between a husband and wife.

with finding suitable partners for their children, not with whether the two people loved, or even knew, each other. In the dialogue *Oeconomicus* by the Greek general and writer XENOPHON, the landowner Ischomachus says this to his bride:

> Do you now understand why it was I married you, and why your parents betrothed you to me? There would have been no difficulty in finding another girl to share my bed: I am quite sure you realize that. No; the decision was only taken after a great deal of thought . . . as to the best helpmeet each of us could find for the care of our home and our future children.

LOVE OUTSIDE OF MARRIAGE.   Just because most people in the ancient world married for reasons other than love did not mean that affection, and even passion, could not grow within a marriage. However, even men who were happily married had little hesitation about finding sex, and frequently romance, outside of marriage. Greek law allowed a married man to have a concubine* in addition to a wife. Since only his wife could produce legitimate offspring, the purpose of the concubine was primarily to satisfy the man's sexual desires.

* **concubine** a woman who lives with a man without being married to him

Many married men developed relationships with courtesans, women who lived independently and entertained male suitors, both married and unmarried. Social custom dictated that Greek wives remain within the household most of the time, while men frequently sought the companionship of well-known courtesans. In fact, romance and passion were considered more appropriate in these more casual relationships than they were in marriage. As the Greek orator DEMOSTHENES said, "We have courtesans for the sake of pleasure, concubines for the daily health of our bodies, and wives to bear us lawful offspring and be the faithful guardians of our homes." (*See also* **Family, Greek; Family, Roman; Helen of Troy; Marriage and Divorce; Prostitution; Women, Greek; Women, Roman.**)

---

## LUCAN

A.D. 39–65
ROMAN POET

* **epic** long poem about legendary or historical heroes, written in a grand style

* **Roman Republic** Rome during the period from 509 B.C. to 31 B.C., when popular assemblies annually elected their governmental officials

* **equestrian order** second rank of the Roman upper class, consisting of wealthy landowners whose social position entitled them to claim eligibility for service in the cavalry

* **philosopher** scholar or thinker concerned with the study of ideas, including science

* **quaestor** Roman financial officer who assisted a higher official such as a consul or praetor

* **augur** Roman religious official who read omens and foretold events

* **republican** favoring or relating to a government in which citizens elect officials to represent them in a citizen assembly

Marcus Annaeus Lucanus, also called Lucan, is best known for his epic* poem *Pharsalia,* also known as *De Bello Civili (Civil War).* The poem comprises ten books and recounts the civil war between Julius CAESAR and POMPEY that led to the fall of the Roman Republic* and the beginning of the Roman Empire. It is generally considered the greatest Latin epic after the *Aeneid* by VERGIL. Lucan's excellent style won him praise in his own time and the attention of the emperor NERO. He wrote much during his brief life and career, but only a few fragments exist of poems other than *Pharsalia.*

Lucan was born in Spain, the son of a Roman equestrian* and nephew of the philosopher* SENECA THE YOUNGER. Nero appointed Lucan to the high offices of quaestor* and augur* at a very young age. In the year A.D. 60, Lucan won a prize at the games called Neronia for a poem that praised the emperor Nero. However, he fell out of favor with the emperor following the publication of the first three books of *Pharsalia* in A.D. 62 or 63. Nero's resentment may have arisen from jealousy, since he himself was an aspiring poet, or because of the openly republican* and anti-imperial sentiments in Lucan's work. Soon, those same sentiments spurred Lucan to join a conspiracy to overthrow the emperor. When Nero discovered Lucan's involvement, he forced the young poet to kill himself.

*Pharsalia* is based on historical events, but Lucan raised the significance of the events and characters to mythic proportions. The principal hero is CATO THE YOUNGER, the Stoic senator who defied Julius Caesar to the end and chose to commit suicide rather than live under Caesar's rule. Cato represented the freedom and glory of the former republic, which Caesar had destroyed by his illegal grab for power. The other hero was Pompey, who led the republican army against Caesar and who symbolized to Lucan the weaknesses of the failing republic. *Pharsalia* ends with

Caesar's victory over Pompey at the Battle of Pharsalus, although the last volume is unfinished. (*See also* **Civil Wars, Roman; Epic, Roman; Literature, Roman; Senate, Roman; Stoicism.**)

## LUCIAN

**BORN ca. A.D. 120**
**GREEK WRITER AND LECTURER**

* **satire** literary technique that uses wit and sarcasm to expose or ridicule vice and folly

* **province** overseas area controlled by Rome

* **rhetoric** art of using words effectively in speaking or writing

* **philosophy** study of ideas, including science

Lucian was a Greek writer and performer renowned for his skill in combining well-known rhetorical and literary techniques to create new literary forms. He was a popular artistic figure in his own time, and his works had a major influence on European writers from the early A.D. 1300s to the late 1700s. Lucian wrote mainly satire*, and his works consistently poked fun at the vanity, self-importance, and folly of human beings. However, his main goal was not social criticism; rather it was to entertain his audience by using familiar literary devices in unique ways to produce a comic or satiric effect.

**LIFE AND EDUCATION.** Little is known for certain about Lucian's life. He was born in the city of Samosata in the kingdom of Commagene, a mountainous area north of the Roman province* of SYRIA. (Today, this area is part of southern Turkey.) His native tongue was Aramaic, and he learned Greek as a second language. From his writings, it is clear that he received a good Greek education in rhetoric*, philosophy*, art, and literature. Much of his success rested on his ability to use his knowledge in these areas. Lucian traveled widely, performing throughout the Roman empire.

**UNDERSTANDING LUCIAN'S WORKS.** Lucian combined four techniques that were normally used as exercises by students of rhetoric: the narrative (story); formal description; comparison; and the encomium (praise). He combined these techniques into a single work, and in doing so created a new literary form.

By examining Lucian's *Herodotus,* one can see his techniques at work. Lucian apparently wrote the work for a tour of Macedonia, the birthplace of the famous general and ruler ALEXANDER THE GREAT. It tells the story of how the early Greek writer Herodotus gained fame and fortune by reading his histories aloud at the Olympic Games. First, Lucian sets up a comparison between himself and the famous historian. He then inserts a description of a painting by Aëtion, who like Herodotus, displayed his work in Olympia. Lucian recalls Macedonia's glorious past as embodied in the figure of Alexander the Great, and he brings these themes together in enthusiastic praise of the Macedonian audience he was addressing. The audience is favorably compared to the audience that heard Herodotus, and Lucian is portrayed as an athlete waiting to be appraised by his critical listeners.

*Herodotus* was one of 11 pieces by Lucian called introductions, designed to establish a relaxed relationship with the audience at the beginning of a performance. Lucian's longer works, one or more of which would have followed the introduction, use the same techniques of combining conventional material in new ways. Some 70 works have been attributed to Lucian, including *Dialogues of the Gods, Dialogues of the Dead, A True Story, The Ass,* and *Banquet.*

Lucian freely took ideas from handbooks of rhetoric and philosophical teachings, as well as from other writers and literary traditions. In creating his own parodies*, he often reworked quotations, dialogues, or scenes from the well-known works of others. Lucian's highly educated audiences would have been familiar with these sources, and much of their enjoyment probably came from recognizing Lucian's clever combinations and references to these other works. His literary techniques were copied by satirists and comic writers for five centuries—from the early A.D. 1300s in Italy to the end of the 1700s in France, Germany, and England. (*See also* **Education and Rhetoric, Greek; Literature, Greek.**)

* **parody** work that imitates another for comic effect or ridicule

---

## LUCRETIUS

ca. 94–ca. 50 B.C.
ROMAN PHILOSOPHER AND POET

* **philosophy** study of ideas, including science

Lucretius, whose full name was Titus Lucretius Carus, is something of a mystery. His only known work is a long philosophical poem called *De rerum natura (On the Nature of Things).* Historians have discovered nothing about his family, his social status, or his life. Even the dates of his birth and death are only estimates based on the few scattered references to him in the writings of later Romans. Although some scholars have suggested that Lucretius was not a Roman, most believe that he was a well-educated Roman from a good family.

Lucretius's poem explains and celebrates Epicureanism, a philosophy* that was based on the teachings of EPICURUS, a Greek thinker of the 300s B.C. Most people of the time believed that the gods controlled or interfered in human affairs and that the soul, which continued to exist after death, could be punished for a person's sins in life. The Epicureans, the people who followed Epicurus's philosophy, departed from these views. They believed that the gods were calm, remote beings who took no interest in the human world, and that the universe, which contained many worlds, was governed by physical or mechanical laws. They also believed that the soul ceased to exist after death. To an Epicurean, the ideal life was one of simplicity and deep thought. Death was nothing to be feared, since it was merely the end of sensation. In his poem, Lucretius praises Epicurus's wisdom, saying that Epicurus "Rescued our life from darkness and rough seas/And rested it in the unclouded light of peace."

*De rerum natura* is 7,400 lines long and divided into six books, each with a prologue, or introductory section. The first two books set forth the basic principles of Epicureanism and the structure of the universe as the Epicureans understood it. Book 2 ends with a declaration that all things, including the world itself, must someday die: "All must age, and fade, and make/ That universal pilgrimage to the grave."

The third and fourth books deal with the human soul and mind. Book 3 tells how the soul is made and how it dies. Lucretius argues that people should accept death as inevitable and not fear it. Those who have enjoyed life should go, when the time comes, "as if leaving after a good dinner." For those who have not enjoyed life, death can bring no additional disappointments, since it is pure nothingness. Book 4 explains such human

## A SENSATIONAL STORY

Although nothing definite is known about Lucretius's life, the early Christian father St. Jerome wrote an account of the poet's death. According to Jerome, Lucretius's wife gave him a love potion that drove him insane. He wrote his great poem *De rerum natura* during brief intervals of sanity between fits of madness, then ended his life by suicide. Not a single piece of evidence confirms this tale, which may have been an attempt to discredit Lucretius, who was one of the most famous poets and thinkers of pagan (non-Christian) Rome.

experiences as dreams, memory, and imagination. It also warns against passionate involvement in love, which, Lucretius states, only leads to jealousy and rejection.

The fifth and sixth books are about the natural world. Book 5 shows how the world and all the beings in it were created according to physical laws. It ends with a description of the growth of human civilization, tracing history from the time of primitive cave dwellers to the rise of mighty civilizations. In Book 6, Lucretius explains lightning, volcanoes, earthquakes, rainbows, and other natural events that have caused people to hold false and superstitious beliefs about the gods. Since earthquakes, for example, can be explained by Epicurean theories about the physical world, there is no reason to imagine that they are caused by angry gods. The poem ends with an account of a plague* that brought intense suffering and death to Athens. It is a reminder that everyone and everything must perish.

Despite his serious subject matter, Lucretius's tone is not gloomy. The poem is a declaration of his faith that people can learn to enjoy happy, calm lives. Some of the most famous lines in *De rerum natura* describe someone who is safe on the shore watching another person struggling in a storm at sea. These lines show the satisfaction of the philosopher who escapes the turmoil of life by understanding the true nature of things:

> How sweet to watch, from land, while winds enrage
> The great sea's waves, another man in trouble!
> —Not taking pleasure in another's pain,
> But seeing what evils you yourself are spared.

(*See also* **Philosophy, Roman; Poetry, Roman.**)

* **plague** highly contagious, widespread, and often fatal disease

# MACEDONIA

* **classical** in Greek history, refers to the period of great political and cultural achievement from about 500 B.C. to 323 B.C.

Macedonia was an ancient kingdom on the northwest coast of the AEGEAN SEA, north of central Greece. The center of Macedonia was a fertile plain crossed by rivers and encircled by rugged mountains. The region produced livestock, wine, fruit, iron, gold, silver, and timber.

The people who lived in Macedonia in prehistoric times had little contact with MYCENAE, the Mediterranean civilization that flourished in southern Greece before the rise of classical* Greek civilization. Later, however, early Greeks migrated north and mingled with the local inhabitants to form the Macedonian people, who lived along the Haliacmon River. Their language was related to the Greek language, and they worshiped the Greek gods. According to one Greek legend, the Macedonians were descended from a son of the god ZEUS.

In the mid-600s B.C., King Perdiccas I of the Macedonians expanded his territory, conquering the fertile central plain. His descendants continued to strengthen and enlarge the kingdom. PHILIP II conquered Greece and united it with Macedonia. Philip's son ALEXANDER THE GREAT defeated the PERSIAN EMPIRE and brought Egypt and much of western Asia under his control. After Alexander's death, however, the empire he had created fell apart. A new

19

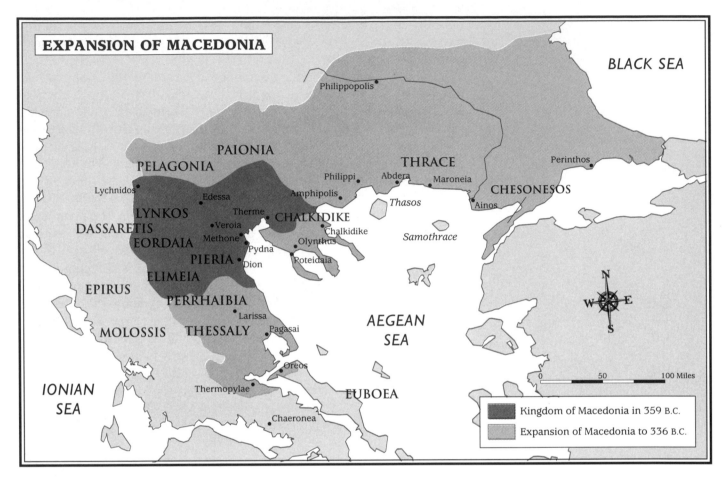

**EXPANSION OF MACEDONIA**

BLACK SEA

Philippopolis

PAIONIA

PELAGONIA

THRACE

Perinthos

Lychnidos

Edessa

Philippi · Abdera · Maroneia

CHESONESOS

LYNKOS

Therme

Amphipolis

Thasos

Ainos

DASSARETIS

Veroia

CHALKIDIKE

EORDAIA

Methone

Chalkidike

Samothrace

Pydna

Olynthus

PIERIA

Dion

Poteidaia

ELIMEIA

EPIRUS

PERRHAIBIA

AEGEAN
SEA

Larissa

MOLOSSIS

THESSALY

Pagasai

IONIAN
SEA

Oreos

50    100 Miles

Thermopylae

EUBOEA

Chaeronea

☐ Kingdom of Macedonia in 359 B.C.

☐ Expansion of Macedonia to 336 B.C.

In 369 B.C. Macedonia was a relatively small kingdom. It took an aggressive and ambitious father-and-son team to transform the state into a powerful empire. Philip II first annexed Greece, and then his son Alexander the Great conquered the Persian Empire.

* **dynasty** succession of rulers from the same family or group

* **city-state** independent state consisting of a city and its surrounding territory

* **province** overseas area controlled by Rome

dynasty* came to power in Macedonia in 277 B.C. During the next century, the kings of this dynasty maintained their grip on most of Greece, despite many uprisings in Athens, Sparta, and other Greek city-states*.

The rising power of Rome soon challenged Macedonia. King Philip V of Macedonia fought two wars against the Romans. He lost the second in 197 B.C., and the treaty that followed stripped Macedonia of its holdings in Greece. Philip's son, Perseus, also waged war against Rome, attempting to free Greece from Roman control. Perseus was defeated, and Rome abolished the Macedonian kingdom, creating four new republics in its place. Two decades later, Rome turned Macedonia into a province* of the Roman Empire. Toward the end of the Roman Empire, in the A.D. 400s, Rome divided Macedonia into two provinces.

In the centuries that followed, Macedonia was invaded by Slavic people from the north, belonged to the kingdoms of Bulgaria and Serbia during the Middle Ages, was conquered by the Islamic Ottoman Empire of Turkey, and eventually was divided between Yugoslavia and Greece. In the 1990s, the formerly Yugoslavian portion of Macedonia became an independent nation.

## MACHINES

See *Technology*.

# MAGIC

* **ritual** regularly followed routine, especially religious

* **deity** god or goddess

oth the Greeks and the Romans believed in and practiced magic. By doing so, they thought they could control the environment and influence the outcome of events. The performance of magic often included complicated rituals* and rites that reflected the religious practices of the times.

There was an important difference between the religious and magical rites that the Greeks and Romans practiced, however. Religion usually involved gods and goddesses who, the ancients believed, controlled nature. These deities* might or might not respond to the prayers of the individual. Magic, on the other hand, bound or constrained nature if certain rituals were performed carefully and in accordance with tradition. Magic usually operated through semidivine "intermediaries"—supernatural forces somewhere between this world and that of the gods. Many of the magical beliefs of the ancients survive to the present as popular superstitions. For example, the belief that a black cat crossing one's path brings bad luck is rooted in the ancient past.

The idea of magic existed from the beginning of human history. The Persian *magus,* or magician, had mysterious (but not necessarily evil) powers. In Greece, the idea of the magus evolved into the evil sorcerer, who was considered a fraud. Greek thinkers, such as PLATO, rejected magic and sorcery and demanded that those who practiced them be punished. Other

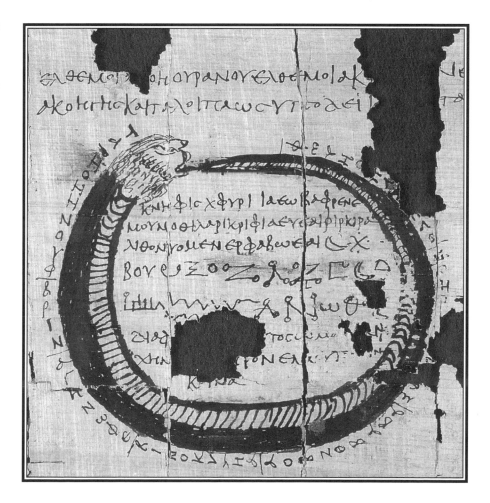

A symbolic snake figure adorns this magical text, which was written on papyrus and preserved from the ancient world. The text may have recorded the ingredients of a spell or the words for a curse.

branches of philosophy such as SKEPTICISM, Epicureanism, and Cynicism also criticized the use of magic. Nevertheless, the practice of magic was widespread in all classes of society in both ancient Greece and Rome.

The Greeks and Romans practiced several forms of magic. The two most common forms were black magic and white magic. Black magic was destructive. It was intended to harm an individual or bring about the destruction of property. A curse was the most obvious kind of black magic, and the Greeks and Romans were masters at devising creative curses for every occasion. Other forms of black magic were potions, poisons, and spells. In most cases, the ancients called upon demonic* spirits to help work black magic. A witch was believed to have extraordinary powers of black magic. Some of the powers attributed to witches included calling on the dead and the powers of the underworld, reversing the flow of water, controlling the weather, and turning people into birds or animals by night.

White magic was the opposite of black magic. It was used to protect an individual against harm, bring good fortune, or cure someone of an illness. The ancients used diverse rituals in white magic. Some of these rituals included purifications (cleansings) with water and fire, the casting of spells and calling out of strange words (incantations), and the use of amulets or charms, often in the form of ornaments that were worn. The preparation of magical potions from herbs and plants was often important to healing. In this respect, white magic came very close to the ritual medicine used by ancient physicians.

Guarding against the "evil eye" was the most widespread type of white magic in ancient times. Parents placed amulets on their babies to keep them from attracting envy or hatred. Farmers were regular users of white magic. They cast spells to bring forth rain, danced special dances to bring forth a bountiful crop, and poured libations, or offerings, into the soil to appease the gods. Thus, magical practices often closely followed the religious rituals performed by priests.

Magic had many dos and don'ts. For example, one was advised to touch the earth when it thundered and to smooth out one's bed on rising. The first was to prevent a lightning strike and the second to prevent the impression of the body from being used to cast a black-magic spell. To avoid misfortune, the Greek thinker PYTHAGORAS warned against eating beans, picking up objects that fell to the floor, and wearing rings. The literature of ancient Greece and Rome is filled with comments on magic. (*See also* **Divinities; Religion, Greek; Religion, Roman; Ritual and Sacrifice.**)

* **demonic** referring to demons or evil spirits

## THAT OLD BLACK MAGIC

Curses written on lead tablets—lead being a heavy, dark metal—and buried in the ground were a common type of black magic. The Roman sports fan who wrote the following curse must have had little faith in his team's chances of winning the weekly chariot race. (The Green and White are the names of chariot teams.)

I invoke you, Spirit, whoever you are, and lay it upon you from this hour, this day, this moment that you torment and destroy the horses of the Green and White, kill and crush the charioteers, . . . leave no breath in their bodies.

## MAGISTRATES

Magistrates (from the Latin *magistratus*) were governmental officials in ancient Greece and Rome. In Greece, magistrates called archons took over many of the functions of the early Greek kings. They controlled the treasury and supervised public works and the AGORA, or marketplace. In early Greek democracies, such as Athens, magistrates were usually elected from a list of names of major property owners. Later on, property qualifications were lowered, and all magistrates were chosen by lot. In the military dictatorship of SPARTA, magistrates, called

* **city-state** independent state consisting of a city and its surrounding territory

* **Roman Republic** Rome during the period from 509 B.C. to 31 B.C., when popular assemblies annually elected their governmental officials

## ARCHONS

In ancient Greece, archons were the highest officeholders of a city-state. They had both lawmaking power and executive duties. In Athens, archons gradually took over the running of the government, while reducing the power of the kings.

There were three types of Greek archons, and each had responsibility for a specific job. The *basileus,* or "king" archon, presided over the Areopagus (council of elders) and religious ceremonies. The *strategos* commanded the army, and the *archon eponymos* was the nominal head of state and had the widest duties. These included the protection of property and the family and the direction of festivals.

* **edict** proclamation or order that has the force of law

ephors, were chosen by voice vote. Not all Greeks could be magistrates. Usually only the well-to-do could afford to take time out from everyday life to serve, although Athens provided a small salary for its magistrates.

At first, magistrates required no special training and performed any and all functions. Gradually, they became more specialized as city-states* grew larger and the administration of government became more complex. Small cities needed only a few magistrates. In the larger cities, boards of magistrates were established. Each magistrate had a particular job and a limited term in office. Magistrates were accountable to the public and to their peers. Greek citizens maintained control of their magistrates by examining their qualifications before they entered office and after they left office. In addition, magistrates in Greece could be prosecuted for misconduct.

During the Roman Republic*, magistrates were elected each year by the people. They served for one year and normally were not reelected, although the SENATE could extend their term of office if necessary as promagistrates. Magistrates received no salary for their work. Hence, only the wealthiest Romans could afford to serve as magistrates and considered it an honor to do so. A Roman magistrate had to be knowledgeable in many areas—administration, finance, law, and military operations for the defense of Rome—yet they were "amateurs," and some made terrible blunders. During the empire, magistrates were elected by the Senate and at the wish of the emperor.

Magistrates in Rome rose to positions of prominence through a hierarchy called the *cursus honorum.* The hierarchy, or career path, was in place by the mid-100s B.C. QUAESTOR was the first level. Then came AEDILE, PRAETOR, and CONSUL. (TRIBUNES were outside the *cursus* because only PLEBEIANS were eligible.) CENSORS, also outside the hierarchy, were elected every five years for a term of 18 months. The level above these magistrates was that of dictator, a position that was intended to be held for 6 months, usually during a period of crisis. Lucius SULLA and Julius CAESAR held that position but stayed in office beyond the allotted 6 months. Senior magistrates had easy access to the members of the Senate. In fact, Rome's Senate was made up of those who had served as senior magistrates. Once former magistrates entered the Senate, they were there for life, unless removed by the censors.

The complexity of running the republic gave rise to distinct magisterial functions. The *praetor urbanus,* for example, was responsible for administering justice in Rome. Four aediles were in charge of the general care of the city, traffic, water and food supply, and market practices. Higher magistrates, such as praetors, administered the laws, issuing at the start of their tenure edicts* stating how they intended to interpret the law during their term of office. Unlike their Greek counterparts, Roman magistrates were not formally accountable to the people who elected them. Rome occasionally attempted to bring actions against certain magistrates, but that was often politically difficult to do. High officeholders were protective of their power and privilege and unwilling to give up either without a fight. This situation gave rise to bloody warfare during the late republic. (*See also* **Government, Greek; Government, Roman.**)

# MAPS, ANCIENT

## A FAMOUS CITY MAP

One of the most famous maps in the ancient world was the *Forma Urbis Romae.* Engraved on 151 slabs of marble, the *Forma Urbis Romae* depicts the city of Rome as it existed in the early A.D. 200s. The map adorned a wall in the Temple of Peace in Rome. Only a portion—about 10 percent—of the map remains, providing scholars with valuable information about life in the ancient city.

The oldest known map, from Babylonia, exists on a clay tablet and dates from around 2500 B.C. The ancient Greeks made the first scientific maps in the 500s B.C. The Greeks were interested in creating maps that accurately depicted the size and shape of the known world. The Romans, however, developed maps that had greater value for military and administrative purposes.

During the 500s B.C., the philosopher* Anaximander of Miletus created the first map of the inhabited world as it was known to the Greeks. The geographer Hecataeus, who was also a scholar from Miletus, improved upon Anaximander's map. Hecataeus thought that the world was a disk and that all the land was surrounded by the river Oceanus. Hecataeus wrote a book called *Journey Around the World,* in which he discussed the places and peoples he encountered on a sea voyage along the shores of the Mediterranean and Black seas. Although the Greek historian HERODOTUS relied on this work when he wrote his *Histories,* he criticized both Anaximander's and Hecataeus's depictions of the earth as being simplistic and naive.

The Greek philosopher PYTHAGORAS, who also lived in the 500s B.C., believed that the earth was a sphere, and by the 300s B.C., most Greek scholars accepted this concept. The philosopher ARISTOTLE provided six different arguments supporting the idea of a spherical earth. His student, Dicaearchus, mapped the Strait of Gibraltar (at the western end of the Mediterranean Sea) and the Himalayas (a mountain range in Asia), both at a similar latitude. He also assumed the existence of an eastern ocean.

In the 200s B.C., ERATOSTHENES, the head of the Library of ALEXANDRIA, used the longitude and latitude of places to determine their distances from each other. Using these figures, he made a remarkably accurate map. Eratosthenes also made a fairly accurate calculation of the circumference of the earth. The Hellenistic* astronomer Hipparchus criticized these measurements and made detailed corrections to Eratosthenes' map.

In the A.D. 100s, PTOLEMY, the mathematician, astronomer, and geographer, created maps that he included in his eight-volume *Geography.* Ptolemy's map of the world extended from Thule (probably in the Shetland Islands near Scotland) to Africa south of the equator. Although Ptolemy's maps contained errors, they were the basis for the maps that were produced over the next few centuries. Ptolemy's most glaring error concerned the location of Asia. On Ptolemy's map, the continent of Asia stretched farther east than it actually does. In the late A.D. 1400s, Christopher Columbus used maps based on those of Ptolemy, and when he landed in the Caribbean, he believed that he was actually in Asia.

The greatest advancement in cartography (mapmaking) in ancient Rome was made as a result of Roman military policy. Roman generals surveyed the lands they conquered, and Roman mapmakers used information derived from road construction to make accurate maps of the empire. Surveyors marked off landholdings in each province*, and maps delineating these landholdings were displayed in the forum* of each city. An official map of the Roman Empire—in effect, a map of the entire Mediterranean basin—was prepared during the reign of the first emperor, AUGUSTUS. Its creator was Marcus Agrippa, Roman general and administrator and most trusted friend of Augustus. The map was displayed on one of the main gates to the city of Rome so that all visitors could see at a glance the full extent of the empire. (*See also* **Astronomy and Astrology; Geography and Geology, Mediterranean.**)

## MARATHON

Marathon, located on the eastern coast of ATTICA, a region in the eastern part of central Greece, was the site of a famous battle. In 490 B.C. Athenian hoplites, heavily armed infantrymen, defeated the larger force of armed troops under the command of King Darius of Persia. This event marked the end of the first phase of the PERSIAN WARS.

Marathon is situated on a coastal plain—about two miles wide and five miles long—northeast of Athens. In 490 B.C. Darius—the king of Persia—invaded Greece. The Athenians were urged by Miltiades, their *strategos,* or military commander, to meet the Persian force at Marathon. There the Athenians, backed up by their Plataean allies, took a defensive position. The combined Greek force of about 10,000 men faced a Persian army twice as large that included infantrymen, archers, and cavalry. The bulk of the Persian cavalry did not participate in the battle, however, and the Athenians, feeling bold, decided to advance. Under Miltiades' command, the Athenians lengthened their lines by thinning the center. When they came within range of hitting their targets, they broke into a run and thrust their long spears into the enemy rather than hurling them.

While the Persians attacked the center of the Athenian force, the stronger ends of the Athenian line valiantly defeated their foes. The victorious end-line Athenian warriors then closed in on the Persian center as it returned from pursuing the Greeks. The Greeks chased the remaining Persians to their fleet, which was waiting in a nearby bay, and captured seven of the Persian ships. The Greeks allegedly killed about 6,400 Persians in the Battle of Marathon but lost only 192 of their own. The Athenian dead were buried under a mound at the site.

The Greek troops had expected help from SPARTA, but it never came. According to the Greek historian HERODOTUS, the Athenians sent a runner named Pheidippides to Sparta to ask for help. He arrived in Sparta the day after he left Athens, having covered a distance of about 125 miles. The Spartans could not come in time because of a religious festival.

Legend has obscured the historian's account, however. According to legend, Pheidippides ran a little more than 26 miles from Athens to Marathon in order to join the battle. He then ran back to Athens to announce the Greek victory to the populace. After announcing the victory, Pheidippides died from exhaustion. His heroism gave rise to the modern-day foot race called a marathon. A marathon was part of the first modern OLYMPIC GAMES, which were held in Athens in 1896. (*See also* **Wars and Warfare, Greek.**)

### "GREEKS TROUNCE PERSIANS AT MARATHON!"

If the ancient Greeks had had newspapers, this headline might have been the most famous one of 490 B.C. The Greek victory over Persia at Marathon was made possible by the valor of the determined and well-coordinated hoplites. Each hoplite was protected by a bronze helmet that covered most of his face. A tough garment made of layers of heavy linen covered the upper body. Bronze shin guards, called greaves, covered the front and back of the lower leg. The hoplite used a large wooden shield to ward off blows and carried a long spear for thrusting into the enemy.

## MARBLE

Marble, a stone that shines when polished to a high degree, was one of the favorite building materials used in the ancient world. The ancient Greeks and Romans also used the term *marble* to refer to granite, porphyry, and other types of polished stones. Glistening white, colored, or veined, marble was used in the construction of temples, government buildings, marketplaces, and other structures throughout ancient Greece and Rome. Sculptors also used marble to create statues of lasting beauty. The elegance and versatility of ancient marble can be appreciated in the numerous edifices and statues that have survived to the present.

Marble was sought after for its color and the ease with which it could be worked. White marble was the most desirable, but gray and green types were also valued. In Greece, the best white marble came from Paros; the best gray marble came from Naxos. The white marble used in the architecture on the Acropolis in Athens came from Mt. Pentelicus in Attica. The marble from Pentelic contained deposits of iron that became visible after years of exposure to the weather. Because of this feature, structures built of Pentelicon marble took on a golden glow after time.

Although marble quarries* existed in Italy from early times, the Etruscans did not use much of it. When Rome became the center of power on the Italian peninsula, the quarrying of marble became an important industry. The finest white marble came from Carrara in Italy. The emperors, especially Augustus, made extensive use of white marble in the monuments and buildings of Rome. Augustus imported several different types of marble from Asia Minor, Egypt, Greece, and northern Africa. Colored marble became fashionable for interior decorations in palaces and villas.

The cutting and transporting of marble were very expensive. For this reason, most buildings were only faced with thin blocks of marble. Sometimes architects used columns of marble or marble embellishments to decorate structures of a less costly type of stone. Despite its cost, marble became extremely popular as a building material throughout the Roman empire. Some people had environmental concerns about the widespread use of marble. The writer Pliny commented that "Mountains were made by nature to serve as a framework for holding together the inner parts of the earth. . . . We quarry them for mere whim." (*See also* **Architecture, Greek; Architecture, Roman; Construction Materials and Techniques; Quarries; Sculpture, Greek; Sculpture, Roman.**)

See color plate 13, vol. 2.

* **quarry** open pit from which stone is removed

## MARIUS, GAIUS

### ca. 157–86 B.C.
### ROMAN GENERAL AND POLITICIAN

* **Roman Republic** Rome during the period from 509 B.C. to 31 B.C., when popular assemblies annually elected their governmental officials

* **hierarchy** order of authority or rank

Gaius Marius, a military commander during the late Roman Republic*, had a long and notable career. He rose through the hierarchy* of Roman government officials to become a consul, or a chief governmental official, six times. Under his generalship, the minimum property qualification for service in the Roman legions was removed. Many men who joined the army had no farm or occupation to which to return after discharge. Hence, they tended to reenlist for military service. In time, these men became semiprofessional soldiers, often loyal to a specific commander.

Marius was born into a family belonging to the equestrian order* and married Julia, the aunt of Julius Caesar. He served in the Roman army in Spain and fought against Jugurtha, king of Numidia, a region in northern Africa. He won the loyalty of his soldiers and gained his first consulship in 107 B.C. Promising a quick end to the war in Numidia, Marius took some immediate steps. He raised an army himself and called for volunteers

* **equestrian order** second rank of the Roman upper class, consisting of wealthy landowners whose social position entitled them to claim eligibility for service in the cavalry

from the landless Roman classes. In return for their service, he offered them victory, glory, and land grants. Although Marius received the credit for the victory over Jugurtha, it was actually Lucius Cornelius SULLA who negotiated the surrender of the Numidian king and who, thereafter, became Marius's rival.

Marius followed the same successful recruiting methods to assemble an army to keep Germanic barbarians from invading Rome. In return for his military prowess, the people of Rome reelected him consul every year from 104 to 100 B.C. His success in battle came from his use of the guerrilla tactics of stealth and surprise and from the unwavering loyalty of his troops.

Marius's skill as a general did not carry over into the political arena, however. On his return to Rome in 100 B.C., he became embroiled in political infighting in the Senate. Marius was the leader of the Populares, a group of senators who supported the popular reforms proposed by Tiberius and Gaius GRACCHUS. On the opposing side were Sulla and the Optimates, or "best men," a group that included and represented the old senatorial establishment. In 88 B.C. both Sulla and Marius wanted to command Rome's army against Mithradates, the king of Pontus in ASIA MINOR. Sulla seized the city of Rome and set out for the east, while Marius and his supporters fled to Africa. Marius returned to Rome to murder his Optimate opponents. He died in 86 B.C., shortly after beginning his seventh consulship. Sulla returned from the east in 83 B.C. and became dictator of Rome two years later. (*See also* **Armies, Roman; Rome, History of.**)

## MARK ANTONY

See *Antonius, Marcus.*

## MARKETS

* **city-state** independent state consisting of a city and its surrounding territory

* **polis** in ancient Greece, the dominant form of political and social organization; a city-state

See color plate 6, vol. 2.

Markets played an important role in the lives of the ancient Greeks and Romans. Each Greek city-state* had an AGORA, or marketplace, where goods were bought and sold. In Rome, the FORUM was originally the main market site for the city.

The first markets appeared in Greece in the 900s B.C., gradually replacing older forms of direct exchange, or barter. With the rise of cities, markets became an important part of urban life. At first, markets were little more than places where sellers set up stalls for the display of their retail goods or farm produce. These makeshift arrangements eventually gave way to more permanent structures. The first shops were built in ATHENS around 500 B.C. The polis* supervised the markets and levied taxes on the merchants. The main concern, however, was to make sure the city had enough food for its inhabitants.

Towns and villages had markets too. Special days—called market days—were regularly set aside for buying and selling. Religious festivals were often held on market days to take advantage of the fact that many people would ordinarily be gathered at the market on those days.

A daily market existed in Rome from 210 B.C. The emporium (a technical term for "shop" or "store"), built in 193 B.C., was the site for most

The traditional ancient market consisted of makeshift booths in the center of town, in which sellers could display their wares. This relief depicts a woman displaying foodstuffs at a butcher shop.

* **aedile** Roman official in charge of maintaining public property inside the city, such as roads, temples, and markets

selling. The markets came under the supervision of the aediles*. Regular markets sprang up in towns throughout the Italian peninsula. There were also regional fairs and estate markets. With improvements in shipbuilding techniques, trade expanded to overseas markets throughout the Mediterranean region, where the ancient system of open-air markets is still in use today. (*See also* **Aedile; Agora; Food and Drink; Ships and Shipbuilding; Trade, Greek; Trade, Roman.**)

# MARRIAGE AND DIVORCE

Marriage was central to the organization of families and of society in both ancient Greece and ancient Rome. The main function of marriage in both cultures was the production of legitimate children—that is, children who were legally recognized as their father's offspring and who would inherit the family's name, status, and property. The Greeks and Romans recognized that marriage was not a perfect institution and allowed people in unsatisfactory marriages to divorce their partners.

GREEK CUSTOMS AND LAWS. The customs and laws that governed Greek marriage varied from place to place and over time. All Greek marriages, however, shared a few basic features. By the 500s B.C., marriage had become patriarchal, or organized around the male line of descent. Upon marrying, a woman left her own family and joined that of her husband. Men arranged marriages. A woman's father—or, if her father was dead, her closest adult male relative—gave her to another man to bear his children. Her consent was not required. Marriages between uncles and nieces or between first cousins were common. Such marriages kept the wealth within a family.

A Greek bride usually brought a dowry* to her marriage. Although a dowry was not necessary to make a legal marriage, men were reluctant to

* **dowry** money or property that a woman brings to the man she marries

accept a bride who did not have one. In such cases, relatives or the state might provide the girl with a dowry. If a marriage dissolved, the husband would return the dowry to his wife's family.

In ATHENS, legal marriage began with *engye,* or betrothal, a formal contract between the bride's guardian and the groom that spelled out the details of the dowry. The wedding followed, sometimes several years later. Women were usually married at the age of 14 or 15, and men were about 30 when they married.

An Athenian wedding was celebrated by rituals* that marked the bride's progress from one stage of life to another. Before marrying, she bathed in water from a sacred spring. Then, a wedding feast took place at either the groom's home or the bride's family's home. Women attended the banquet but sat separately from the men. Afterward, a procession of friends and relatives escorted the bride to the groom's house. They carried torches, sang marriage hymns, and played music—all to attract the attention of as many people as possible, who would serve as witnesses to the wedding. The groom's mother welcomed the bride to her new home, and the guests showered the couple with nuts and dried fruits, which were symbols of fertility. The first food that the bride ate in her new home was a quince, a fruit that also symbolized fertility. If the marriage did not go well, a husband could divorce his wife simply by shutting her out of the house. A wife who wanted to divorce her husband, however, had to obtain permission from the government to end her marriage.

* **ritual** regularly followed routine, especially religious

The main function of marriage in ancient Greek and Roman society was the production of legitimate children to inherit the father's name, status, and property. Customs regarding women's rights varied from city to city, however. A marriage scene is depicted here.

## MARRYING FOREIGNERS

The Greeks and Romans regulated marriage between citizens and foreigners so that people outside the state could not acquire citizenship simply by marrying citizens. Around 450 B.C., the Athenians passed a law stating that only children of two citizens would be considered citizens. This discouraged Athenians from marrying outsiders. Over the centuries, the Romans created a complex web of laws that defined categories of people who could, or could not, enter into legal Roman marriages. In general, if one partner in a marriage was a noncitizen, the children could not be Roman citizens.

*See color plate 3, vol. 3.*

Marriage customs in SPARTA were quite different from those elsewhere in Greece. Women and men generally married when they were about 18 or 20 years old. Spartans sometimes followed a tradition called marriage by capture, in which a group of young people in a dark room chose their mates at random. In the early stages of marriage, a bride remained in her family's home. As a sign that she had married, she cut her hair and temporarily dressed in men's clothing.

According to Greek myth, Cecrops, the first king of Athens, invented marriage as a punishment for women. Before marriage existed, said the myth, women were the political equals of men, but the institution of marriage imposed limits on their power. The Greeks expected that all women—except slaves—would marry. There was no respectable place for unmarried women in Greek society. Over time, however, Greek ideas about marriage changed. By the 200s B.C., marriage was a more equal partnership, and women could obtain divorces as easily as men. Perhaps more important, marriage eventually became a matter of personal choice. Greek culture began to accept love as a motive for marriage.

ROMAN CUSTOMS AND LAWS.   Roman marriage was organized around the orderly transfer of property, rank, and CITIZENSHIP rights from one generation to the next. People regarded it as the normal duty of both sexes to marry and have children. The state encouraged marriage, and laws passed in 18 B.C. and 9 B.C. levied fines on unmarried people. In addition, unmarried people were not allowed to inherit, and people who were married but childless received only half of their inheritance.

The Romans recognized two basic types of marriage. In marriage with *manus,* or control, a woman left her family and entered her husband's family. Marriage with *manus* was sometimes celebrated with a ritual that symbolized the sale of the bride to the groom. All of the bride's property became her husband's upon marriage, but she became one of his heirs and could inherit, along with his children, a share of his property if he died before her. In free marriage, or marriage without *manus,* a married woman remained either under her father's guardianship or free and in control of her own property. Free marriage did not change a woman's legal status. Although she continued to own property, she was not recognized as her husband's heir.

Customs and laws set limits on Roman marriage. No marriage was valid without the consent of both parties, not just on the wedding day but every day. A marriage lasted only as long as both partners continued to agree to be married to each other. The minimum age of consent for girls was 12. Some girls younger than 12 married to cement alliances between wealthy or upper-class families, but they did not legally become wives until they came of age. Boys could marry at 14, but they rarely did so before the age of 16 or 17. Senators generally married at 21 or 22.

The Romans celebrated both forms of marriage with traditional rituals. Brides parted their hair into six locks and tied the locks with wool. They dressed in long white robes, flame-colored shoes, and a flame-colored veil. In the bride's father's house, with friends of both families

* **sacrifice** sacred offering made to a god or goddess, usually of an animal such as a sheep or goat

* **Roman Republic** Rome during the period from 509 B.C. to 31 B.C., when popular assemblies annually elected their governmental officials

gathered around, the couple declared their consent to the marriage and joined their right hands. They asked for the blessings of the gods by sacrificing* an animal, often a pig. After a banquet, the guests marched to the groom's house in a procession. The bride's attendants or the groom carried her across the threshold of her new home. This ritual ensured that she would not stumble on the doorstep, which would bring bad luck to the marriage.

Most brides entered marriage with dowries, which usually consisted of land, slaves, money, or other property. If the husband died or divorced the wife, she regained the dowry, which guaranteed her enough money to live on or to remarry. By the end of the Roman Republic*, divorce was simple and fairly common. It required no legal formalities. Either partner could divorce the other with either a spoken declaration or a written notice. Children of a divorced couple normally remained with the husband. Christian rulers during the late Roman Empire made laws to discourage divorce, which became less acceptable after the A.D. 100s. (*See also* **Family, Greek; Family, Roman; Women, Greek; Women, Roman.**)

## MARS

Second in power only to Jupiter, Mars was the highly respected Roman god of war. Festivals were held in his honor to mark the start and finish of military campaigns. Soldiers also made sacrifices to him during battle.

Mars was the Roman god of war. In early mythology, Mars was a god of farmers and farming. He fought off drought and flood, the two main enemies of farmers. He was second in power and authority, after JUPITER, and was greatly honored and respected.

The month of March was named for Mars, and it was the first month of the early Roman calendar. His festivals—accompanied by horses, trumpets, and other symbols of war—were held during March and they marked the beginning of military campaigning. Another festival for Mars was held in October at the end of the campaigning season. At this time, weapons were blessed and put away for the winter. Mars had his own priest and his own sacred animals—the wolf and the woodpecker. The Campus Martius, a field in Rome where men practiced warrior skills, was named after Mars. Before a battle, soldiers offered sacrifices to Mars and to the goddess Bellona, who was at various times described as his wife, sister, or daughter.

According to an ancient Roman legend, Mars was the father of ROMULUS AND REMUS, the mythical founders of Rome. Although a fierce god of war, Mars had a softer side—he was in love with VENUS, the goddess of love. Artists and sculptors often show them together as "Love" and "Strife."

Ares, the Greek god of war, was not as popular as his Roman counterpart, Mars. Introduced into Greece from THRACE, Ares was the only son of ZEUS and HERA. Ares is featured in Homer's epic poem the *Iliad,* in which he supports the Trojans. But his character, warlike and loud, is hardly noble. In Homer's *Odyssey,* Ares is in love with APHRODITE, the Greek goddess of love. Together they have twins, Phobos (Panic) and Deimos (Fear). In Athens, the meeting place of the Council of Elders was the Areopagus, or Hill of Ares. (*See also* **Divinities.**)

ca. A.D. 40–ca. 104
ROMAN POET

* **epigram** short poem dealing pointedly, and sometimes satirically, with a single thought

* **patron** special guardian, protector, or supporter

The poet Martial (born Marcus Valerius Martialis) lived in Rome during the reigns of the emperors NERO, VESPASIAN, TITUS, and DOMITIAN. Martial's fame comes from the numerous short poems and epigrams* he wrote. His epigrams—powerful, often obscene, and generally humorous—reveal much about Roman society, manners, and morals.

Martial was born in Bilbilis, Spain (in the present-day province of Saragossa). His father was a wealthy knight. In A.D. 64 Martial traveled to Rome to seek a career. There he came under the guidance of SENECA THE YOUNGER, Nero's political adviser. Seneca tried to promote the young man's political career. Martial served as a military TRIBUNE, but his political career ended abruptly when Nero turned on Seneca. Cut off from the support of his patron*, Martial turned his attention elsewhere. In his mid-20s, he began to write poems for a living and quickly learned that his favorite mode of expression was the epigram. In the course of his career, he became the greatest writer of epigrams the ancient world would know.

The word *epigram* comes from the Greek word for inscription. The short statements inscribed on tombstones gradually evolved into short poems marking special occasions in a person's life, commemorating real and imaginary events, or making a verbal attack on an enemy. The Romans adopted the Greek epigrammatic tradition and turned it into a popular form of SATIRE. The Roman epigrammatists drew attention to human failings and expressed their disapproval of their subjects in language that was often vivid and obscene, and—at its most effective—concise and elegant, with a sharp bite. CATULLUS, the first Roman poet to write epigrams, was secure enough to poke fun at such famous Romans as CICERO and CAESAR. Martial followed Catullus a century later in this same tradition, but his targets tended to be the less powerful people—never the emperor or one of the emperor's favorites.

Martial's early works of epigrams are titled *Liber Spectaculorum* (Book of Public Entertainments), *Xenia* (Gifts), and *Apophoreta* (Party Favors). The *Liber Spectaculorum* was written to celebrate the opening games at the new amphitheater, the COLOSSEUM, built by the emperor Titus. *Xenia* and *Apophoreta* are works of short verses to accompany gifts. His chief work is the *Epigrams,* written in 12 books over a period of 18 years. The *Epigrams* consists of short poems about all aspects of daily life. They provide a vivid picture of the loves and the follies of Roman society in the first century A.D.

Many of Martial's poems are addressed to a person, sometimes to the type of individual he liked to poke fun at—a fortune hunter, a glutton, a drunk, a hypocrite, a lawyer, a barber, an innkeeper, or a surgeon. "Dialus had been a surgeon. Now he is a mortician. He has begun again where he left off." Martial was careful not to use real names in his epigrams, however. His ultimate goal was to attack folly and stupidity as he saw them in humanity in general and to do so in as elegant a way as possible. Martial's vulgar language may offend some modern readers, but as the poet stated: "Prudish reader, quit this book"—his epigrams are not for everyone. He spent his final days in retirement in Spain, and with few regrets. He had been wined and dined in the greatest city in the world, had met everyone he considered worth meeting, and had recorded his observations with biting wit that set a standard that few satirists and epigrammatists in later literature would equal. (*See also* **Poetry, Roman; Rome, History of.**)

# MATHEMATICS, GREEK

* **philosophy** study of ideas, including science

## A ROUND WORLD

The ancient Greeks knew that the world is round. In a work called *On the Heavens,* Aristotle listed reasons to support the idea that the earth is a sphere. For example, he pointed out that the earth's shadow, cast across the face of the moon during lunar eclipses, is clearly the shadow of a round object. Some Greek mathematicians tried to measure the size of the spherical earth. Eratosthenes may have come within a few hundred miles of an accurate measurement, but there is no way to know for sure because he gave his result in *stadia,* units of distance that had at least three different values in the ancient world.

athematics covers a broad range of operations from simple counting to complex theories and calculations. Among other things, it includes algebra, a system of examining the relationships among numbers; and geometry, which deals with shapes, areas, and volumes of space. The Greeks knew about all of these aspects of mathematics. The works of Greek mathematicians are the oldest known writings on mathematical subjects.

The Greeks, however, were not the first people to develop a sophisticated understanding of mathematics. That honor goes to the Egyptians and to the Babylonians, who developed numerical systems early in their history. The Egyptians created the decimal system (the counting system based on 10) and were pioneers of geometry. By about 1700 B.C., the Babylonians had created their own counting system (based on groups of 60) and had surpassed the Egyptians in algebra and basic geometry. Many modern scholars believe that much of the Babylonians' mathematical knowledge made its way to the Greek world, although they do not know exactly when or how it did so.

We know very little about the origins of mathematics among the Greeks. According to ancient Greek historians, mathematics arose as a branch of philosophy* concerned with speculations about the meaning and relationships of numbers and forms. Tradition suggests that two early Greek mathematician-philosophers of the 600s and 500s B.C., THALES OF MILETUS and PYTHAGORAS, were said to have introduced geometry to the Greeks. Neither of them left any writings, however, and modern researchers are unable to determine the extent of their mathematical knowledge, or what and whom they taught. The first person to write a book about mathematics was Hippocrates of Chios, who was active in Athens in the mid-400s B.C. Several generations of mathematicians perpetuated his work. Only fragments of their work have survived, mostly in the form of references in later writings.

Around 300 B.C., EUCLID summarized Greek knowledge of mathematics in a volume called *Elements of Geometry,* which is the oldest surviving mathematical textbook. Euclid's work—and Greece's single greatest contribution to mathematics—was based on the proof. In mathematics, a proof is a series of logical steps that prove, or demonstrate, that a statement is true. The statement to be proven is called an axiom, or premise. Euclid's mathematics, and Greek mathematics in general, introduced deductive reasoning, which became one of the principal Greek contributions to philosophy and science. Deductive reasoning is an orderly system of thought in which each step in a particular proof is firmly based on previously proven conclusions.

Greek mathematicians of the 200s B.C. produced several significant works on mathematics, especially geometry. In the centuries that followed,

Greek thinkers applied Euclid's method of deductive reasoning to various scientific challenges, such as measuring the size of the earth, creating more accurate sundials, and drawing maps that accurately represented the surface of the earth. Scholars such as ARISTOTLE, ARCHIMEDES, ERATOSTHENES, and PTOLEMY applied mathematical principles to astronomy, geography, and practical mechanics.

The works of Greek mathematicians had little influence on the early Christian world. Translated into Arabic, though, they helped fuel a great burst of intellectual activity in the Islamic world after the A.D. 800s. During the Renaissance*, when Europeans "rediscovered" the ancient Greek and Roman civilizations, the works of Euclid and Aristotle formed the basis for mathematical study for many years. (*See also* **Philosophy, Greek and Hellenistic; Science.**)

* **Renaissance** period of the rebirth of interest in classical art, literature, and learning that occurred in Europe from the late 1300s through the 1500s

## MECHANICS

See *Technology.*

## MEDEA

Medea was a character in Greek mythology. According to ancient writers, her name meant "cunning," and she was skilled in witchcraft. All of the stories about Medea portray her as a treacherous schemer who betrayed or murdered even the people closest to her. The Greek poet PINDAR and other Greek writers recorded several versions of her colorful story.

Medea came from a distinguished family. Her grandfather was said to be the sun, and her father was Aeëtes, king of Colchis and owner of a great treasure that was known as the GOLDEN FLEECE. When a handsome Greek warrior named Jason arrived in Colchis to capture the fleece, the gods caused Medea to fall in love with him. She used her magical skills to help Jason steal the fleece and escape. According to one version of the story, she murdered her younger brother and scattered pieces of his body so that her father, stopping to gather them, would be unable to catch her and Jason as they fled. In another version, her brother was older, and Medea helped Jason kill him when he followed them to reclaim the fleece.

Violence also marked the later events in Medea's life. Medea learned that Jason planned to divorce her and marry the young daughter of the king of Corinth. Medea was so jealous that she not only murdered the Corinthian princess with a poisoned wedding dress but also killed her own and Jason's children to punish him. With the help of her grandfather the sun, Medea escaped from Corinth—according to legend, in a chariot drawn through the sky by winged snakes. These events are dramatized in EURIPIDES' tragedy *Medea,* produced in 431 B.C.

Medea later married Aegeus, the king of Athens, and bore him a son, Medus. When Theseus, the king's son by an earlier marriage, arrived in Athens to claim his inheritance, Medea tried to kill him. Medea left Athens with Medus and returned to her homeland of Colchis. The later years of her life are shrouded in mystery, but some accounts say that she and

Medus gained control of Colchis, and that Medus later conquered the region known as Media, part of present-day Iran, and named it after himself.

# MEDICINE, GREEK

The most important contribution of the Greeks to medicine was the introduction of a scientific approach to health, illness, and treatment. Some Greeks, instead of blaming the gods or other supernatural forces for disease, looked to the natural world for explanations of wellness and illness. Greek medical theories influenced Roman thinkers, and Greek and Roman medical theories and practices set the course of Western medicine long after the fall of the Roman Empire.

DOCTORS IN ANCIENT GREECE.   The medical practices of the ancient Greeks were very different from modern practices. For instance, anyone could be a physician, or medical doctor, since there were no medical schools or certification procedures. People generally treated themselves, their family members, and their slaves. They used traditional or folk remedies for everyday illnesses and injuries, such as colds and sprains. For more serious problems, they called in a physician. A physician's training consisted of anything from simply watching another healer at work to studying scientific and philosophical texts about drugs, surgery, and medical theory. Some physicians traveled from place to place, selling their skills along the way. Although some Greek city-states* hired official public physicians, ancient records do not indicate the duties these doctors performed.

* **city-state** independent state consisting of a city and its surrounding territory

Greeks made important contributions to medicine with their scientific approach to illness. They sought explanations from the natural world rather than the supernatural one, a practice that set the stage for later Western medicine. In this relief sculpture, a physician is shown treating a patient.

Greek medicine never consisted of a single theory, approach, or set of treatments. A variety of medical theories always existed, each with its own group of followers. Gradually, however, leading physicians and medical writers came to share certain basic concepts. These concepts formed the basis of the medical knowledge that the Greeks transmitted to the Romans.

**TEMPLE MEDICINE.**   Early Greek ideas about medicine were linked to religious beliefs. Like the Egyptians, the Mesopotamians, and other ancient peoples of the Mediterranean and western Asia, the early Greeks believed that events in the human world were caused by supernatural forces. The gods caused people to become injured and sick, and the deities also cured disease, healed wounds, and restored good health. The treatment of illness involved religious practices such as prayers, sacrifices*, and rituals*. This type of medicine, linked to religious and magical beliefs, is called temple medicine. It remained a powerful force throughout the ancient period, even after the rise of scientific medical theories.

Temple medicine enabled people to ask for help from a variety of gods and goddesses. By the 400s B.C., one of the most popular of the healing gods was ASCLEPIUS, believed to be the son of the god APOLLO. Shrines and TEMPLES devoted to him were scattered throughout the Greek world. One of the largest of these temples was in the Greek city of EPIDAURUS. People seeking help from Asclepius spent the night sleeping in his shrine. They believed that the god would appear to them while they dreamed and tell them how they could be cured. The Greeks used this process, called incubation, to seek advice from many of their gods. In the case of Asclepius, many patients were satisfied with the advice they received. At many shrines, they presented tablets thanking the god for curing them of such conditions as lameness, blindness, baldness, and snakebite.

Shrines and temples to healing gods continued to flourish, even after scientific medical thinking had become well established. Archaeologists have found many stone and clay models of body parts at the sites of Greek and Roman temples. The models were left as tokens of gratitude to the gods who, patients believed, had cured their ailments.

**SCIENTIFIC MEDICINE.**   A new approach to medicine arose in the 400s B.C. Philosophers* and scientists from the Greek city of MILETUS had begun to explain the world in terms other than those of religion, mythology, magic, or superstition. They believed that supernatural forces did not necessarily explain how the natural world works. This belief inspired a later generation of thinkers and physicians to take a similar approach to understanding the human body. Instead of simply asking the gods for a cure, these physicians tried to understand how a healthy body works, so that they could restore a sick body to a state of health.

This scientific approach to medicine is called Hippocratic medicine, named after HIPPOCRATES, a physician who was active around 425 B.C. Ancient writers believed that Hippocrates was the source of a collection of medical texts—numbering about 60—which scholars call the Hippocratic corpus*. Evidence suggests that he may not have actually written any of them and that they were likely the work of his followers.

* **sacrifice** sacred offering made to a god or goddess, usually of an animal such as a sheep or goat

* **ritual** regularly followed routine, especially religious

* **philosopher** scholar or thinker concerned with the study of ideas, including science

* **corpus** the complete works of an author

36

However, the works provide a record of ideas that he introduced into Greek medicine. At the center is the belief that health, illness, and medicine can be understood in natural physical terms, like any other branch of science. The texts in the Hippocratic corpus cover a wide range of subjects, including diet, anatomy\*, surgery, and the medical uses of drugs and herbs. Some works discuss the proper relationships between doctor and patient and the role of the physician in society.

The concept of balance was central to Hippocratic medicine. Hippocratic physicians believed that good health resulted from a balance within the body of different qualities, such as wet and dry or hot and cold. The Hippocratic physicians also believed that disease resulted from an imbalance among the humors, or fluids, of the body. Although they originally disagreed about how many humors existed, the Hippocratic physicians eventually settled on four—blood, phlegm, yellow bile, and black bile. This theory was similar to the one proposed by earlier philosophers, which suggested that the world consisted of four elements—air, water, fire, and earth. Blood became associated with the element of air and the season of spring, phlegm with water and winter, yellow bile with fire and summer, and black bile with earth and autumn. After examining a patient's symptoms, a physician prescribed medications, changes in diet, exercise, or other treatments to bring the humors back into balance.

In the centuries after Hippocrates, physicians continued to spread Hippocratic ideas, and they also extended medical knowledge into new areas. Many physicians and scientists wrote texts on medications, poisons, and medicinal plants. In the 200s and 100s B.C., the city of Alexandria in Egypt, a center for many kinds of learning, produced much new medical activity. Herophilus and Erasistratus, two Greek physicians of the 200s B.C., pioneered the study of anatomy. Most people of the time, including most physicians, believed that dissecting\* human corpses dishonored the dead and was against their religion. Herophilus and Erasistratus moved beyond this belief. They were the first to carry out systematic dissections of human corpses, discovering the existence of the nervous system.

Five hundred years after Hippocrates, another Greek physician became the supreme medical authority of his time. GALEN of PERGAMUM studied in various Greek and Asian cities, later becoming the physician to the imperial\* family in Rome, where he spent the latter part of his life. He wrote many books on medical subjects, combining Hippocratic ideas with the philosophies of PLATO and ARISTOTLE and the insights he had gained from his years of treating patients and studying anatomy. To the Hippocratic theory of the four humors, Galen introduced Plato's idea that each person has three souls—a rational soul in the brain for reason and motion, a choleric soul in the heart for energy, and a vegetative soul in the liver for nutrition. Like the Hippocratic physicians, Galen believed that good health was a result of a balance among forces in the body, and that a physician's job was to restore and help the patient maintain that balance. After A.D. 200, people throughout the Roman Empire turned to Galen's writings as their primary source of medical theory and information. (*See also* **Medicine, Roman.**)

* **anatomy** structure of a living organism and its parts

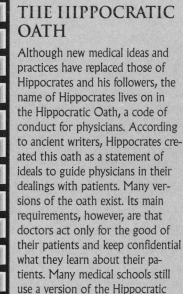

## THE HIPPOCRATIC OATH

Although new medical ideas and practices have replaced those of Hippocrates and his followers, the name of Hippocrates lives on in the Hippocratic Oath, a code of conduct for physicians. According to ancient writers, Hippocrates created this oath as a statement of ideals to guide physicians in their dealings with patients. Many versions of the oath exist. Its main requirements, however, are that doctors act only for the good of their patients and keep confidential what they learn about their patients. Many medical schools still use a version of the Hippocratic Oath in their graduation ceremonies for new doctors.

* **dissect** to cut apart an animal or plant for the purpose of examining its structure

* **imperial** pertaining to an emperor or empire

See color plate 11, vol. 3.

# MEDICINE, ROMAN

* **Roman Republic** Rome during the period from 509 B.C. to 31 B.C., when popular assemblies annually elected their governmental officials

* **sacrifice** sacred offering made to a god or goddess, usually of an animal such as a sheep or goat

* **epidemic** disease that affects a large number of people or animals

* **oratory** art of public speaking

* **rhetoric** art of using words effectively in speaking or writing

* **philosophy** study of ideas, including science

* **aristocrat** person of the highest social class

## THE LONG-LIVED THEORY OF HUMORS

Galen taught that the body had four humors, or vital fluids—a theory he borrowed from the earlier Greek school of Hippocratic medicine. According to this theory, illness resulted from an excess or shortage of one of the humors. This idea persisted for centuries. As late as the A.D. 1890s, physicians and their patients still spoke of imbalances in the humors. In addition, the humors came to be associated with certain personalities or moods. For example, an angry person was thought to have too much blood. Too much black bile, on the other hand, made a person melancholy, or "in a black humor."

The Romans, like other ancient peoples of the Mediterranean, had a long tradition of folk medicine. Throughout much of their history, the Romans healed themselves, needing little help from professional physicians. Beginning in the late Roman Republic*, the Romans adapted many features of Greek scientific medicine. The most influential doctor and medical writer of the Roman Empire, GALEN of PERGAMUM, spent much of his career in Rome.

Much of early Roman medicine was based on the belief that the gods or other supernatural forces caused illnesses and injuries, which could be treated with prayers, chants, the wearing of charms, or by making animal sacrifices* and performing other rituals. Such magical or religious acts, it was believed, won the favor of the gods, who then healed the wound or cured the disease. Folk medicine also used remedies, such as herbs, that had been tested over many generations and often had real medicinal value.

Folk medicine also reflected the rural values that shaped Roman thought, even after Rome had become a large city. Looking fondly back to the sturdy farmers who made up early Roman society, traditional Romans took pride in being able to care for themselves without the help of physicians.

In 293 B.C., when Rome was in the midst of an epidemic*, the Romans began to worship ASCLEPIUS, the Greek god of healing. They built a shrine in his honor, calling him by his Latin name, Aesculapius. After this time, the Romans learned more about Greek medicine and medical practice, although they did not always like what they discovered. According to legend, a Greek doctor named Archagathus of Sparta set up a surgical practice in Rome in 219 B.C. Because he was such a bad surgeon, Archagathus soon earned the nickname *carnifex,* or butcher. Asclepiades, a physician who arrived in Rome a century later, made a better impression. He prescribed mild remedies and very little surgery. Asclepiades' approach to treatment appealed to the Romans in the first century B.C., when a Greek philosophy known as Epicureanism was popular in Rome. (The Epicureans asserted that people should strive for tranquility in their lives and should not fear the gods, who, they believed, took no interest in human affairs.)

By the early Roman Empire, the topics of a traditional Roman education—war, law, agriculture, and politics—were expanded to include other fields influenced by Greek learning—oratory*, rhetoric*, philosophy*, architecture and art, and medicine. Cornelius Celsus, writing in A.D. 14–37, compiled an encyclopedia of these topics, and the section on medicine has survived. Although Celsus was a Roman aristocrat*, he nursed slaves as well as members of his own family back to health in a *valetudinarium,* or sick bay, a special room set aside for medical treatment. He called in a physician only when an illness or injury exceeded his skills. Celsus's work indicates that he had direct experience performing surgical procedures, while his discussion of drugs and medications is largely borrowed from Greek sources. The Roman writer PLINY THE ELDER used Celsus as a source of information when he composed his *Natural History,* a 37-volume work on science and other topics.

Many of the physicians working in Rome were Greeks or Greek-speaking Asians. Their ideas were rooted in Greek medicine, especially in the writings

Although early Roman medicine tended to rely on the supernatural, the Romans eventually learned from the Greeks to adopt more scientific practices. Here is a collection of ancient surgical tools, some of which actually bear a remarkable resemblance to today's equipment.

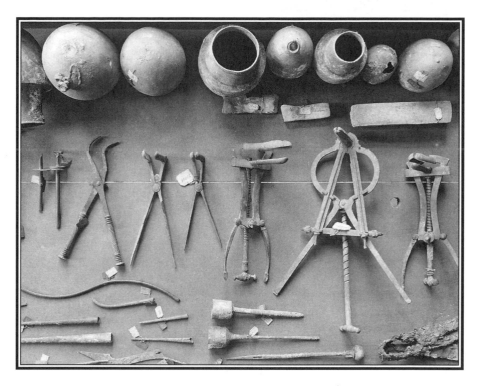

\* **dissect**  to cut apart an animal or plant for the purpose of examining its structure

of the Hippocratic school. These works were based on the teaching of a Greek physician named HIPPOCRATES, who claimed that illnesses had natural causes, not supernatural ones. There were many different versions of Hippocratic medicine, however. Differences in philosophical or scientific theories gave rise to rival branches of medicine. At the same time, folk medicine was still used, and throughout the Roman empire, people continued to visit temples, wear charms, perform rituals, and pray to the gods for cures.

The physician Galen, educated in Greece, Egypt, and western Asia, arrived in Rome around A.D. 162. He had friends and patients in aristocratic circles, and he soon became the personal physician of the emperor and his family. However, Galen's importance in the history of medicine lies not in his own practice but in the dozens of books he wrote on a wide range of medical topics. In his book *On Anatomical Procedures,* for example, Galen discussed the dissecting\* technique that he had perfected on apes and compared the bodies of these apes with human bodies. One of his works discusses the place of the physician in Roman society; another is a storehouse of information about Hippocrates and other early Greek physicians; and a third is a handbook on wellness, or how to stay healthy. Galen adopted the Hippocratic concept that the body contains four humors, or fluids—blood, phlegm, yellow bile, and black bile. He added to this Plato's concept of three souls, with one soul responsible for thought and motion, another one for energy, and the third for digestion. According to Galen, good health was a state of balance among the humors, the souls, and other elements that gave the human body life.

Although Galen had no students, by the A.D. 300s scholars had organized his writings into a system that physicians and philosophers continued to study and follow for hundreds of years. The teachings of the

Hippocratic physicians and the writings of Galen dominated Western medical thought for the next 1,500 years. (*See also* **Medicine, Greek; Philosophy, Greek and Hellenistic; Philosophy, Roman.**)

# MEDITERRANEAN SEA

See map in Geography and Geology, Mediterranean (vol. 2).

## ACROSS THE MEDITERRANEAN

Travel across the Mediterranean was slow in ancient times. The prevailing winds, blowing from north to south, made travel in that direction the quickest. The voyage from Neapolis (Naples) to Alexandria on the coast of Egypt—about 1,000 nautical miles—took about nine days. The return trip might have taken as long as two months. On the return trip, ships had to sail all around the Mediterranean coast in search of a wind strong enough to fill their sails.

---

\* **galley** large, open ship, propelled chiefly by oars, that was used for war and commerce throughout the ancient Mediterranean; Roman galleys also used sails

The Mediterranean Sea is the most significant geographical feature of southern Europe, the region that includes present-day ITALY, SPAIN, and France. Greece, Turkey, and the other nations of the Balkans, the Middle East, and North AFRICA all have borders on or near the Mediterranean Sea. The ancient civilizations of Greece and Rome developed around the Mediterranean Sea. The ancient Romans were so proud and possessive of this body of water that they called it *mare nostrum,* which means "our sea."

The Mediterranean Sea covers an area of about 970,000 square miles. Almost completely surrounded by land, it is an inland sea. It extends for about 2,232 miles eastward from the Strait of Gibraltar (separating Spain and Morocco) to the Levantine coast (present-day Syria, Lebanon, Israel, and the Sinai Peninsula). It reaches 680 miles from the northern end of the Adriatic Sea—an arm of the Mediterranean—to the coast of Libya in northern Africa. The average depth of the Mediterranean is about 4,920 feet.

The Mediterranean Sea is divided by the Strait of Sicily into western and eastern basins, or depressions in the earth's surface that are filled by the ocean. These basins are dotted with numerous islands. The largest island in the Mediterranean is SICILY, which is located off the boot tip of the Italian peninsula. The major islands in the western basin are Sardinia, Corsica, and Majorca. Islands in the eastern basin include CYPRUS and CRETE, as well as the smaller island of Malta. The AEGEAN SEA, an eastern arm of the Mediterranean, contains hundreds of islands, the largest of which are Lesbos, RHODES, Chios, and Samos.

Water from the Atlantic Ocean flows into the Mediterranean Sea through the Strait of Gibraltar. The Nile River, the longest in the world, flows through Egypt into the Mediterranean from its headwaters in Africa. The Ebro River (in Spain) and the Rhône (in France) also flow into the Mediterranean Sea. In Italy, both the TIBER RIVER, which goes through Rome, and the Arno flow into the Mediterranean Sea.

The numerous inlets and bays of the Mediterranean coastline led to the development of transport and trade from earliest times. Both the Greeks and Romans used the Mediterranean Sea as a waterway for the shipment of grain, wine, olive oil, and other products. Early ship captains learned how to sail their galleys\* through the sea's unpredictable and often stormy waters. They raised their square sails when winds blew fair. Greek and Roman shippers tried to limit their activity to the period from late spring to early fall, when the weather was most settled and seas were generally calm. Shipping did not stop in the winter, however; it only slowed down.

The main purpose of Mediterranean shipping in ancient times was to transport cargo, not passengers. Ancient cargoes included fish sauce, olives, nuts, and honey, in addition to sacks of grain and jugs of wine and olive oil. Stone was the most difficult cargo to handle. It had to be moved by means of

* **quarry** open pit from which stone is removed

wagons, rollers, and ramps from quarries* in Africa and elsewhere to barges and then onto ships. Clay jars containing wine and oil also presented problems to ancient shippers. The fragile jars—standing more than three feet tall and weighing about 50 pounds each—could be broken during loading and unloading or from being tossed about during a storm. HARBORS dotted the Mediterranean coastline. Among the busiest and most famous of these were DELOS in Greece, ALEXANDRIA in Egypt, and OSTIA near Rome.

The numerous ships going across and around the Mediterranean Sea were easy prey for pirates. PIRACY began as another way for poor people in coastal villages to make a living, but it soon developed into a full-scale industry. Pirates were aided by the many coves and out-of-the-way bays of the Mediterranean that were ideal for hiding out and preparing for ambush. Throughout the ancient world, piracy was regularly supressed by various governments. The most famous enemies of pirates were the Romans. Such leaders as Julius CAESAR and POMPEY made names for themselves by successfully eliminating this scourge of the sea. (*See also* **Quarries; Ships and Shipbuilding; Trade, Greek; Trade, Roman.**)

# MEDUSA

### MYTHOLOGICAL MONSTER

* **hero** in mythology, a person of great strength or ability, often descended from a god

* **mortal** human being; one who eventually will die

In early Greek mythology, Medusa was one of three monstrous sisters called the Gorgons. She is sometimes called Gorgo. The Gorgons were so hideous that one glimpse of them turned a person to stone, although according to some versions of the myth, only Medusa was this ugly.

The Greek hero* Perseus was ordered to kill Medusa, who was the only one of the three sisters who was mortal*. The goddess ATHENA and the god HERMES prepared Perseus for his attack by giving him a pair of winged sandals, a helmet of invisibility, and a special blade with which to behead the Gorgon. By gazing at Medusa's reflection in his bright shield, Perseus successfully obtained her head and escaped from her angry sisters. He

A she-monster with a face that could turn a person to stone, Medusa was a central character in the Perseus and Andromeda myth. In addition to her ferocious ugliness, she is most commonly depicted with snakes for hair.

then used the head to turn one of his enemies to stone. Perseus gave Medusa's head to Athena, who mounted it in the center of her shield, where it appears in many sculptures and paintings of the goddess.

Medusa was the lover of POSEIDON, the sea god, and was pregnant when Perseus cut off her head. PEGASUS, the winged horse of Greek legend, arose either from Medusa's head or from one of the drops of blood that fell from her body.

Early Greek art depicted Medusa with snakes for hair, the fangs of a wild boar, and a ferocious grin. Around the 400s B.C., the image of the Gorgons began to change. No longer were they said to be hideous, but rather they were portrayed as beautiful women. (*See also* **Myths, Greek.**)

See color plate 9, vol. 3.

# MENANDER

ca. 342–ca. 291 B.C.
GREEK PLAYWRIGHT

* **philosophy** study of ideas, including science

Menander was one of the leading Greek comic playwrights of his time. His work was a model for Roman playwrights, who imitated his comedies. These Roman comedies, in turn, influenced later European writers, including William Shakespeare. Menander's comic tradition is alive today. Many of the situations and characters in modern television and movie comedies can be traced back to situations and characters in Menander's plays.

Little is known about Menander's life. He was born into a distinguished family in Athens and studied philosophy*. He began writing at an early age. Like other playwrights of his time, he wrote plays for the dramatic competitions that were part of regular festivals in ATHENS and elsewhere in Greece. Menander produced his first play when he was about 20 years old, and it won first prize. Over the next 30 years he wrote another 107 plays. According to tradition, Menander drowned while swimming at Piraeus, the port of Athens.

Sadly, Menander's huge literary output did not survive into modern times. The texts of his plays were lost, and only two sources of information about his work remained. One source was the imitations of Menander's plays by the Roman comic playwrights PLAUTUS and TERENCE. The other source consists of the 900 references to Menander in ancient Greek and Roman texts. Some of these references include quotations from Menander's plays, but no quotation is longer than 16 lines.

* **archaeologist** scientist who studies past human cultures, usually by excavating ruins

* **papyrus** writing material made by pressing together thin strips of the inner stem of the papyrus plant

It was thought that Menander's work would remain forever unknown to the modern world. Beginning in the early A.D. 1900s, however, archaeologists* found scraps of Menander's plays on pieces of papyrus*. Scholars have now recovered large portions of six plays and smaller parts of a dozen more. Their most valuable find is a complete play called *Dyskolos,* which means "The Grouch" or "The Bad-Tempered Man." It is the story of a city boy who falls in love with a country girl, the daughter of a cranky old man who distrusts everybody and talks to no one. After misunderstandings and mishaps involving family members and servants, the young man saves the life of the old grouch, who then gives the boy permission to marry his daughter. The play ends with a double wedding, and the clever servants even force the old man to join the wedding feast.

*Dyskolos* provides an example of the themes that Menander used in many of his plays: conflict between city and country ways of life, mistrust between rich and poor people, the importance of chance and good luck, and the triumph of love and family ties over difficult circumstances. Focusing on these themes, Menander helped create a style of Greek drama that is called New Comedy. Earlier Greek comedies, such as the plays of ARISTOPHANES, were filled with social or political satire. These plays, called Old Comedy, often had fantastic settings and plots. New Comedy, on the other hand, was concerned with private family life and was set in the everyday world. Characters did not travel to the heavens or the underworld*, as in Old Comedy, but remained firmly planted on earth, generally in their own neighborhoods. New Comedy was meant to entertain its audience, but the plays of Menander and other New Comedy writers also had a moral message. In these plays, selfishness and deceit were punished, while generosity, tolerance, and good humor were rewarded.

Another feature of New Comedy was the stock character. This was a character who would be instantly recognized by the audience because he or she had certain predictable traits. Among the stock characters that Menander used were the boastful soldier, the servant who outsmarts the master, the miser, and the innocent young lovers. Although he used familiar stock characters, Menander gave them original twists. For example, instead of boasting about his military adventures, a soldier brags about his girlfriend's wardrobe. Menander gave full and distinctive personalities to his characters—even to servants and women, whom other playwrights generally ignored. Menander's insight into human nature won him high praise in the ancient world, and his plays remained popular long after his death. In the A.D. 100s, the Greek biographer PLUTARCH wrote, "For what other reason, truly, would an educated man go to the theater, except to see a play by Menander?" (*See also* **Drama, Greek; Drama, Roman.**)

* **underworld** kingdom of the dead; also called Hades

---

## MERCURY

See *Hermes.*

---

## METAMORPHOSES

See *Apuleius; Ovid.*

---

## MIDAS

LEGENDARY KING

According to Greek legend, Midas was a king of Phrygia, a kingdom in central ASIA MINOR (present-day Turkey). The Greeks told several stories about Midas, and in them he appeared rather foolish. The most familiar tale, that of his golden touch, illustrates the motto "Be careful what you wish for."

According to this story, Midas captured Silenus, a companion of the god DIONYSUS, either by getting Silenus drunk or by luring him into a magnificent rose garden. Midas later released Silenus. In gratitude for Silenus's freedom, Dionysus granted Midas a wish. The king immediately wished that everything he touched would turn to gold. Midas's excitement over his new ability was short-lived, however, when he discovered that he could neither eat nor drink—everything he tried to consume turned to gold. To rid himself of the golden touch, Midas bathed in a magical river. From that day forward, that river's sands contained gold dust.

Midas had a second unfortunate encounter with the gods when he judged a music contest between APOLLO and PAN. The king declared Pan the better musician. This outraged Apollo—who was, among other things, the god of music—and the angry god replaced Midas's ears with the ears of a donkey. The embarrassed Midas wore a turban to cover his disgraceful ears, and only his barber knew about them. Desperate to tell the secret, the barber finally whispered it into a hole in the ground. But reeds grew over the hole, and whenever the wind blew, the reeds whispered the king's secret: "Midas has donkey's ears."

A real king named Midas or Mita ruled Phrygia in the late 700s B.C. Greek storytellers may have attached his name to their comic tales. The stories of Midas lived on for centuries, and OVID, a poet of the early Roman Empire, retold them in his book *Metamorphoses.* (*See also* **Gold; Myths, Greek.**)

## MIGRATIONS, EARLY GREEK

* **dialect** form of speech characteristic of a region that differs from the standard language in pronunciation, vocabulary, and grammar

* **classical** in Greek history, refers to the period of great political and cultural achievement from about 500 B.C. to 323 B.C.

* **archaeological** referring to the study of past human cultures, usually by excavating ruins

* **artifact** ornament, tool, weapon, or other object made by humans

The first Greek-speaking people migrated to Greece as early as 2000 B.C. Eventually, their culture spread throughout the country, their language evolving into several different dialects*. During the 1100s B.C., more migrations occurred, as the DORIANS, a people from northern Greece, moved into the southern part of the country. Later still, the Dorians and other Greeks migrated from the Greek mainland across the AEGEAN SEA. Some of these migrants settled on the Aegean islands, and others started settlements on the coast of ASIA MINOR.

Evidence for early Greek migrations comes from several sources. Among these sources are the writings of Greek historians and classical* authors, many of which were based largely on oral traditions. Archaeological* artifacts* sometimes reveal material traces of the arrival of migrants in an area. INSCRIPTIONS may also provide evidence for migrations by showing the introduction of a new language or dialect in a given area. Since evidence gathered from the different sources does not always agree, the details of early Greek migrations are still unclear. As new evidence comes to light, scholars adjust their interpretations of these migrations as well.

THE FIRST GREEK MIGRANTS.   Scholars believe that Greek-speaking people first moved into the region no later than the 1400s B.C., and perhaps as early as 2000 B.C. The earliest date is based on the appearance of new styles of pottery probably introduced by Greek-speaking migrants from the north. A change in burial customs around 1700 B.C. has also been interpreted as evidence of the arrival of Greek migrants. Inscriptions in an early Greek form of writing, called Linear B, have been found on clay tablets in CRETE, and these tablets have been dated to about 1400 B.C. This is now believed to be the latest possible date for the appearance of Greek speakers in both Crete and mainland Greece.

Regardless of when Greek-speaking people first arrived in Greece, by the 1200s B.C. most people spoke Greek, thought of themselves as Greek, and shared a common Greek culture. By the 1200s B.C., the region in southern Greece around the ancient city of MYCENAE had reached an especially high level of cultural development. In fact, the Mycenaeans might have eventually controlled all of Greece under one centralized government had it not been for the migration into southern Greece of the Dorians near the end of the 1100s B.C.

THE DORIANS.   The Dorians are believed to have come from the Doris region of central Greece, although they may have originated from farther north. The Dorians spoke a dialect of Greek called Doric, and they probably herded livestock for a living. The Dorian migration into southern Greece in the 1100s B.C. is associated with the decline of Mycenaean civilization and a shift from centralized government to the independent city-state*.

The archaeological record indicates that many of the main settlements in southern Greece, including Mycenae itself, were destroyed during the 1200s B.C. After this destruction, most of the settlements were rebuilt, some with increased fortifications. A second phase of destruction occurred in the 1100s B.C. This time the earlier settlements were abandoned and replaced by new ones. Cultural changes and a decline in the standard of living followed this second phase of destruction.

* **city-state** independent state consisting of a city and its surrounding territory

Over thousands of years, the active migration and colonization of diverse groups of people contributed to a rich and varied civilization in Greece.

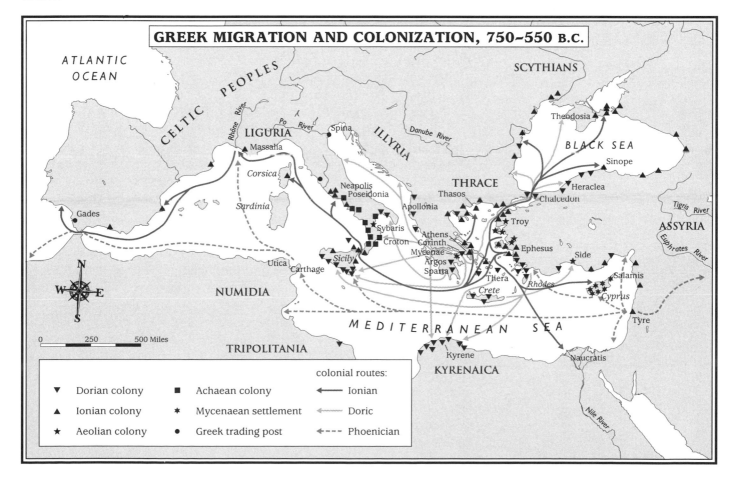

**GREEK MIGRATION AND COLONIZATION, 750–550 B.C.**

ATLANTIC OCEAN

CELTIC PEOPLES

SCYTHIANS

Rhône River

LIGURIA

Po River

Spina

ILLYRIA

Danube River

Theodosia

BLACK SEA

Massalia

THRACE

Corsica

Neapolis
Poseidonia

Thasos

Sinope

Heraclea

Chalcedon

Sardinia

Apollonia

Troy

Tigris River

Gades

Sybaris

Athens

Ephesus

ASSYRIA

Croton

Corinth
Mycenae

Side

Euphrates River

Sicily

Argos
Sparta

Salamis

Utica

Carthage

Thera

Rhodes

Cyprus

NUMIDIA

Crete

Tyre

N W E S

MEDITERRANEAN  SEA

0    250    500 Miles

TRIPOLITANIA

Kyrene

Naucratis

KYRENAICA

Nile River

colonial routes:

▼ Dorian colony      ■ Achaean colony      ← Ionian

▲ Ionian colony      ✶ Mycenaean settlement      Doric

★ Aeolian colony      ● Greek trading post      ◄--- Phoenician

## HERACLES AND THE DORIAN INVASION

According to Greek tradition, the Dorian migration was a military invasion led by descendants of Heracles, the Greek hero known for his great strength. When Heracles died, his sons were exiled from the city of Mycenae, and they took refuge with the Dorian people in northern Greece. Hyllos, one of the sons, became king of a Dorian tribe. Hyllos's grandsons led a Dorian invasion to regain control of Mycenae and win lands for their followers. Whether or not the story is true, it is clear that the Dorians became established throughout southern Greece around that time, and soon afterward settled throughout the Mediterranean.

Scholars are uncertain whether the Dorian migrants invaded and conquered southern Greece in the 1100s B.C., or whether they were able to absorb the Mycenaean civilization because it was already declining for other reasons. Early Greek historians apparently believed the traditional accounts that the Dorian migration was a military invasion, perhaps led by descendants of the hero HERACLES. The historians HERODOTUS and THUCYDIDES wrote more realistic accounts of a Dorian invasion of southern Greece, and Thucydides gave the date of the invasion as 1120 B.C.

While archaeologists believe that Mycenaean civilization was torn apart by violence during the last decades of the 1200s B.C. and fell into total decline toward the end of the 1100s B.C., nothing links this destruction to Dorians invading and conquering southern Greece. Even if the collapse of Mycenaean civilization was a result of other causes, Dorian migrants apparently took advantage of it. By the end of the 1100s B.C., they had moved into the area in large numbers. The development of the city-state form of government accompanied the settlement of Dorians in the area. The Dorians had small, tightly knit tribal groups in which each individual played a role. This sense of group identity contributed to the development of the early city-state.

Although all of the migrants who moved into southern Greece during the 1100s B.C. were probably not Dorians, the Dorians were likely the first to arrive, and they probably arrived in larger numbers than the rest. As a result, their name came to be associated with the migrants as a whole.

LATER MIGRATIONS. Following the Dorian migration—or invasion—other migrations occurred in Greece. These migrations involved groups of people leaving Greece to establish new settlements elsewhere. Most of the settlements later developed into city-states, as had the earlier Dorian settlements in southern Greece.

Soon after the Dorians moved into southern Greece, some of them left mainland Greece to settle on the islands of the Aegean Sea. Herodotus wrote that this occurred during the same generation that the Dorians arrived in southern Greece, perhaps as early as 1115 B.C. These Dorian migrations are also documented by archaeological evidence. By 1000 B.C., Dorian settlements appeared on the western coast of Asia Minor. These settlements have been identified from their pottery. In addition, Dorians apparently settled on the island of RHODES in the Aegean Sea and on the island of Crete in the Mediterranean, probably sometime during the 900s B.C.

By 1000 B.C., Greece had five different regional dialects. In addition to Doric, these included Aeolic, Ionic, Arcado-Cyprian, and Northwest Greek. Although scholars once believed that different waves of migrations into Greece from the north explained the existence of these different dialects, the dialects likely evolved after the first Greek speakers arrived. Each dialect was associated with a specific geographic region. Aeolic was spoken in the eastern part of Greece, and Ionic was the dialect in and around Athens. The various dialects were similar but distinctive. A person speaking the Aeolic dialect would be understood by a person speaking the Ionic dialect. Yet, each would be recognized as coming from a different region by variations in speech and vocabulary. Similarly, people today in the United States and Great Britain speak different dialects of modern English.

According to Greek tradition, from about the 700s B.C. onward Greeks speaking these dialects migrated from Greece, probably because of pressure from tribes from northern Greece. They traveled across the Aegean Sea to settle on the Aegean islands and along the western coast of Asia Minor, as the Dorians had a few centuries earlier. Aeolic speakers from eastern Greece settled near TROY on the western coast of Asia Minor and Ionic speakers in nearby Smyrna. The nature of the Greek dialects spoken in these and other places by the 400s B.C. corresponds to this pattern of migration. (*See also* **Archaeology of Ancient Sites; Colonies, Greek; Ionians; Languages and Dialects; Peoples of Ancient Greece and Rome.**)

# MIGRATIONS, LATE ROMAN

* **barbarian** referring to people from outside the cultures of Greece and Rome, who were viewed as uncivilized

* **imperial** pertaining to an emperor or empire

* **nomadic** referring to people who wander from place to place to find food and pasture

* **subsidy** financial aid given to a person or group by a government

## BRITAIN AND THE BARBARIAN MIGRATIONS

Although Britain was not invaded by the Vandals, it did have its share of barbarian invasions. Beginning in the A.D. 300s, the Roman province of Britain was repeatedly invaded by migrating barbarian tribes—Angles from present-day Denmark, Saxons from Germany, and Picts and Scots from the northern British Isles. After Roman imperial power collapsed in Britain in A.D. 409, the country was ruled by tyrants from barbarian tribes. Many of the Britons who survived these attacks migrated to northwestern Gaul. This part of France is still called Brittany.

An "age of migrations" began in A.D. 376 when a barbarian* tribe called the HUNS chased the German-speaking VISIGOTHS to the northern frontier of the Roman Empire. The Visigoths and other Germanic tribes had repeatedly attempted to cross the northern imperial* border, but each time the Romans had driven them back. This time, with the Huns in pursuit, the Romans allowed the Visigoths to escape across the frontier into the empire.

Admitting the Visigoths was a turning point in the Western Roman Empire. It marked the beginning of three great phases of barbarian migration across Europe. Within 200 years, German tribes established kingdoms in every part of the western empire and helped bring about its collapse. These migrations also resulted in a blending of the Germanic cultures with that of the Romans, which included the adoption of CHRISTIANITY by the barbarians.

FIRST PHASE OF MIGRATIONS. No one knows for certain who the Huns were or where they came from, except that they were nomadic* herders who practically lived on horseback. (They were even rumored to sleep on their horses.) The Huns moved westward from east of the Black Sea in the A.D. 300s, overthrowing tribal kingdoms as they went. The Huns overran the OSTROGOTHS in the Ukraine and then pushed the Visigoths to the edge of the Roman frontier.

The Romans accepted the Visigoths into the empire because they hoped they would fight for the Roman army. However, Roman officers treated the Visigoths very badly, and the Visigoths rebelled. The Visigoths defeated the army of the Eastern Roman Empire, which gave them some leverage within the Roman government. When THEODOSIUS came to power in A.D. 379, he gave some imperial lands and annual subsidies* to the Visigoths in return for their help in defending the empire against the Huns. This was the first time in Roman history that an entire barbarian tribe had been allowed to settle within the empire while remaining under the control of its own leaders. Furthermore, the Visigoths were not subject to Roman law. But the Romans were unable to control the Visigoths, and the empire was soon overrun by other invading tribes.

When Theodosius died in A.D. 395, the Roman government stopped paying subsidies to the Visigoths. Under their leader, Alaric I, the Visigoths attacked the Romans and occupied the city of Rome in A.D. 410.

47

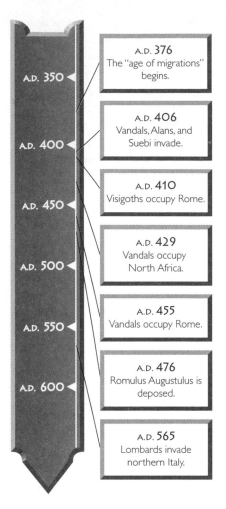

A.D. 350

A.D. 400

A.D. 450

A.D. 500

A.D. 550

A.D. 600

**A.D. 376**
The "age of migrations" begins.

**A.D. 406**
Vandals, Alans, and Suebi invade.

**A.D. 410**
Visigoths occupy Rome.

**A.D. 429**
Vandals occupy North Africa.

**A.D. 455**
Vandals occupy Rome.

**A.D. 476**
Romulus Augustulus is deposed.

**A.D. 565**
Lombards invade northern Italy.

* **booty** riches or property gained through conquest

* **pyre** pile of wood used to burn a dead body

They carried off booty* but spared the treasure at St. Peter's Basilica, as well as the lives of any who sought refuge in a Christian church. (The Visigoths were themselves Christian.) Although the Visigoths managed to hold Rome for only a few days, this marked the first time the city had fallen to a foreign enemy in 800 years. Finally, in A.D. 418, the Roman government agreed to give the Visigoths their own kingdom on the southwestern coast of GAUL.

Once settled in Gaul, the Visigoths became federates of the Roman Empire. This meant that they had their own laws and courts, leaders, and churches, but they had no control over Roman citizens in the region. The Visigoths quickly expanded their kingdom, and by the end of the A.D. 400s, they had pushed into Spain. In A.D. 507, the Visigothic kingdom in Gaul was overthrown by the Franks, who gained control of almost all of Gaul. The Visigoths continued to live in Spain until the early A.D. 700s, when they were defeated by Moors and Arabs from North Africa.

THE SECOND PHASE OF MIGRATIONS. The second phase of migrations began in A.D. 406 when the VANDALS and their allies, the Alans and the Suebi, broke through the northern imperial frontier and entered Gaul. Like the Visigoths, the Vandals and the Suebi were Germanic tribes who fought on foot. The Alans, like the Huns, were nomadic herders who fought on horseback. Like the Visigoths before them, the three tribes may have been pushed to the Roman frontier by the Huns.

Once they crossed the imperial frontier, the Vandals and their allies turned northwest toward the Strait of Dover that separates BRITAIN from the rest of Europe. Fearing that the Vandals were about to invade, the people of Britain panicked. They declared their leader an emperor, and with a large fighting force crossed the strait into France. The Vandals and their allies, perhaps never intending to attack Britain in the first place, fled to the southwest.

The Vandals moved toward the Pyrenees Mountains instead, causing much damage as they went. One writer at the time described Gaul as a vast funeral pyre*. The Vandals and their allies destroyed almost everything they encountered as they cut a huge path across the middle of Gaul. (The modern word *vandalism* is derived from their name.) In A.D. 409, the Vandals crossed into Spain.

Less than a decade after they entered Spain, the Alans were overrun by the Visigoths, who were acting on behalf of Rome. The Suebi established a kingdom in Spain, which was overrun by the Visigoths in A.D. 585. The Vandals settled in western Spain and then crossed the Strait of Gibraltar into Africa in A.D. 429. Once there, they marched eastward and captured what is now Tunisia, which was Rome's prime source of grain and oil.

The occupation of North Africa contributed significantly to the fall of the Western Roman Empire. The occupation deprived Rome of its main food supply, and it also challenged Rome's control of the central Mediterranean region. In A.D. 439, the Vandals captured CARTHAGE, the city of the empire that was second in importance only to Rome. The Vandals began a long series of sea raids on the central Mediterranean coast. They occupied the city of Rome for two weeks in A.D. 455, the second time in less than half a century that the great city had fallen to a foreign enemy.

The Vandals also interrupted the flow of grain from EGYPT to CONSTANTINOPLE. The Eastern Roman Empire tried, without success, to drive the Vandals out of Africa. In A.D. 468, the eastern empire launched a huge expedition from Constantinople that nearly emptied its treasury, but it also ended in failure. It was not until A.D. 534, after a brilliant campaign led by the general Belisarius, that the Eastern Roman Empire was able to overthrow the Vandal kingdom in Africa.

THIRD PHASE OF MIGRATIONS.    A third major invasion of Germanic tribes began in A.D. 455. This time it was primarily the Ostrogoths who threatened the security of the Eastern Roman Empire. The Ostrogoths had been overrun and oppressed by the Huns since the A.D. 300s, and the Roman government had allowed them to settle on imperial lands. However, the Ostrogoths wanted more land and government subsidies as well. In A.D. 476, the Roman army, which was composed almost entirely of barbarians, rebelled and deposed* the last Roman emperor in the West, Romulus Augustulus. They replaced him with Odoacer, an Ostrogoth leader. Odoacer's rule was peaceful, until the Ostrogoths attacked northern Italy. Theodoric, the

* **depose** to remove from high office

---

The movement of various barbarian tribes into the Roman empire contributed to a blending of cultures. The migrations were often the result of wars, invasions, and expansions that forced people to leave their homelands and settle in foreign places.

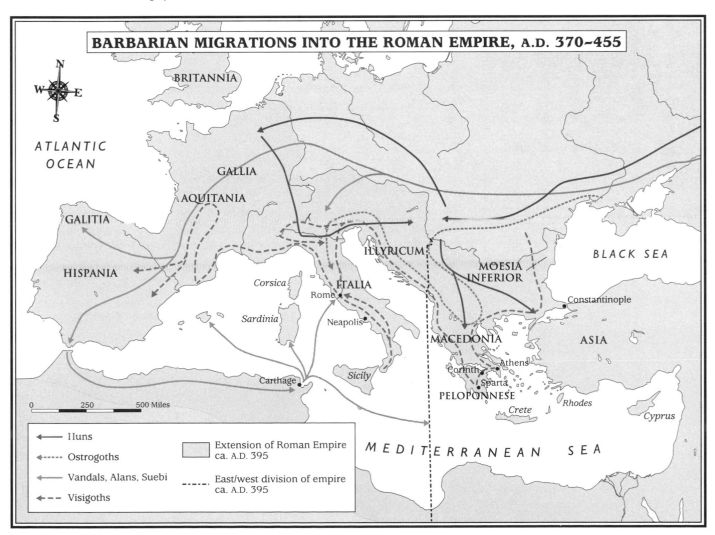

**BARBARIAN MIGRATIONS INTO THE ROMAN EMPIRE, A.D. 370–455**

Huns
Ostrogoths
Vandals, Alans, Suebi
Visigoths

Extension of Roman Empire ca. A.D. 395
East/west division of empire ca. A.D. 395

king of the Ostrogoths, killed Odoacer with his own hands in A.D. 493. Theodoric's reign was an era of peace and prosperity for Italy. However, when Theodoric died in A.D. 526, relations between the Ostrogoths and the Romans broke down, and hostilities were renewed.

In A.D. 536, Belisarius, after conquering the Vandals in Africa, fought the Ostrogoths in Italy. This devastating war nearly eliminated the Ostrogoths. There was incredible destruction of life and property, and for a while, Rome was almost uninhabited for the first time in more than a thousand years. At the end of the war, JUSTINIAN I, the great Roman emperor in the East, made Italy part of his domain.

In A.D. 565, the Lombards, a final group of Germanic invaders, entered Italy. They pushed down from central Europe and attacked the Romans, who were unable to prevent them from settling in the northern part of the country. The Lombardy region of northern Italy takes its name from this last group of migrants. (*See also* **Armies, Roman; Germans; Wars and Warfare, Roman.**)

## MILETUS

**M**iletus was a leading Greek city of ASIA MINOR (present-day Turkey). It was located on the west coast of the Anatolian peninsula, near the mouth of the Maeander River. The city's fame came from its busy harbor and extensive trade. Milesians (the people of Miletus) founded trading colonies in EGYPT and ITALY and along the shores of the Black Sea. The city was also home to such great thinkers as THALES and ANAXIMANDER.

Miletus was founded by IONIANS, early Greeks who had migrated from the Greek mainland to Asia Minor around 1000 B.C. Miletus was one of 12 such cities founded by mainland Greeks. Other settlements included EPHESUS and the island of SAMOS. Miletus's fleet and trade rivaled those of Lydia, a kingdom in western Asia Minor. By 546 B.C. Miletus and other Greek cities in Asia Minor were under the rule of the Persians. In 499 B.C. the Milesians led an unsuccessful revolt against the Persians, in which their city was destroyed. About 20 years later, Miletus joined Athens in the Delian League against the Persians.

Displeasure at Athenian control of the league prompted Milesians to revolt against Athens in 412 B.C., during the PELOPONNESIAN WAR. Miletus had a brief alliance with SPARTA, which ended when the Persians took possession of Miletus in 386 B.C. Persian rule ended in 334 B.C., when Miletus was captured and then liberated by ALEXANDER THE GREAT. Following the death of Alexander in 323 B.C., Miletus came under the influence of the PTOLEMAIC DYNASTY of Egypt and the SELEUCID DYNASTY of Syria. Both dynasties tried to annex* the city to their own empires.

Miletus became part of the Roman empire in 129 B.C., and its importance diminished. The harbors became clogged with silt*, leaving the city several miles from the sea. Attacks by barbarian* Gothic tribes in the A.D. 300s further weakened the city's importance. (*See also* **Cities, Greek; Greece, History of; Trade, Greek.**)

* **annex** to add a territory to an existing state

* **silt** fine particles of earth and sand carried by moving water

* **barbarian** referring to people from outside the cultures of Greece and Rome, who were viewed as uncivilized

# MILITARY ENGINEERING

Military engineering is the process of designing and building war machinery. It also includes developing the means to transport these war machines and to communicate between military sites. Inventors and engineers in ancient Greece and Rome created several impressive war machines. Sometimes, they improved on earlier devices, but they also invented new devices to solve particular problems encountered during wartime.

Much of ancient military technology involved producing devices to attack the defenses of a city during a siege*. The Greek historian THUCYDIDES described one clever invention. In 424 B.C., the Boeotians mounted a siege against the city of Delium. The defenders of Delium had strengthened part of their city wall with wood. To attack this section of the wall, the Boeotians created a device that may have been the first flamethrower. They sawed a long pole in half lengthwise, cut a groove along each half, and then put the halves back together to form a long hollow pipe. From one end of the pipe they hung a kettle. They mounted the other end of the pipe on wagons and attached a leather bellows* to it. They then wheeled the pipe to the wooden section of the wall, poured burning charcoal and tar into the kettle, and worked the bellows. The blast of air from the bellows produced a great wall of flame that drove the defenders back and destroyed part of their defenses.

Besieging forces also used movable, fortified towers equipped with battering rams and other weapons to break down a city's walls. In the late 300s B.C., a visiting engineer named Kallias told the people of RHODES that he could defend the city with a crane that could lift off the ground any attacking siege tower, rendering the tower useless. The Rhodians were so impressed that they fired their military engineer, Diognetos, and hired Kallias.

This detail from Trajan's Column depicts ancient soldiers building fortifications. In wartime, towers were fortified not just for defense but also for offense. Battering rams and weapons were often incorporated into these sturdy structures.

See
color plate 9,
vol. 2.

Soon, an enemy attacked Rhodes with a 160-ton siege tower that was 125 feet high and 60 feet wide. Only then did Kallias inform the dismayed Rhodians that he could not build a crane to handle this monstrous tower. The Rhodians begged Diognetos for help, and he came up with a simple but effective scheme. Working secretly at night, he made holes in the wall where the tower was expected to attack, sticking sloping wooden chutes through the holes. The entire population of Rhodes then poured mud, water, and sewage down these chutes. The next day, when the tower rolled forward, it bogged down in the muddy cesspool the Rhodians had created.

The most impressive military technology of the Greeks and Romans was the catapult—an instrument that hurled stones, arrows, or pointed shafts called bolts. The earliest such device was the crossbow, a handheld weapon that used a mechanism to draw back the bowstring on a heavy, stiff bow. The crossbow shot an arrow much farther and more forcefully than an ordinary bow. Military engineers developed new and more efficient kinds of crossbows during the 300s and 200s B.C. The largest known bow measured 15 feet from tip to tip and threw a 40-pound stone ball from a sling of leather or woven hair. Catapults used springs that consisted of a bundle of cords made from a flexible material to increase the amount of force created. At first, military engineers used cords made from plant fibers, but they later used the tissues of oxen or other animals. These cords were flexible and strong and could hold a great deal of tension.

Large catapults were not intended for use by individual soldiers. Teams of men positioned and operated them. Catapults that threw bolts were fairly accurate against targets up to 250 yards away, while those that hurled stones had a range of about 150 yards. With such devices, an army could attack oncoming soldiers, throw rocks over city walls to smash buildings and people on the other side, or hurl flaming arrows into a besieged city.

Some of the military engineering works built by the Romans still stand today. Across their empire, the Romans fortified their military towns with ramparts* and ditches. They built BRIDGES and straight, interconnecting ROADS so that their troops could march quickly from town to town. During the PUNIC WARS with Carthage, Roman engineers also became skilled at building naval defenses, including harbors, lighthouses, and coastal forts, to guard themselves from invasion by sea. (*See also* **Technology; Wars and Warfare, Greek; Wars and Warfare, Roman; Weapons and Armor.**)

* **rampart** earth or stone embankment, often topped with a low wall, built to protect soldiers from enemy fire

## MINERALS

See *Geography and Geology, Mediterranean; Mining.*

## MINING

* **alluvial** referring to earth, sand, and other substances deposited by running water from rivers and streams

The ancient Greeks and Romans obtained many different metals by mining. GOLD and silver were mined because of their value. Copper, tin, iron, and lead were mined because of their usefulness. The Greeks and Romans developed various methods of mining metal ores, including sifting through alluvial* deposits, mining mineral deposits in open pits at the earth's surface, and digging mines deep underground.

The Greeks primarily sifted through river beds and streams to obtain metal ores. Once these sources were used up, the Greeks turned to underground mining. One of the most productive mining areas was around Laurium in southeastern ATTICA, the region in which ATHENS is located. Rich in lead, zinc, and silver deposits, Laurium was mined from as early as 1500 B.C. until 103 B.C., when a slave revolt brought a halt to the mining there. Another productive Greek mining area was Siphnos in the CYCLADES islands, where abundant deposits of gold and silver were located. The Greeks also mined gold and silver in northern Greece, MACEDONIA, THRACE, and on the island of Thasos.

Italy had few precious metals. Therefore, the Romans traded with CARTHAGE in North Africa and with the kingdoms in the eastern Mediterranean for gold and silver. As the empire expanded, however, the Romans acquired the metals that were mined in the conquered lands. The Romans controlled vast mineral resources in Iberia (Spain), GAUL (France), BRITAIN, ASIA MINOR (Turkey), and in the provinces* near the Danube River. While the Romans did not develop new mining areas, they greatly expanded the mining that was done in existing regions and extracted a greater variety of ores from them. Production at the major Roman mines reached its peak during the first 200 years of the Roman Empire. Starting in the A.D. 200s, Germanic tribes invaded the empire, disturbing mining production in many areas.

Although the Romans adopted the tools and techniques of the Greeks, Egyptians, and other peoples they conquered, they also made their own advances in mining technology. Since only gold and copper existed in a natural state, the Romans developed better methods for turning metals that occurred naturally as mixed compounds—such as silver, lead, and tin—into usable materials. The Romans also constructed mines that were deeper than those of the Greeks. Since some deep mines extended below the underground water level, draining water from the mines was a serious problem. Although some Roman mines used men to bail out water, others used pumps or water-lifting wheels. Miners used iron picks, hammers, and chisels. They placed ore in buckets, which they then hauled to the surface by hand or by pulley.

Providing adequate ventilation in mines was also a major problem. Both the Greeks and the Romans constructed mine shafts in pairs, with connecting passages between the two shafts that facilitated the movement of air. Sometimes fires were lit in one shaft to cause a down draft in the other. Wherever the shape of the land allowed, openings were made at different levels to increase air flow in the mines. Still, many workers died from inhaling poisonous fumes or from suffocation.

Working in a mine was grueling and dangerous work. The Greeks primarily used slaves. The Romans used slaves, criminals, and, in the late Roman Empire, Christians to work in the mines. Many slaves, chained underground, did not see daylight for months at a time. Many were forced to work until they died. By the A.D. 100s, forced labor was in short supply, and miners were often skilled free men. (*See also* **Construction Materials and Techniques; Quarries; Slavery.**)

* **province** overseas area controlled by Rome

**Remember:** *Consult the index at the end of Volume 4 to find more information on many topics.*

## MINOS

### LEGENDARY KING

* **dynasty** succession of rulers from the same family or group

According to Greek legend, Minos ruled the Mediterranean island kingdom of Crete before the time of the Trojan War. The Bronze Age culture that developed at Knossos, Crete's capital city, around 1600–1400 B.C. is called Minoan after King Minos. Some scholars think the name *Minos* is the title of a dynasty* rather than the name of an individual king. Minos was believed to be the son of Zeus and Europa, a Phoenician princess.

While competing for the chance to be king of Crete, Minos prayed to Poseidon, the god of the sea, to send him a bull to sacrifice. The god sent the bull, but the animal was so beautiful Minos could not kill it. This refusal angered Poseidon, who retaliated by causing Pasiphaë, the wife of Minos, to fall in love with the bull. The Minotaur, half-human, half-bull, was born from their union. Minos hired the famous inventor Daedalus to build a labyrinth—a maze—in which to keep the Minotaur. The labyrinth may have been part of Minos's palace at Knossos.

The legends about Minos suggest that he was the favorite son of Zeus, who made his kingship possible. According to Plato, Minos retired from his position every nine years to visit with Zeus for the purpose of renewing their friendship and his kingship. Minos allegedly gave the first laws to human beings and served as judge for both the living and the dead. Some myths about Minos emphasize his cruelty. According to one, he forced Athens to send a yearly gift of seven young men and women to be sacrificed to the Minotaur. The sacrifices ended when the hero Theseus killed the Minotaur. The story of Theseus and the Minotaur was a popular theme in early Greek art.

Minos died a violent death. He had imprisoned Daedalus, who escaped to Sicily and the protection of King Cocalus. Minos followed Daedalus to Sicily, where he was scalded to death by the king's daughters. (*See also* **Bronze Age, Greek; Crete; Myths, Greek.**)

## MINTS

See *Coinage.*

## MITHRAS

* **cult** group bound together by devotion to a particular person, belief, or god

* **initiate** one who is just learning the rites of worship

* **hierarchy** order of authority or rank

Mithras was the chief god in an Indo-Persian mystery cult* that appeared in Rome during the late republic. Membership in the cult was restricted to men. Cult members believed that Mithras was their savior who offered rebirth and eternal life. The Romans worshiped him as a sun god. At its peak, during the A.D. 100s and 200s, the cult attracted soldiers especially, but it was also popular with minor government officials, slaves, and freedmen. In time, the cult spread throughout the empire. The emperor Julian the Apostate was the most famous initiate* in the cult of Mithras.

Small groups of members met secretly in dwellings they called caves. These were either actual caves, underground rooms, or hidden chambers. There the initiates were ranked in a hierarchy* of seven levels. Initiates passed through each level, approaching, but never reaching, actual priesthood. The celebration of a meal together was an important ritual in the cult of Mithras.

Inscriptions on monuments hint at some of the beliefs and rituals of the cult. Mithras is often shown killing a bull whose tail looks like a shaft of wheat. He is generally accompanied by various animals as well as two lesser gods and by images of the sun and moon. Some scholars believe that the killing of the bull was intended to represent the sacrifice that Mithras made to save the world. Others interpret the slaughter of the bull and the presence of the sun and moon as an astrological allegory* for the heavenly journey of the soul.

Important cult centers were located in Rome and its port city of OSTIA. Traces of the cult have been found in every part of the Roman empire, from Britain to the mouth of the Danube River. Mithraism never attracted the Roman upper classes, however, and its size remained small in comparison to other religions. (*See also* **Christianity; Cults; Eleusinian Mysteries.**)

* **allegory** literary device in which characters represent an idea or a religious or moral principle

## MONARCHS, GREEK

* **city-state** independent state consisting of a city and its surrounding territory

A ruler in Asia Minor, Mausolus extended his rule over Greek coastal cities in the mid-300s B.C. During this time, monarchy had reemerged as the dominant form of Greek government after a long period of displacement by democracies, oligarchies, and occasional tyrannies in the various city-states.

Monarchies, or governments run by kings or queens, were common in Greece between the 1600s and 1100s B.C., a period of Greek history called the Mycenaean age. Later, most Greek city-states* became democracies or oligarchies*, although sometimes they were ruled by tyrants*. By the 400s B.C., most Greeks knew about kingship only from myths or as a form of government common among barbarian* peoples. After the reign of ALEXANDER THE GREAT, monarchy reemerged as the dominant form of government in the Greek world.

Greek monarchies faded after the Mycenaean age as nobles challenged the one-man rule of kings. The nobles who replaced the kings were, in turn, challenged by the lower classes, and many aristocracies* were overthrown by tyrants. The strong-armed tactics of tyrants and the unlawful manner in which they came to power caused deep resentment. Lack of support from their subjects only made tyrants even more oppressive. By the 400s B.C., most Greek city-states had deposed* their tyrants, replacing them with more democratic governments. ATHENS is probably the best-known example of a Greek city-state that successfully made the transition to democracy.

Even after most of the tyrants were gone, monarchies continued to rule in such places as SPARTA, SICILY, MACEDONIA, and the Cimmerian Bosporus. Sparta was the only city-state on the mainland that kept its monarchy throughout the classical* period. Two generals from old Spartan families ruled the city-state jointly as kings. Most city-states in Sicily, which the Greeks had colonized early in its history, never achieved enough stability to become democratic. The Sicilian cities of Gela, Akragas, and SYRACUSE were all under the rule of tyrants. On the fringe of the Greek world was the kingdom of the Cimmerian Bosporus. The kingdom was located on land on both sides of the straits that connect the Black Sea and the Sea of Azov. The state was formed in the 480s B.C. by a prominent Greek family that had organized other Greek settlers for protection against their Scythian neighbors.

Although the monarchs of Macedonia claimed to be descended from Greeks, most Greeks ridiculed them, especially their language. In the 400s and 300s B.C., Macedonian kings organized a national army, modernized the kingdom, and brought Greek artists to their capital of Pella. King PHILIP II

* **oligarchy** rule by a few people

* **tyrant** absolute ruler

* **barbarian** referring to people from outside the cultures of Greece and Rome, who were viewed as uncivilized

* **aristocracy** rule by the nobility or privileged upper class

* **depose** to remove from high office

* **classical** in Greek history, refers to the period of great political and cultural achievement from about 500 B.C. to 323 B.C.

* **imperial** pertaining to an emperor or empire

* **dynasty** succession of rulers from the same family or group

* **annex** to add a territory to an existing state

* **province** overseas area controlled by Rome

strengthened and enriched the kingdom. He defeated the Greek forces in battle and gained control of Greece. Philip's title in Macedonia was king, but in other regions he conquered his title differed. He became the *hegemon* (leader) of the Panhellenic Congress of Greece, he assumed the title of pharaoh in Egypt, and he took the imperial* title when he conquered Persia. Philip's son, Alexander the Great (designated Alexander III of Macedon), conquered the PERSIAN EMPIRE and extended Macedonian power to INDIA.

Wars between Alexander's generals followed his death in 323 B.C., and dynasties* were established in the lands that Alexander had conquered. In Egypt, the PTOLEMAIC DYNASTY ruled until the death of CLEOPATRA in 30 B.C., when the kingdom was annexed* by the Roman Empire. The SELEUCID DYNASTY, which was based in Syria and Mesopotamia, controlled an empire that was larger and more loosely organized. This dynasty fell to the Romans as well, who divided the kingdom into provinces*. Monarchies were also established in ASIA MINOR and in northern Afghanistan. The monarchies that existed earlier in Syracuse, Macedonia, and the Cimmerian Bosporus continued. Unlike the monarchies in Asia Minor that became Roman provinces, the kingdom of the Cimmerian Bosporus survived as a monarchy controlled by Rome until the 300s B.C. (*See also* **Democracy, Greek; Government, Greek; Greece, History of; Mycenae; Tyrants, Greek.**)

# MONEY AND MONEYLENDING

**M**oney is any object that is used to purchase goods and services. Throughout history, many different types of objects have been used as money, but coins made from precious metals have been the most common. Because money was useful for buying items, people in ancient Greece and Rome often needed to borrow money from individuals or institutions, such as TEMPLES or banks. For much of classical antiquity, the coin itself was worth what it weighed. Fiduciary money, which we use today (in which the object itself is not actually worth its agreed-on value), was rare.

* **classical** in Greek history, refers to the period of great political and cultural achievement from about 500 B.C. to 323 B.C.

* **Hellenistic** referring to the Greek-influenced culture of the Mediterranean world during the three centuries after Alexander the Great, who died in 323 B.C.

**MONEY IN ANCIENT GREECE AND ROME.** By about the 800s B.C., most Greek communities had adopted official units of money, usually in some form of precious metal. Lydia, in western ASIA MINOR, was the first nation to mint coins, in about 635 B.C., and the practices of minting and using coins spread rapidly. After about 400 B.C., Rome was also using coins as money. Coins were stamped with a particular design to show that they were of uniform size. This saved people the trouble of having to weigh each coin individually. Although most coins were used in the region in which they were produced, the coins of Athens during the classical* period and the coins of ALEXANDER THE GREAT and his successors in the Hellenistic* period were made in large quantities and used over a wide area.

The first coins were made only of precious metals, especially electrum, a naturally occurring mixture of GOLD and silver. Later silver was used widely, and gold coins were introduced by PHILIP II, the king of Macedonia, in the 300s B.C. After Philip, a combination of gold and silver was used in most coins. Because southern Italy and Sicily had a limited supply of precious metals, these areas began producing bronze coins, which had less value as metal. By the 300s B.C. most Greek city-states, including Athens, adopted bronze coins. However, most city-states continued to use gold and silver in addition to bronze, believing that coins of high value must be made of good metal.

Although coins were widely used in Greek and Roman cities, coins were less important or not used at all in large areas of the Mediterranean. Instead, people bartered* agricultural produce or other goods as they always had. Money was not even necessary for overseas trade.

**MONEYLENDING.** Although the practice of lending money is older than the use of coins in ancient Greece and Rome, coins made moneylending easier. In Greece, most moneylending occurred between individuals, although temples and banks also made loans. Wealth, for the most part, consisted of land and the goods produced from the land. Wealthy people could be cash poor, and they borrowed money from one another to maintain their social standing or to influence political decisions. Poor people also borrowed money from wealthier people, usually at high rates of interest.

Small businesses run by merchants controlled moneylending during the Roman Republic*. Instead of coins, these merchants used bills of exchange, which were written orders from one person to pay a certain amount of money to another. This system spread throughout the empire. During the later years of the Roman Empire, the business of moneylending gradually shifted from merchants to the wealthy owners of large estates. It was customary for Roman moneylenders to charge interest on the loans they made. (*See also* **Banking; Coinage; Economy, Greek; Economy, Roman; Taxation; Trade, Greek; Trade, Roman.**)

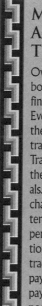

## MONEYLENDING AND OVERSEAS TRADE

Overseas traders often needed to borrow large sums of money to finance their trading expeditions. Even if they owned their own ship, they still needed to buy cargo for trade and supplies for the trip. Traders often borrowed the money they needed from wealthy individuals. These moneylenders frequently charged extremely high rates of interest—sometimes as high as 30 percent—because trading expeditions were very risky. Unless the trader was shipwrecked, he had to pay back the loan. If he failed to repay it, the moneylenders could take possession of his ship and its cargo.

* **barter** to exchange goods and services without using money

* **Roman Republic** Rome during the period from 509 B.C. to 31 B.C., when popular assemblies annually elected their governmental officials

# MOSAICS

* **artisan** skilled craftsperson

* **Hellenistic** referring to the Greek-influenced culture of the Mediterranean world during the three centuries after Alexander the Great, who died in 323 B.C.

* **terra-cotta** hard-baked clay, either glazed or unglazed

osaics are a type of decoration found in ancient Greek and Roman buildings, both public and private. Artisans* called mosaicists arranged small pebbles or colored stones into intricate geometric designs, or they used a more sophisticated technique called tessellation to create scenes of flowers, animals, gods, and mythological heroes. Art historians are uncertain as to the origin of mosaic art. Some think it originated with the patterned pebble floors that were used in the Near East as far back as the 700s B.C., although the remains of unpatterned pebble floors have been found in the Bronze Age ruins of the Minoan and Mycenaean civilizations (1500–1200 B.C.). Mosaics developed into a highly skilled art form during Greece's Hellenistic* period.

The earliest Greek mosaics were made from rounded pebbles set in a layer of fine cement. Strips of lead or terra-cotta* were used to outline and reinforce the design of the natural pebbles. At first, mosaics were utilitarian. They were used in private homes to cover floors with a smooth, water-resistant surface. Designs were either geometric shapes or two-dimensional figures placed against a dark background. By the late 400s B.C., the use of floor mosaics had spread throughout Greece. Artisans began to use a wider range of colors and shades in an attempt to make figures more realistic.

# MOSAICS

The Romans adopted Greek mosaic techniques and used this colorful art form to decorate their palaces and other important buildings. In this mosaic from Pompeii, actors are shown preparing for a performance.

See color plate 11, vol. 1.

See color plate 11, vol. 1.

## THE BEST IN THE WORLD

The Roman tradition of vault and wall mosaics reached its peak during the early Christian era of the Roman Empire. Mosaics with backgrounds of dark blue and gold covered church interiors in Ravenna and Milan, Italy, and in Thessalonika, Greece. The most glorious mosaics were the work of Byzantine artisans. They used tesserae (small cubes of gold, colored glass, and stone) as covering for church domes, vaults, and walls in the most important churches of the empire. One of the largest and most magnificent of these buildings was Hagia Sophia in Constantinople. Built by the emperor Justinian in the A.D. 500s, it originally contained more than four acres of golden tesserae.

The finest Greek mosaics date from the 300s B.C. and come from the Macedonian city of Olynthus. The rectangular floor mosaics from this region of Greece depict scenes from Greek mythology surrounded by a border of flowers, vines, or stylized waves.

Around the 200s B.C., artisans developed tessellation. This is the technique of cutting glass, stone, or terra-cotta into small cubes (called tesserae) and closely fitting them into a bed of mortar. The technique resulted in designs of astounding beauty. Artists used tesserae to create pictures of birds, animals, mythological scenes, theatrical scenes, and historic events. By the 100s B.C., artists had mastered the arrangement of many tiny pieces of colored stone in patterns so complex that they closely resembled the effects of painting. The technique of tessellation changed the way in which mosaics were produced. Artists assembled the largest pieces of the scene in panels, called *emblemata,* in their workshops. Once assembled, the panels were laid into a floor. Outstanding examples of tessellated mosaics have been found in the great Hellenistic cities of ALEXANDRIA (in Egypt) and PERGAMUM (in Asia Minor). Considered the masterpiece of tessellation, the Alexander Mosaic from the southern Italian city of POMPEII shows Alexander the Great and the Persian king, Darius III, during the battle of the Issus River.

There is little distinction between Greek and Roman mosaics. The Romans adopted Greek techniques and applied them to mosaics on walls

* **vault** arched ceiling or roof

* **province** overseas area controlled by Rome

and the vaults* of buildings. During the Roman Empire, mosaics were mass-produced for use in private houses, apartments, and tombs and in large public BATHS. Each province* of the Roman Empire developed its own favorite designs and color preferences. In the A.D. 300s, Christians adopted the use of mosaics for the decoration of their churches. (*See also* **Architecture, Greek; Architecture, Roman; Bronze Age, Greek; Construction Materials and Techniques; Household Furnishings.**)

## MUSES

* **philosophy** study of ideas, including science
* **Titan** one of a family of giants who ruled the earth before the Olympian gods

In ancient Greek mythology, the Muses were the goddesses of the fine arts, music, and literature. In Roman times, they were associated with all intellectual pursuits, such as history, philosophy*, and astronomy. The Muses were extremely popular with poets, who dedicated works to them and invoked their names for inspiration.

The Muses were the daughters of ZEUS and Mnemosyne, a Titan*. The Muses lived on Mt. Olympus with the other gods and goddesses. There were originally three Muses: Melete (Practice), Mneme (Memory), and Aoede (Song). In his work the *Theogony,* the Greek poet HESIOD increased their number to nine and assigned each a name. Their specialties or attributes were further developed during Roman times.

Each Muse presides over a particular science or art. They are Calliope (epic poetry), Clio (history), Euterpe (flute playing), Terpsichore (lyric poetry and choral dance), Erato (lyric poetry and songs), Melpomene (tragedy), Thalia (comedy), Polyhymnia (hymns and pantomime), and Urania (astronomy). APOLLO, the god of music and prophecy, presided over the Muses. The ancient Greeks believed that they danced with him and other deities at festivals on Mt. Olympus.

The Muses are significant figures in the art, literature, and philosophy of Western civilization. The Greek philosopher PLATO wrote that "possession by the Muses" was a form of "divine madness" and necessary for creative pursuits. The Muses often appear in ancient Greek and Roman sculpture, paintings, and MOSAICS. The word *museum* originally meant "a place of the Muses." (*See also* **Divinities; Poetry, Greek and Hellenistic.**)

## MUSIC AND MUSICAL INSTRUMENTS

* **philosophy** study of ideas, including science

Music, for the ancient Greeks, included poetry, dance, song, instrumental music, and other art forms. To say that someone was unmusical meant that that person did not understand or appreciate the arts. The Greeks considered music a link to the gods, as well as a branch of the highest forms of human thought, such as philosophy* and mathematics. The Romans had a somewhat more limited definition of music, regarding music as just one of many art forms and not necessarily the most interesting or the most important. Still, music played a part in Roman public and private life, just as it had among the Greeks.

**MUSIC IN SOCIETY.** Music was highly valued throughout Greek history. The Greeks told myths in which their gods and goddesses created the first

# MUSIC AND MUSICAL INSTRUMENTS

The Greeks broadly defined music to include a range of art forms. They actively learned about, made, and used a variety of instruments; one of the most popular instruments was the stringed lyre shown here.

See color plate 3, vol. 4.

* **chorus** in ancient Greek drama, a group of actors whose singing or dancing accompanies and comments upon the action of a play

* **city-state** independent state consisting of a city and its surrounding territory

music and musical instruments. They believed that music had many powers, including the power to communicate with the gods. From earliest times, music was a central part of religious ceremonies. Soloists or choruses* sang hymns of praise to the gods. Greek drama most likely grew out of these religious festivals. The OLYMPIC GAMES and the other great games that were held regularly in Greece included competitions for solo singers, choruses, and instrumentalists, as well as for athletes.

Music was closely linked to poetry and dance. Poet-composers created both the words and the music of their compositions, and the Greeks would not have understood the idea of writing music to accompany the words of someone else. These poet-composers often worked for royal or noble households and wrote music on demand. Some were employed by the Greek city-states* to create music for special occasions, such as a celebration of an important victory by a local athlete or a victory in war.

Folk songs and traditional music were part of everyday life. People sang at weddings, harvest celebrations, and other occasions. Shepherds sang or played pipes to their flocks in the fields, rowers sang to keep time as they worked the oars, and women sang as they performed their domestic tasks. Soldiers and athletes trained to musical accompaniment. Among the most valuable slaves were skilled musicians. Most citizens were expected to have some musical training and ability, and Athenian youths attended dancing classes as part of their education. Although party guests often listened to music provided by hired entertainers or slaves, they sometimes made their own music by singing and playing instruments.

Some Greek thinkers saw a close connection between music and philosophy. In the 500s B.C., the philosopher and mathematician PYTHAGORAS claimed that the world and the human soul were organized in mathematical relationships similar to those between musical notes. Pythagoras's belief in the concept of a "music of the spheres" was shared by Plato, one of the most influential thinkers of classical Greece. Plato believed that music had a direct effect on a person's soul and actions, and he called philosophy "the greatest music."

Most scholars think that music was less important in Roman society and education than in Greek life. To the Romans, poetry and music were not part of a single art form as they were for the Greeks. However, music did have many roles in Roman life. Romans of various classes sang traditional folk songs, wedding songs, and work songs. Songs and instrumental music were a necessary part of religious ceremonies, public games, and funeral processions. The Roman armies used horn players to relay signals over great distances. Musicians played an important role in Roman theater, which featured song and dance performances between plays or sections of plays. Pantomime and mime, two popular forms of Roman theater, depended upon singers and players. Although some knowledge of music was part of a good Roman education, no Roman citizen would consider making a career as a professional musician, since music making was something fit only for foreigners and slaves.

**MUSICAL INSTRUMENTS.** Although the Greeks knew about many kinds of instruments, including ones that were developed in western Asia or Egypt, most Greek musicians relied on two main instruments, the aulos and the lyre. The aulos was a reed instrument similar to the modern oboe. In its most common form, the aulos consisted of two pipes with holes along each pipe that the player covered with his or her fingers to create different tones. The pipes were joined at one end to a round, hollow bulb. The player blew across a piece of reed into this bulb, producing whistling, flutelike sounds, as well as a deeper-toned booming sound. The Greeks also played a similar instrument called the syrinx. The syrinx, or pan pipes, consisted of a set of small pipes of varying lengths. The player blew across the tops of the pipes to produce different tones.

The lyre was a wooden frame with strings stretched across it. Although all of the strings were the same length, each had a different thickness and tightness, so that each made a different tone when plucked. The musician usually played the lyre by bracing the bottom of the frame against his or her waist. The kithara was a larger type of lyre that produced a greater variety of sounds. The musician plucked the kithara strings with a plectrum, or pick, which was usually a small piece of horn or ivory. While the Greeks rarely used brass horns or percussion instruments, such as handheld drums, cymbals, and wooden clappers, the Romans played these instruments. The Romans also developed a water organ that used water pressure to force air through pipes of different lengths, producing loud sounds. In general, the Romans were more tolerant of foreign musical styles and instruments than the Greeks, and they were quicker to adapt foreign elements to their own use.

Only a few fragments of written music from Greece and Rome survive, and little is known about how this music sounded. But the Greeks and

## MUSIC AND WAR

The ancient Greeks saw a connection between music and war, and that connection was dancing. Some festivals featured dances in which the performers carried weapons or acted out battles. Such performances were also part of cultural life in the city-state of Sparta, a highly military society. Good dancers were agile and strong, qualities that made them good at sports—and at war. The philosopher Socrates supposedly said that the best dancers were also the best fighters.

See color plate 9, vol. 4.

Romans contributed to the development of music in a number of ways. The Greeks conceived of a mathematical basis for music. They devised musical scales, called modes, which in Roman times were replaced with a standard diatonic (seven-note) scale. The Greeks also created a system of musical notation. The heritage of Greek music and Hebrew liturgy* blended in the Roman world and influenced the music of the early Christian church. (*See also* **Drama, Greek; Drama, Roman; Poetry, Greek and Hellenistic.**)

* **liturgy** form of a religious service, including spoken words, songs, and actions

## MYCENAE

* **hero** in mythology, a person of great strength or ability, often descended from a god
* **epic** long poem about legendary or historical heroes, written in a grand style

Mycenae was a city on a hill in the northeastern part of the Peloponnese, the peninsula that forms the southern part of mainland Greece. Mycenae was the main center of civilization in Greece during the late Bronze Age, which lasted from the 1600s to the 1100s B.C. Historians refer to that era of Greek history as the Mycenaean period. Legends about Mycenaean heroes* and kings survived to become the basis of HOMER's *Iliad* and *Odyssey,* the epic* poems about the Trojan War, which was believed to have taken place at the end of the Mycenaean period.

The Mycenaean period began when wealthy kingdoms appeared in southern Greece around 1600 B.C. Most modern historians believe that the groups that came to power were local people, but other scholars claim that invaders took control of the region. These new rulers established dozens of rival kingdoms, each with a central fortress and palace. The largest of these capitals was Mycenae.

In the 1400s B.C., the Mycenaeans probably conquered the rich Minoan civilization that existed on the island of CRETE. For the next few hundred years, Mycenae was a major power in the eastern Mediterranean, controlling cities on the Greek mainland and on islands in the AEGEAN SEA. The Mycenaeans also developed a trade network that linked all the lands around the Mediterranean. The Mycenaeans shipped their pottery and olive oil to other lands in exchange for luxury goods, such as perfumes, wool, and bronze swords. Remnants of Mycenaean pottery have been found in many regions of the Mediterranean.

Mycenae reached its peak of wealth and power in the 1300s and early 1200s B.C. During that period, the city had a palace surrounded by fortress walls that also enclosed a cluster of shrines. Most people lived in a large settlement outside the walls. Around 1250 B.C., Mycenae was damaged by fire, perhaps during an enemy attack, and the city's importance declined. By 1100 B.C., Mycenae was only a village. Several centuries later, Mycenae again flourished, with carved stone water tanks, baths, and a temple dedicated to either ATHENA or HERA. For a brief period in the 400s B.C., Mycenae was an independent city-state*. However, after the classical* period, Mycenae once again decayed as its inhabitants drifted away. By the time the Greek geographer Pausanias visited the area in the A.D. 100s, little remained of once-great Mycenae.

* **city-state** independent state consisting of a city and its surrounding territory
* **classical** in Greek history, refers to the period of great political and cultural achievement from about 500 B.C. to 323 B.C.

The modern discovery of the Mycenaean civilization began in 1876, when Heinrich Schliemann, a German excavator, uncovered prehistoric graves at Mycenae. Some of the graves contained treasures and appeared to be royal tombs. In one tomb, Schliemann found a golden mask of a king or warrior, and he mistakenly believed that he had discovered the burial place of AGAMEMNON, the legendary king of Mycenae and hero of the Trojan War. However, since Schliemann's time, archaeologists* have found several tombs at the bottom of wells, or shafts. Some contained bronze weapons and precious artwork, such as a bowl of rock crystal with a handle in the shape of a duck's head. The people of Mycenae buried their honored dead in beehive-shaped chambers or vaults made of stone blocks. The most famous chamber tomb is the Treasury of Atreus. These tombs contained richly decorated weapons and vessels of precious metal. The warlike character and love of hunting is reflected in the contents of these tombs. Items found in these graves are scholars' chief source of information about ancient Mycenae.

* **archaeologist** scientist who studies past human cultures, usually by excavating ruins

Although little remains of the temples, houses, palaces, or fortress walls of ancient Mycenae, the main entrance of the city's citadel* can still be seen today. The Lion's Gate is a huge stone threshold containing a sculpted relief of two lions standing beside a column, a symbol of the city's once great palace. Scholars have also uncovered evidence of the Mycenaean language, an early form of Greek, in Mycenaean ruins. (*See also* **Archaeology of Ancient Sites; Bronze Age, Greek; Death and Burial; Greece, History of;** *Iliad;* **Languages and Dialects; Monarchs, Greek;** *Odyssey.*)

* **citadel** fortified place or stronghold that commands a city

## MYSTERIES

See *Cults; Eleusinian Mysteries; Religion, Greek; Religion, Roman.*

## MYTHS, GREEK

The word *myth,* which comes from the Greek *muthos,* originally had the general meaning of "word" or "speech." By the fifth century B.C., myth began to refer specifically to an entertaining, though not necessarily truthful, spoken story. However, myths were far more than just entertaining stories to the Greeks. Myths provided the early Greeks with a sense of their identity and origins, as well as an understanding of their place in nature and their relationship to the gods. By retelling myths from one generation to the next, the Greek people maintained their connection with their past and passed on this heritage to their children.

Most of what is known about Greek myths comes from early Greek literature. Much of the epic* poetry of HOMER, for instance, was based on or referred to myths. The works of the poet HESIOD, especially his *Theogony* and *Works and Days,* are especially rich sources of myth, as are the odes* of PINDAR. The great dramatists of the classical* period—AESCHYLUS, SOPHOCLES, and EURIPIDES—also used traditional myths as the basis of their tragedies.

Most myths center on one or more basic aspects of human existence—family, society, religion, and nature. However, the characters, setting, and plot vary greatly from one myth to another. Some Greek myths give an account of how the universe came about or how the gods were born, while others describe the origin of early humans or their culture. Still others are simple tales of adventure, sometimes recounting the deeds of ordinary people, sometimes of well-known heroes*. Frequently, myths are about deities*, and many myths feature fantastic creatures, such as giants or monsters.

* **epic** long poem about legendary or historical heroes, written in a grand style

* **ode** lyric poem often addressed to a person or an object

* **classical** in Greek history, refers to the period of great political and cultural achievement from about 500 B.C. to 323 B.C.

* **hero** in mythology, a person of great strength or ability, often descended from a god

* **deity** god or goddess

Greek pottery often depicted scenes from mythology. This amphora illustrates the last of Heracles' Twelve Labors, in which he was required to capture Cerberus, the three-headed watchdog of Hades. The king who ordered the task hides fearfully in a jar as Heracles returns with the beast.

**THE ORIGIN OF THE UNIVERSE.** According to Hesiod, the first things to exist were Void (which the Greeks called *Chaos,* meaning a "yawning" or a "gaping"), Earth *(Gaia),* and Desire *(Eros).* Void produced Darkness *(Erebos)* and Night, which in turn created Light and Day. Earth produced Sky *(Uranus)* and Water and, together with Sky, created several other beings. These included the 12 Titans, giants who went on to give birth to the gods; the three CYCLOPES, one-eyed giants who created thunder and lightning and gave them to the gods; and three monsters called the Hundred-Handed, who helped the gods overpower and imprison the Titans.

Rhea and Cronos, two of the Titans, produced several gods as their offspring, including ZEUS, HERA, DEMETER, and POSEIDON. These gods then fought their parents and the other Titans for supreme power. The battle between the gods and the Titans lasted for ten years, according to myth, until Zeus released the Hundred-Handed from the chains in which their father, Sky, had bound them. With the help of these monsters, the gods won the battle against the Titans, who were imprisoned in the underworld* and guarded by the Hundred-Handed.

After this victory over the Titans, according to the myth, Earth advised the gods to ask Zeus to be their king. They agreed, and Zeus in turn gave his siblings their specific rights and privileges. For example, Zeus gave HADES authority in the underworld. These gods then gave birth to other gods, such as ATHENA, the goddess of war and wisdom, who burst forth from Zeus's head. Zeus, Hera, Demeter, Hades, Poseidon, and all of their offspring are the subject of many Greek myths. One of the best known is the myth of Demeter, the goddess of agriculture, and her daughter, PERSEPHONE. According to this myth, Persephone was kidnapped by Hades and taken to the underworld. Demeter was so filled with grief that she caused the earth's crops to fail, threatening the destruction of human life. Zeus convinced Hades to return Persephone, although she was required to spend part of the year in the underworld as the wife of Hades.

* **underworld** kingdom of the dead; also called Hades

## EASTERN INFLUENCES

Greek myths show considerable influence from the Near East. This is not surprising, since the Greeks had extensive contact with Asia Minor as early as 1600 B.C. Several Near Eastern myths are strikingly similar to Greek myths about gods and heroes. For example, the myth of Demeter—whose anger causes crops to stop growing while her daughter Persephone remains with Hades in the underworld—is almost identical to the Hittite myth of Telepinus and is similar to the Mesopotamian myths of Inanna-Ishtar. Several major Greek gods are thought to have been imported from the Near East, including Apollo, Artemis, Aphrodite, and Dionysus. In addition, Greek and Mesopotamian myths share the concept of an underworld where mortals go after they die.

* **mortal** human being; one who eventually will die

**MYTHS OF HUMANS AND HEROES.** The primary source for myths about early humans is the poetry of Hesiod. A major theme of many of these myths is the downfall of humans from an earlier carefree existence. According to one story, PROMETHEUS, the son of two Titans, stole fire from Zeus and gave it to humans. Angered by this, Zeus punished the mortals* by creating woman. She was named Pandora ("all gifts"), because each god gave to her a plague for mankind as a "gift." When Pandora's curiosity led her to open the jar filled with these gifts from the gods, they were unleashed onto mankind. (Only "hope" remained in the jar.) For this reason, the earth and sea are full of evils, and endless troubles afflict mankind.

There are also many myths about Greek heroes. These are tales about characters who were believed to have played an important role in the past. Some of the best known of these heroic myths were told by Homer in his epic poems. In the *Iliad,* Homer described the deeds of the hero ACHILLES during the Trojan War, which is the subject of several other myths as well. In the *Odyssey,* he told of the journey home from the Trojan War of the mythical hero ODYSSEUS. Both Achilles and Odysseus also fit into the modern category of legendary heroes. Legends take place in relatively modern times, instead of the remote past when the universe was created. Legendary heroes also demonstrate personal qualities admired by the society from which they spring.

The most important Greek hero was HERACLES, who was believed to protect humans from all kinds of evil. He was worshiped all over Greece and was the only hero to be given the status of a god. (*See also* **Divinities; Epic, Greek; Poetry, Greek and Hellenistic.**)

# MYTHS, ROMAN

* **Roman Republic** Rome during the period from 509 B.C. to 31 B.C., when popular assemblies annually elected their governmental officials

* **hero** in mythology, a person of great strength or ability, often descended from a god

* **epic** long poem about legendary or historical heroes, written in a grand style

Although the Romans did not have a large body of myths, several important Roman writers adapted Greek myths for use in their writings. Indeed, the Roman poet OVID is the best source for many Greek myths, since he used many of them in his well-known poem the *Metamorphoses.* Other Roman writers mixed Greek myths with Roman history to create lasting traditions regarding the origin of Rome and the development of the Roman Republic*.

One of the most important Greek myths borrowed by Roman writers is the myth of the Trojan prince Aeneas. According to early Greek writers, Aeneas was a hero* of the Trojan War who traveled to Italy when the war was over. Writing in the 200s B.C., the Roman poet Naevius drew upon the Greek myth of Aeneas for his epic* poem the *Punic War,* in which he described the founding of Rome. About 200 years later, the Roman poet VERGIL made Aeneas the main character of his great epic the *Aeneid,* and the historian LIVY used the Aeneas myth to begin his history of Rome.

Vergil's *Aeneid* tells of the destruction of the city of Troy by the Greeks and of Aeneas's escape with a small band of Trojans. It includes the story of the Trojan horse, by which the Greeks were able to defeat the Trojans. The Greeks built a huge wooden horse, which they climbed inside and then moved outside the walls of Troy. A Greek prisoner in Troy persuaded the

## GREEK AND ROMAN GODS

Unlike the Greeks, the Romans did not create many myths. This may be because they did not think of their gods in human terms as did the Greeks. This changed in the 100s B.C., when the Roman poet Ennius adapted the myths associated with the Greek gods for the principal Roman gods. For example, the Roman goddess Juno was given the myths that had been associated with Hera, the queen of the Greek gods. Similarly, Ennius represented Ares (the Greek god of war) as Mars, and Poseidon (the Greek god of the sea) as the Roman god Neptune. Ennius also added to the list of major Roman gods the Greek god Apollo, who had no Roman counterpart.

Trojans that the horse was sacred and would bring the Trojans good luck from the gods, so the Trojans pulled the horse within the city's walls. At night while the Trojans slept, the Greeks climbed out of the horse and opened Troy's gates so that the rest of the Greek forces could enter. Most of the Trojans were killed, and the city was burned. Aeneas and his small band of Trojans escaped, however. They then wandered to Italy and fought for land upon which to settle and start a new life. By the end of the poem, Aeneas has become successfully established in Italy and is soon to marry Lavinia, the daughter of a local king.

Livy also describes Aeneas's arrival in Italy in book 1 of his history of Rome. Many generations later, Livy added, a female descendant of Aeneas named Rhea Silvia had twin sons fathered by the Roman god MARS. Amulius, Rhea's uncle, left the twins in the TIBER RIVER to drown, but they were found and nursed by a mother wolf at the site of what was to become the city of Rome. The twins were soon discovered by a shepherd, who named them ROMULUS AND REMUS and raised them as his sons.

When they became adults, Livy continued, Romulus and Remus were told that they were the descendants of Aeneas. They established a new settlement in the region where they had been found as infants. During an argument over who should rule this new city, Romulus killed Remus. He named the city Rome, after himself. According to Livy, this was how Rome was founded. Livy continues by describing how Romulus founded the Senate and other institutions of the Republic. (*See also* **Aeneid;** **Epic, Roman; Literature, Roman; Myths, Greek; Poetry, Roman.**)

# NAMES, ROMAN SYSTEM OF

NAMES, ROMAN SYSTEM OF

* **Roman Republic** Rome during the period from 509 B.C. to 31 B.C., when popular assemblies annually elected their governmental officials

* **patrician** member of the upper class who traced his ancestry to a senatorial family in the earliest days of the Roman Republic

The Romans, as well as other peoples of Italy, had a system of names in which the most important element was the *nomen,* or family name. Most Roman men had three names—a *praenomen,* or first name; a nomen; and a *cognomen,* or third name. All Roman citizens—men and married women—used the nomen of the father. The nomen ended in *-ius* for men and *-ia* for women. Thus, the son of Tullius would have the nomen Tullius, and the daughter would have the nomen Tullia.

The praenomen, the Roman first name, distinguished an individual male within the family. By the late Roman Republic*, 18 *praenomina,* or first names, were commonly used. The most popular of these were Gaius, Lucius, Marcus, Publius, and Quintus. A Roman's praenomen was usually abbreviated: for instance, Quintus was abbreviated Q., Marcus shortened to M., and Gaius was written as C. (the early Roman letter that represented both the *c* and *g* sounds).

A cognomen was an additional name that helped identify an individual as a member of a particular branch of a family or clan. Cognomens were usually derived from such family characteristics as physical traits, occupation, or place of origin. A Roman noble usually inherited a cognomen along with his nomen to indicate the branch of the larger family to which he belonged. One seldom simply chose a cognomen for one's children, although it was done at times. Originally, only a patrician* used a cognomen, but beginning in the later Roman Republic, almost all Romans included at least one cognomen in their name.

Roman women usually did not use a praenomen, and they did not change their names when they married. Slaves and other noncitizens generally had only a single name. When a slave gained his freedom, he took the nomen and the praenomen of his liberator and used his original name as his cognomen. (*See also* **Alphabets and Writing; Family, Roman.**)

# NARCISSUS

* **nymph** in classical mythology, one of the lesser goddesses of nature

* **seer** person who foresees future events; a prophet

In Greek mythology, Narcissus was the son of the river Cephissus in Boeotia and the nymph* Liriope. Narcissus was a very beautiful young man—so beautiful, in fact, that he fell in love with his own reflection and died. The English words *narcissism* and *narcissistic,* meaning "excessive love for oneself," come from his story.

When Narcissus was an infant, his mother wanted to know what the future held for her son. She asked the prophet Tiresias if the boy would live a long life. As was often the case with mythological seers* and prophets, Tiresias gave an answer that was not easily understood. He said that Narcissus would live a long life if he never knew himself. The meaning of this answer did not become clear until after Narcissus had met his fate.

Narcissus grew into a young man so beautiful that many people fell in love with him. He rejected them all, causing many broken hearts. One of the saddest of these rejected lovers was the nymph Echo, who had already been punished by the goddess Hera for chattering too much. Hera had rendered Echo unable to speak. Echo could only repeat the last word of what someone else said. When Echo failed to win the love of Narcissus, she faded away until nothing was left of her but her sad voice, endlessly repeating other people's words—an echo.

Another lover rejected by Narcissus prayed to Nemesis, the goddess of vengeance. Nemesis then brought upon Narcissus the fate about which Tiresias had warned. She condemned him to look at his own reflection in a pool on Mt. Helicon in central Greece. As he looked at his face reflected in the water, Narcissus fell more and more deeply in love with himself. Unable to tear himself away from the beloved image of himself, he wasted away and died at the pool's edge. The gods turned him into the narcissus flower, which often blooms on the shores of ponds and pools.

Many ancient writers retold the story of Narcissus. The Roman poet OVID gave one of the most detailed accounts of Narcissus and his fate. In the A.D. 100s, the Greek travel writer PAUSANIAS claimed to have visited the pool on Mt. Helicon. Pausanias argued that Ovid's version of the story was nonsense. According to Pausanias, Narcissus loved his twin sister, who died, and he simply looked at his own reflection to remind himself of her. Still, the story of Narcissus and Echo was often repeated in the Middle Ages as a warning of the dangers of vanity, or having too high an opinion of oneself. Even in the modern age, writers and artists continue to use Narcissus as a subject for poems, paintings, and sculpture. (*See also* **Myths, Greek; Myths, Roman.**)

## MYTHOLOGY AND PSYCHOLOGY

Some stories from classical mythology, repeated by many writers over the centuries, have become part of modern Western culture. The story of Narcissus is one example. Narcissus became a symbol for anyone who was more interested in himself or herself than in anything else in the world. When modern psychologists needed a word to describe that kind of personality, they turned to the story of Narcissus. In psychology, narcissism means an unhealthy or excessive self-interest.

# NAVAL POWER, GREEK

* **city-state** independent state consisting of a city and its surrounding territory

* **classical** in Greek history, refers to the period of great political and cultural achievement from about 500 B.C. to 323 B.C.

* **maritime** referring to the sea

* **tribute** payment made to a dominant power or local government

* **booty** riches or property gained through conquest

* **privateering** wartime activity in which a government authorizes privately owned and manned ships to engage in attacks on an enemy

The creation of a navy was an expensive undertaking for any ancient state. Building and maintaining warships was costly, and naval crews had to be paid since they consisted of free men rather than slaves. Navies were important, however. They not only defended the coastlines of city-states* from enemy invasions, but they also protected trade and commerce from attacks by pirates.

The earliest Greek naval vessels were rowed by 30 or 50 oarsmen in a single level. These ships had armed men on deck who stood ready to board enemy ships. Later Greek ships added more tiers of rowers to produce faster, more powerful, and more maneuverable vessels that were capable of ramming enemy ships. The most important type of warship in classical* Greece was the trireme, which had 170 rowers in three levels. In addition to protecting coastlines and commerce, warships also transported army troops, who sometimes rowed the ships themselves. Because of the close coordination between land and sea operations, Greek naval forces were usually commanded by an army general. Sparta was one of the few city-states in classical Greece to have the position of admiral.

Athens had the most powerful navy in the eastern Mediterranean during the 400s B.C. After the defeat of the Persian fleet at the Battle of Salamis in 480 B.C., Greek maritime* states formed an alliance called the Delian League, which was dominated by Athens. The crews of the League's ships consisted of Athenian citizens and the citizens of allied states. Silver mined in the area around Laurium in ATTICA helped finance the navy, as did tribute* payments from Athens's allies and the donations of wealthy citizens. The strength of the Athenian navy protected coastal communities as well as ships on the high seas from attacks by pirates in search of booty*.

During the PELOPONNESIAN WAR (431–404 B.C.), the Athenian fleet became occupied with military duties. The war sparked widespread privateering* and PIRACY in the eastern Mediterranean, which continued to flourish for some 30 years after Athens was defeated in the war. Eventually the Athenians were able to rebuild their navy and establish a second maritime league

Early Greek naval vessels consisted of one level of oarsmen and armed warriors on deck who were prepared to board enemy ships. In time, more tiers of men were added to produce faster ships and more powerful naval forces.

## DANGEROUS WATERS

Serving in the navy of Rhodes meant fighting the thousands of pirate ships that roamed the Mediterranean. The inscription on a gravestone that once stood over the tomb of three brothers indicates that each was killed in a different battle against pirates. One brother was killed in the strait between Crete and Greece near Cape Malea, a favorite place for pirates to ambush other ships. Greek sailors considered the strait so dangerous that they had a proverb: "Round Malea and forget about getting home."

* **tyrant**  absolute ruler

* **Hellenistic**  referring to Greek-influenced culture of the Mediterranean world during the three centuries after Alexander the Great, who died in 323 B.C.

* **catapult**  military device for hurling missiles, such as stones

to protect ships from pirate attacks. Despite a lack of manpower and funds, the Athenian navy continued to operate well until 322 B.C., when it was defeated by the Macedonian navy at the Battle of Amorgos in the CYCLADES, islands in the Aegean Sea.

Other Greek city-states also developed powerful navies. During the reign of the tyrant* Polycrates in the 500s B.C., the island of SAMOS built a strong navy with the help of the Egyptians. During the Peloponnesian War between Athens and Sparta, the Persian king helped the Spartans maintain a navy in the Aegean Sea to combat the Athenians. Toward the end of the 200s B.C., the island of RHODES emerged as the strongest naval power in the eastern Mediterranean. The Rhodian navy freed the region of pirates for almost a century. However, with the decline of Rhodes, piracy returned to the Mediterranean in full force.

The Hellenistic* kings rivaled each other in their attempts to build stronger navies by constructing more and bigger ships. Since these larger vessels could not rely on speed, they required more oars and rowers and more armed men on board for protection. Rather than ramming enemy ships, Hellenistic warships used catapults* and stationed troops on deck to fight against enemies who tried to board. Although the PTOLEMAIC DYNASTY of Egypt used its navies to establish and protect overseas possessions, no single Hellenistic navy dominated the Mediterranean prior to the emergence of Roman naval power. (*See also* **Armies, Greek, Economy, Greek; Naval Power, Roman; Persian Wars; Ships and Shipbuilding; Trade, Greek; Wars and Warfare, Greek.**)

# NAVAL POWER, ROMAN

See map in Rome, History of (vol. 4).

Rome became a major naval power when it began to expand its territory beyond ITALY. Since the Romans preferred fighting on land to battles at sea, the Roman navy never became as important as the army. However, Rome used its fleets to transport troops, support land campaigns, and protect its ports. The navy also protected trade by fighting PIRACY. During the first 200 years of the Roman Empire, Roman naval power kept the Mediterranean Sea virtually free of pirates.

Rome built its first large navy during the PUNIC WARS against CARTHAGE in the 200s and 100s B.C. Despite disasters resulting from the inexperience of its sailors, the Roman navy performed well against Carthage, partly because Rome built more and larger ships than its rival. The Romans preferred heavy ships equipped with bridges that allowed Roman troops to board Carthaginian vessels, where they fought as they did on land.

After the Punic Wars, the Roman navy declined in strength and importance. Rome relied instead on the ships of its Greek allies for naval operations. As a result, piracy increased dramatically. By the first century B.C., pirates roamed the Mediterranean Sea unchecked. They raided trading vessels, attacked ports and coastal communities, and even went ashore to kidnap wealthy Romans and hold them for ransom.

When the pirates of the Mediterranean threatened the empire's food supply, Rome decided to take action. In 67 B.C., the Roman Senate appointed POMPEY commander of a large operation against the pirates, and

## CAESAR'S REVENGE

When the young Julius Caesar sailed for Rhodes to study law, a gang of pirates captured him and held him for ransom. The pirates were amused by the young man's arrogance. When they set the ransom price at 20 talents—a huge amount of money—Caesar told them he was worth at least 50 talents. He even had the audacity to order the pirates to keep quiet while he took his afternoon nap. The pirates were especially amused when Caesar promised to return after his release and crucify them all.

Caesar, however, was true to his word. After the ransom was paid, he hired a fleet in nearby Miletus. He then returned and crucified every pirate he found.

* **Roman Republic** Rome during the period from 509 B.C. to 31 B.C., when popular assemblies annually elected their governmental officials

he received almost unlimited authority. Pompey raised a massive fleet by seizing the naval forces of Rhodes and other smaller states. His forces attacked all the pirate strongholds in the Mediterranean at the same time, while Pompey himself led a fleet that forced pirate ships from west to east. His successful three-month campaign ended when he attacked the main pirate headquarters at Cilicia on the coast of Asia Minor and forced the last pirates to surrender.

During the civil wars of the late Roman Republic*, the Roman fleets were revived. Sextus Pompeius, the son of Pompey, used his fleets in an attempt to gain control of the Roman world, but Octavian (the future emperor Augustus) defeated him at sea. Octavian's victory at the Battle of Actium in 31 B.C. marked the end of the civil wars and the beginning of the Roman Empire.

Because of the role of the navy in the civil wars, and especially at the Battle of Actium, the emperor Augustus understood the importance of naval power. He moved quickly to establish permanent fleets. Two major fleets—one based at Ravenna on Italy's east coast and one based at Misenum (near present-day Naples)—guarded the coasts of Italy. Augustus also stationed a fleet at Alexandria in Egypt. Later Roman emperors maintained fleets in North Africa, Britain, on the Rhine and Danube rivers, and on the Black Sea. These fleets prevented pirates from returning until the A.D. 200s. In the A.D. 300s, the emperor Constantine divided the fleets into smaller squadrons but by this time Rome's fleets were declining, and Roman naval power eventually disappeared. (*See also* **Armies, Roman; Civil Wars, Roman; Economy, Roman; Naval Power, Greek; Ships and Shipbuilding; Trade, Roman; Wars and Warfare, Roman.**)

**NEPTUNE**

See *Poseidon.*

**NERO**

A.D. 37–68
ROMAN EMPEROR

* **Praetorian Guard** elite and politically influential corps that served as the emperor's bodyguard

**B**orn Lucius Domitius Ahenobarbus, Nero was emperor of the Roman Empire from A.D. 54 to 68. Although an enthusiastic supporter of art and architecture, Nero is best remembered for his lavish lifestyle, his cruelty to those who opposed him, and the downfall of his government.

When Nero was a boy, his mother, Agrippina, married the emperor Claudius, and Claudius adopted him soon after. In A.D. 53, Nero married Claudius's daughter, and the following year he succeeded Claudius as emperor. Just 17 years old, Nero was considered too young to govern, and he was advised during the first several years of his reign by his tutor, Seneca the Younger, and Burrus, the prefect, or commander, of the Praetorian Guard*. Burrus and Seneca were capable leaders, and later Romans considered these years a golden age of good government. While his advisers governed the empire, Nero enjoyed entertainments, such as chariot races and performances of poetry and drama. He often gave public performances and entered competitions himself. Nero lived an

An emperor of extremes, Nero was notorious for his extravagant lifestyle and his cruelty towards those who opposed him. While his love of the arts inspired some great art and architecture, his suspicion and paranoia resulted in the murder of family members to protect himself.

extravagant and outrageous lifestyle, sometimes even roaming the streets in disguise.

After the death of Burrus in A.D. 62, Nero took full control of the empire himself and forced Seneca into retirement. However, Nero was still more interested in entertainment and the arts than in the responsibilities of leadership, and his government quickly fell apart. A suspicious man, Nero arranged the murder of anyone he believed opposed him, including his own mother and wife. In A.D. 68, the army rebelled against him, no longer willing to support an emperor who was more interested in playing music than visiting them in their camps. Although Nero could have retained power had he responded quickly to the revolt, he panicked instead, fled from Rome, and committed suicide.

Nero's death ended one of the most colorful periods in Roman history. Roman art and architecture reached their peak during Nero's rule, and his coins are considered to be the most beautiful ever produced by the Romans. He is also admired for rebuilding Rome after much of the city was destroyed in a great fire. (*See also* **Architecture, Roman; Palaces, Imperial Roman; Rome, History of.**)

# NOVEL, GREEK AND ROMAN

* **prose** writing without meter or rhyme, as distinguished from poetry

* **Hellenistic** referring to the Greek-influenced culture of the Mediterranean world during the three centuries after Alexander the Great, who died in 323 B.C.

* **Byzantine** referring to the Eastern Christian Empire that was based in Constantinople

The novel—or long, fictional, prose* story—was a late addition to Greek and Roman literature. The Greeks, in particular, had a long tradition of story telling, and their novels were similar to some other forms of literature, such as histories and dramas. However, ancient Greek and Roman literary critics believed that novels were a less exalted form of literature than were other forms, perhaps because they were considered neither serious works of art nor accurate portrayals of history. Nonetheless, by at least the first century A.D., novels were popular reading among the educated elite in both Greece and Rome.

GREEK NOVELS. The Greek novel developed during the Hellenistic* era. The earliest novels are now lost, but their plots centered around such traditional stories as the Trojan War and Jason and the Argonauts. The five ancient Greek novels that survive in their entirety were written during the first 400 years A.D. These novels inspired the writers of Byzantine* novels in the A.D. 1100s, and Europeans in the 1500s and 1600s continued to read them for enjoyment.

The first of these novels was *Chaireas and Kallirhoë,* written by Chariton in the first century A.D. It is a love story about the daughter of a famous general. The plot is complicated, and the characters move from one part of the world to another. Chariton's skillful handling of the twists and turns of the story line is evidence that novels were already a well-developed literary form by his time.

The other existing Greek novels were written by Xenophon, Longus, and Achilles Tatius in the A.D. 100s and Heliodorus in the A.D. 200s or 300s. Of the works of these four writers, the novels that were most admired were Longus's *Daphnis and Chloe* and Heliodoros's *Aithiopika. Daphnis and Chloe* relates the story of two adolescents coping with the first stirrings of love and sexuality. *Aithiopika* is a mystery involving an exiled Egyptian priest. It has a carefully crafted plot set on two continents and involves people from three different cultures.

All of these early Greek novels share several common features. They have similar plots, usually involving a teenaged boy and girl who fall in love. In most of these books, just before the couple is to be married, the young lovers are separated. Traveling to distant lands, they suffer storms and shipwrecks, and evil characters imprison and torture them. These novels all have happy endings.

The characters in the early Greek novels are usually from the aristocratic* ranks of society. (Although the two main characters in *Daphnis and Chloe* at first appear to be exceptions, the two young people turn out to be wealthy after all.) Most of the novels take place in the historical past, and some of the action seems far-fetched. The author sometimes makes it quite clear in the beginning that what he narrates did not actually take place. Longus, for example, states that *Daphnis and Chloe* was inspired by a painting he once saw.

Many modern literary critics fault these early Greek novels for having unconvincing characters. While the characters are usually morally upright and admirable, they are often flat and predictable. Nonetheless, the writing in these early Greek novels is skillful and even elegant.

**LATIN NOVELS.** The novel as a literary form was less popular among Latin writers. Only two examples of the Latin novel exist today—the *Satyricon* of PETRONIUS Arbiter, which was written before A.D. 100, and the *Metamorphoses,* or *The Golden Ass,* written in the A.D. 100s by APULEIUS. No earlier Latin works of fiction are known.

Although only parts of the *Satyricon* survive, it was a very long work that filled at least 16 books. The novel relates the humorous adventures of a homosexual couple. As its name suggests, it is a satire*, mostly of the conventional Greek romance novel. The *Satyricon* also contains literary and social criticism. In one famous scene, Trimalchio, a rich and crude former slave, holds a pretentious and vulgar dinner party, which was intended to ridicule contemporary Roman society.

Apuleius's *Golden Ass* is the only complete Roman novel to survive from this period. Filling 11 books, it tells the story of a young man who is changed into a donkey. The novel describes the boy's comic adventures before he is changed back into a human being by the goddess ISIS. Apuleius weaves traditional folktales into the plot, the most famous of which is the tale of CUPID AND PSYCHE, which takes up two entire books of the novel.

Although both Petronius and Apuleius adopted the literary form of the Greek novel, they changed it in typically Roman ways. For example, they both made fun of the Greek emphasis on young love among the aristocracy by focusing on low-life realism and base humor. Both Roman writers also applied complex literary techniques to their works, such as using several narrators to tell the tale. (*See also* **Books and Manuscripts; Literature, Greek; Literature, Roman.**)

* **aristocratic** referring to people of the highest social class

* **satire** literary technique that uses wit and sarcasm to expose or ridicule vice and folly

## ROMANCE IN FACT AND FICTION

In the early Greek novels, young people fall in love, and their love inevitably leads to marriage. This romantic ideal of love and marriage was strictly the stuff of fiction. In reality, marriage in the Mediterranean world was almost never the result of love. Instead, marriage was a carefully negotiated business arrangement between clans and families. Thus, romance was a literary convention, not a fact of life.

## NUMBERS

See *Mathematics, Greek; Roman Numerals.*

OCTAVIAN

See *Augustus, Caesar Octavianus.*

ODYSSEUS

* **hero** in mythology, a person of great strength or ability, often descended from a god

* **epic** long poem about legendary or historical heroes, written in a grand style

* **abdicate** to give up the throne voluntarily or under pressure

Odysseus was one of the most prominent heroes* in Greek mythology. He is best known from Homer's epic* poem the *Odyssey,* which relates Odysseus's ten-year journey home after the Trojan War. Odysseus was a popular subject for other Greek writers as well, and his exploits were frequently featured in Greek works of art. The Romans referred to him as Ulixes, from which his English name, Ulysses, is derived.

Odysseus was the only son of Laertes, the king of Ithaca, and his wife, Anticleia. He married Penelope, the daughter of the king of Sparta, who bore him a son, Telemachus. After Laertes voluntarily abdicated* his throne, Odysseus became king. When the Trojan War began, Odysseus, accompanied by 12 shiploads of men, reluctantly joined his fellow Greek warriors in their battle against the Trojans.

Odysseus also plays a prominent role in the *Iliad,* Homer's epic about the events of the Trojan War. Here Homer portrays him as a skilled and

One of the most famous heroes of Greek mythology, Odysseus was a popular subject for both writers and artists. At the end of his long journey, Odysseus is said to have returned to his wife, Penelope, in disguise and unrecognized, as this sculpture suggests.

## ODYSSEUS AND THE CYCLOPS

On his way home to Ithaca, Odysseus was blown off course and landed on the island of the Cyclopes, who were one-eyed giants. One of the giants, named Polyphemus, captured Odysseus and his men in a cave and blocked their exit with a huge rock. Odysseus told the giant that his name was Outis, which means "Nobody." After making the giant drunk, Odysseus blinded Polyphemus with a hot stake. The giant cried out for help, but since he said that Nobody was attacking him, the other Cyclopes ignored him. The next morning the blinded giant opened the entrance of the cave, and Odysseus and his men escaped.

* **siege** long and persistent effort to force a surrender by surrounding a fortress with armed troops, cutting it off from aid

courageous fighter and a man known for his diplomacy and wisdom. In the *Odyssey,* however, Odysseus more frequently uses cunning and deceit to defeat stronger opponents, such as the one-eyed, giant CYCLOPS. He not only resorts to tricks and lies to escape trouble, but he seems to tell tall tales simply for enjoyment.

Odysseus's cunning is best illustrated by the story of the Trojan horse. The Greeks had laid siege* to Troy for ten years without success. Odysseus suggested the idea of building a hollow wooden horse large enough for Greek warriors to hide inside. The horse was left outside the gates of Troy, supposedly as a religious offering. When the curious Trojans pulled the horse inside the gates of Troy, the Greek warriors emerged from the horse, opened the gates, and captured the city.

At the beginning of the *Odyssey,* Telemachus praises his father as the ideal king who must return home to Ithaca to reestablish peace and order. Homer portrays Odysseus as a noble, strong, enduring man, who has been loyal to his wife for 20 long years. In many other early Greek poems and plays, however, Odysseus is presented in a much less favorable light. In one poem, Odysseus pretends to be insane in order to get out of his responsibility to fight in the Trojan War, and he is a villain in the play *Philoctetes* by SOPHOCLES. The Roman poet VERGIL (who idealized the vanquished Trojans) referred to Odysseus in a similar way. Odysseus appears in many later works of literature, almost always playing the role of a trickster. (*See also* **Homer;** *Iliad;* **Literature, Greek; Literature, Roman; Myths, Greek;** *Odyssey.*)

## ODYSSEY

* **hero** in mythology, a person of great strength or ability, often descended from a god

* **nymph** in classical mythology, one of the lesser goddesses of nature

The *Odyssey* is an epic poem about the Greek mythic hero* ODYSSEUS. It was composed by HOMER in the 700s B.C. The *Odyssey* has always been an extremely popular work of literature. Among ancient books, only the Bible has been read more than the *Odyssey.*

Organized into 24 books, the *Odyssey* is a very long poem, containing about 12,000 verses. The poem relates Odysseus's ten-year voyage back to his native island of Ithaca after fighting in the Trojan War, which lasted ten years. Homer describes Odysseus as a "resourceful man," one who possesses courage, determination, and endurance. The story itself is basically a folktale with typical folk themes, such as romance, adventure, and the triumph of virtue over evil. It is a masterfully crafted work with descriptive language that lends beauty and grace to the narrative.

The epic begins *in medias res,* a literary technique in which a story opens in the middle of the action and then returns to the start. As the epic begins, Odysseus has left Troy for his journey homeward, but he is a prisoner of Calypso, a sea nymph* who has held him captive for more than seven years. During Odysseus's long absence from Ithaca, his wife Penelope and son Telemachus have awaited his return. A group of suitors, each of whom hopes to marry Penelope and obtain the throne for himself, pursues her and tries to convince her that Odysseus is dead. They also scheme to find ways to get rid of Telemachus. The goddess ATHENA intervenes to protect Odysseus and his household. She counsels Telemachus to banish the suitors from his home and to leave Ithaca to seek news of his father.

Eventually, the god Hermes forces Calypso to release Odysseus, and Calypso helps him build a makeshift raft in order to set sail for home. But he is blown off course by a storm sent by the sea god, POSEIDON, and he washes up on the shore of the Phaeacians. While there, Odysseus tells the Phaeacians about the adventures he and his crew have encountered since leaving Troy.

First, he tells them about the land of the lotus eaters, whose food cures one of homesickness. Some of Odysseus's men ate the food and wanted to remain there, but Odysseus forced them to continue on their journey. Next, Odysseus and his crew found themselves on the island of the CYCLOPES, the one-eyed giants. They were held captive there by the Cyclops Polyphemus, and Odysseus tells how he and some of his men escaped after blinding the giant. Their next stop was on the island of Aeolia, where the Lord of the Winds gave Odysseus a bag containing all the winds except the west wind, which continued to blow in order to help them sail home. Odysseus's sailors, however, thinking the bag contained gold, opened it, and the winds escaped, blowing the men off course yet again.

Soon they arrived at the land of the Laestrygonians. The Laestrygonians were man-eating giants who crushed ships with large rocks and ate the crews. Odysseus escaped with just one ship, which he sailed to the island of Circe, a powerful witch who changed Odysseus's few remaining men into pigs. Circe later transformed the crew back into human beings, but she told Odysseus that in order to reach his home, he would first have to visit the underworld*. There Odysseus saw the ghosts of his mother and several heroes of the Trojan War. He also saw how sinners were punished. While in Hades, Odysseus met a prophet who told him the best route to take to Ithaca.

But Odysseus's adventures were far from over. He and his men sailed past the island of the SIRENS, sea nymphs whose beautiful singing was said to lure sailors to their death. Circe had warned Odysseus about the Sirens, so he plugged the ears of his men with beeswax and had himself tied to the mast until they were out of earshot of the Sirens' song. Circe had also told

* **underworld** kingdom of the dead; also called Hades

The adventures and exploits of the Greek mythological hero Odysseus are best illustrated in Homer's epic poem the *Odyssey*. A work of monumental proportions, the epic tells the tale of the hero's ten-year journey home after fighting for ten years in the Trojan War. This scene shows Odysseus's men in the land of the Laestrygonians.

them how to sail past the sea monsters Scylla and Charybdis. Just as they had avoided these dangers and home seemed near, some of Odysseus's men ate the sacred cattle of the sun god. As punishment, a thunderbolt struck the ship and the crew drowned. This time only Odysseus survived, and he found himself on Calypso's island.

Moved by his tale, the Phaeacians take Odysseus home to the shores of Ithaca. There Athena appears to him, warning him of the suitors in his palace. She advises Odysseus to disguise himself as a beggar and instructs him to go to a swineherd's hut in the countryside before returning to the palace. There Odysseus and his son are reunited, and they plot vengeance on Penelope's suitors. Odysseus's old dog, Argos, recognizes his master in spite of his disguise. Penelope, believing Odysseus to be dead, is about to choose a new husband. She announces a competition, and she says that she will marry the winner. The man who can string her husband's bow and perform a very difficult feat of archery will be her new husband. Odysseus enters the competition and wins. Odysseus cries victoriously, "Now I shoot at another mark, and let Apollo aid me," and, with the help of his son and two servants, massacres all of the suitors. With peace restored, Odysseus finally reveals his true identity to Penelope, and he and his faithful wife are reunited.

The *Odyssey* is both a simpler and more complicated poem than the *Iliad*. It is simpler because it tells the story of only one man and his companions. But it is more complex in that it moves forward and backward in time and across many regions of the mythological world. Little is known about the author of this great work. Homer may have been a bard who sang or recited his work at the palace of an ancient king or nobleman. He and other poets of his day sang about an idealized past—an age of heroes and close communion with the gods. It is not known if Homer wrote down the verses himself or if others, long after his death, wrote down the verses that had been preserved by the Greek tradition of public recitations. (*See also* **Epic, Greek; Literature, Greek; Myths, Greek.**)

# OEDIPUS

* **epic** long poem about legendary or historical heroes, written in a grand style

Oedipus was a legendary king of the Greek city of Thebes. The literature of the ancient Greeks includes several versions of his life story, in each of which he is the victim of terrible misfortune. In the most famous account, Oedipus killed his father and married his mother.

The earliest account of Oedipus is in the epic* poems of HOMER. The *Iliad* mentions Oedipus only as a king of Thebes who most likely died in battle. The *Odyssey* provides a few more details, mentioning that Oedipus unknowingly married his mother, who killed herself when his identity became known.

Other epic poems contained longer, more detailed versions of the story of Oedipus. Although these poems are now lost, references to them in other works indicate that they presented Oedipus as an outcast who was doomed by an ancient curse. The lost epics helped create the image of Oedipus and his family that appears in the tragic dramas of three great Greek playwrights. SOPHOCLES told the most detailed version of the tale in three of his plays: *Oedipus the King, Oedipus at Colonus,* and *Antigone*. AESCHYLUS and EURIPIDES also wrote plays about the life of Oedipus.

## THE OEDIPUS COMPLEX

"Oedipus complex" is a term for an unconscious desire for the exclusive love of the parent of the opposite sex. It was first used by Sigmund Freud, the Austrian physician who helped to pioneer the field of psychiatry in the early A.D. 1900s. He took the name from the legendary Greek tragic figure, Oedipus.

Freud believed the Oedipus complex was a stage in normal development between the ages of two and six, when a child begins to experience the conflicting emotions of love and hate, yearning and jealousy, and fear and anger. Freud believed most people outgrew the Oedipus complex, but that a few did not.

* **oracle** priest or priestess through whom a god is believed to speak; also the location (such as a shrine) where such utterances are made

* **plague** highly contagious, widespread, and often fatal disease

According to Sophocles' version of the story, King Laius of Thebes kidnapped the son of an enemy. This act brought upon Laius a curse that was to torment several generations of his family. After Laius married a woman named Jocasta, an oracle* warned Laius that if his wife bore a son, that son would kill Laius. Jocasta did indeed have a son, and King Laius took the baby to a mountainside, drove a spike through his ankles, and left him there to die. A shepherd from CORINTH rescued the baby and named him Oedipus, which means "swollen feet." King Polybus of Corinth, who had no children, adopted the infant.

When Oedipus became a young man, people pointed out that he resembled neither King Polybus nor his wife. Curious about his real parents, Oedipus questioned the oracle at DELPHI. The oracle replied that Oedipus was doomed to kill his father and marry his mother. Thinking that the king and queen of Corinth were his parents, the horrified Oedipus decided not to return there. As he wandered toward Thebes, he argued with a stranger at a crossroads and killed him. Upon reaching Thebes, Oedipus learned that King Laius had just been killed and that the Sphinx, a creature with the body of a lion but a human head, was terrorizing the city. The Sphinx challenged people with a riddle: "What walks on four legs in the morning, two legs at noon, and three legs in the evening?" The creature killed all those who answered the riddle incorrectly. Oedipus defeated the Sphinx by giving the correct answer to the riddle. The answer was: "A man, who crawls as a baby, walks when grown, and leans on a stick when old." Happy to be rid of the Sphinx, the people of Thebes made Oedipus their king, and he married Jocasta, the widow of King Laius.

Oedipus and Jocasta had four children. A plague* then struck Thebes, and, according to the oracle at Delphi, the city would be saved only if the people drove out Laius's murderer. Oedipus investigated the matter, and he soon realized that the man he had killed at the crossroads was King Laius. He also learned that Laius was his father. Just as the oracle at Delphi had predicted, Oedipus had killed his father and married his mother. Shocked and horrified at this revelation, Jocasta hanged herself. Oedipus blinded himself with pins and left Thebes as an outcast and a victim of fate.

The Greek playwrights composed various accounts of later events in Oedipus's life. In most versions, he cursed his sons, who later went to war against each other. In Sophocles' *Oedipus at Colonus,* Oedipus's daughter Antigone leads the aged, blind man to a sacred grove of trees near Athens, where he dies. His ghost was said to protect Athens from any attack by Thebes. (*See also* **Drama, Greek; Epic, Greek; Myths, Greek.**)

## OLIGARCHY

Oligarchy is a Greek word meaning "rule by the few." In an oligarchy, some of the free population is excluded from having basic political rights and from holding office. Participation of citizens in government is severely restricted, and control of the government is turned over to a small group of individuals who, because of their birth, wealth, or special abilities, are viewed as best able to control government. The Greek philosopher Aristotle defined oligarchy as the rule

* **aristocracy**  rule by the nobility or privileged upper class

* **tyranny**  rule by one person, usually obtained through unlawful means

* **city-state**  independent state consisting of a city and its surrounding territory

* **Hellenistic**  referring to the Greek-influenced culture of the Mediterranean world during the three centuries after Alexander the Great, who died in 323 B.C.

of the rich. Some political theorists maintain that aristocracy* is a better term for oligarchy.

There were several types of oligarchies in the ancient world. Some oligarchies were actually tyrannies*; others were early forms of federal or representative government. The city of CARTHAGE, on the coast of North Africa, was the largest oligarchy in the Mediterranean region. In the fifth century B.C., its government changed from that of one-man rule to an oligarchy in which a small group of individuals held the power. This group was made up of magistrates (called *sufets*), generals, and a council of nobles.

Oligarchies existed in most Greek city-states* before the 500s B.C., although they were not then called by that name. In the 500s, some city-states began moving toward democracy. While ATHENS became the most successful Greek democracy during the 400s B.C., SPARTA was the most powerful oligarchy. Sparta was governed by five officials (called *ephors*) and the *gerousia*, a council made up of 28 elders and the two Spartan kings. In the mid-400s, the cities of the region of Boeotia, north of Athens, freed themselves from Athenian control and established a type of oligarchic government. Full citizenship in each city was based on the ownership of a specified amount of property. Those who had full citizen rights were organized into four councils. Decisions were passed by all four groups. Each city was divided into wards, or sections, with representation based on population. The citizens of each ward elected a magistrate, council members, soldiers, and jury members. The members of the Boeotian League (as the member cities called themselves) met at the city of THEBES in a council of 660.

At the end of the fifth century B.C., some Athenians revolted against democracy. The regime of the Four Hundred in 411 B.C. proposed a constitution that reflected the ideas of the Boeotian constitution. However, the Four Hundred never consolidated their rule sufficiently to establish a true constitution. They quickly dissolved into a wider, and more democratic, body known as the Five Thousand, which eventually merged back into a democracy. For a brief period, from 404–403 B.C., the Thirty Tyrants established an oligarchy in Athens. In the Hellenistic* period, the distinctions between oligarchy and democracy became even less clear, since even democratic states tended to be governed by the rich. States calling themselves democratic were really oligarchic. (*See also* **Democracy, Greek; Greece, History of; Tyrants, Greek.**)

## OLIVES

Along with grain and wine, olives were one of the basic foods of the peoples of the Mediterranean region. Because olive trees generally yield a crop every other year, farmers usually grew olive trees along with other tree crops, or they combined olive growing with sheepherding. Cultivation of olives in Greece dates from the BRONZE AGE. By 600 B.C. the olive was well established in Italy.

Olives are native to the dry, warm regions of Greece, Italy, Spain, France, the Balkan Peninsula, Asia Minor, northern Africa, and the countries of the eastern Mediterranean region. Because olives do not grow from seeds, the ancients developed many techniques for cultivating olive

* **graft** to insert a shoot or bud from one kind of tree into a slit in a closely related tree so that it will grow there

trees. These techniques included planting cuttings from mature trees to make new trees and grafting* one kind of tree onto another.

Olives are harvested in autumn and winter and are used both as table food and for their oil. The ancients thought green olives produced the best olive oil. These olives were harvested early for crushing and pressing. Ripe, black olives contain more oil than green olives. The ancients also packed olives in salt for future use, cured them in wine or vinegar, cooked them with other foods, and ground them into a mash.

The ancient peoples had many uses for olive oil other than for cooking and eating. It was used as medication—it was believed to cure an earache when poured into the affected ear. Olive oil was also used as fuel for lighting, as a base for perfumes and cosmetics, and as a lubricant for the body. Wrestlers coated themselves with olive oil before a wrestling match. The finest olive oil was offered as a gift during religious FESTIVALS or awarded to an outstanding athlete. (*See also* **Agriculture, Greek; Agriculture, Roman; Bread; Food and Drink.**)

## OLYMPIA

* **Peloponnese** peninsula forming the southern part of the mainland of Greece

* **sanctuary** place for worship

* **cult** group bound together by devotion to a particular person, belief, or god

Located in the northwestern Peloponnese*, Olympia was the legendary home of the Titans, the mythical giants who ruled the earth before the Olympian gods (who resided at the unrelated site of Mt. OLYMPUS). It later became the site of the main sanctuary* of the Greek god ZEUS. Pilgrims from all parts of the Greek world traveled to Olympia to worship at his shrine. Olympia is also important as the site of the first Olympiad, or OLYMPIC GAMES, held in 776 B.C.

Around 1200 B.C. the Greeks established the cult* of Zeus at Olympia, which survived into the A.D. 300s. The most famous building at Olympia was the temple of Zeus, completed around 457 B.C. Inside the temple stood a colossal statue of the god sculpted by PHIDIAS, a well-known sculptor from Athens. The gold and ivory statue—one of the Seven Wonders of the Ancient World—presented Zeus seated on a throne. The Roman emperor CALIGULA was so impressed by the statue that he planned to take it back to Rome. However, the ship intended to carry it was struck by lightning, perhaps a sign from the god himself.

Olympia's importance as a sanctuary declined for a time under the Romans but then revived under the emperors TIBERIUS and NERO. In A.D. 426 the emperor Theodosius ordered the destruction of the temple. In the A.D. 500s, the entire temple area of Olympia was buried under debris from an earthquake. The debris preserved the ancient objects for future generations. (*See also* **Divinities; Festivals and Feasts, Greek; Festivals and Feasts, Roman.**)

## OLYMPIC GAMES

The Olympiad of 776 B.C. was the first major athletic festival of the ancient world. The Olympic Games, as they are known today, were begun in OLYMPIA, in Greece, to honor the god ZEUS. The games were held every four years for about 12 centuries. They ended in the late A.D. 300s on the order of the emperor THEODOSIUS. The destruction of Olympia by an earthquake may have hastened their demise. The Greek writer PINDAR credits

## MILO THE MAGNIFICENT

The Olympic Games produced many famous athletes whose names and accomplishments have been preserved in the annals of the athletic competition. No ancient athlete impressed the Greek public more than the wrestler known as Milo of Croton, from southern Italy. He won at least six Olympic olive crowns and reigned as Olympic wrestling champion from 532 to 512 B.C. His 20-year record has never been broken.

Milo was over 40 when he was finally forced to retire. But his technique, balance, and strength became legendary. Greeks said he could stand on a greased discus and no man could push him off.

* **hero** in mythology, a person of great strength or ability, often descended from a god

* **city-state** independent state consisting of a city and its surrounding territory

The first Olympiad, an organized international competition that drew participants from throughout the Greek world, inspired sportsmanship, goodwill, and community pride—ideals that are still valued in today's Olympics. The discus throw, which is still included in the Olympic Games, is shown here.

the mythic hero* HERACLES with the inspiration for the Olympic Games—to celebrate his cleaning of the Augean stables, one of his famous Twelve Labors.

The Olympic Games were held around mid-August or mid-September, after the harvest was in. The athletic competitions were open to male citizens from all parts of the Greek world. There were no amateurs or women participating in the events. Competitors were either aristocrats (who had the time and money to train) or professional athletes. The prizes for winning an event were a crown of wild olive, immense prestige, and sometimes political advancement. Winners often were able to build on their success at Olympia in terms of military advancement as well. In fact, the athletic contests were, in a sense, "war games" in which city-states* displayed the might and skill of their male citizens.

The first and only competition at the Olympic Games for many years was the *stadion,* a footrace of about 200 yards. It was run in the stadium, a place with a track for the runners and seats for observers. By the mid-600s B.C., a core of events had been established. In addition to the stadion, the other events included the double stadion, a 5,000-yard footrace, a pentathlon (a five-event competition consisting of a discus throw, a standing jump, a javelin throw, a footrace, and wrestling), boxing, a chariot race, a horse race, and a *pankration,* which was an extreme, "anything goes" wrestling match. The games lasted about five days, during which time there were religious ceremonies, social events, and a parade of champions on the final day.

The Olympic Games were remarkable for several reasons. They were an organized, international event whose participants came from every part of the Greek world. The games also provided a respite from the almost

constant WARS AND WARFARE. To ensure that war would not interfere with the games or with travel to and from Olympia, a truce of one to three months was instituted. During this period, participating states were forbidden to take up arms against each other. The truce guaranteed athletes and spectators safe passage. The truce was violated in 364 B.C. by the Arcadians, a Greek people from the central Peloponnese*. The decline of the games may be traced to that date. In 80 B.C. the games were transferred to Rome.

The modern Olympic Games began in 1896 in Athens. They were revived by a French educator, Pierre de Coubertin. (*See also* **Festivals and Feasts; Games, Greek.**)

* **Peloponnese** peninsula forming the southern part of the mainland of Greece

---

## OLYMPUS, MT.

* **deity** god or goddess

Rising above the AEGEAN SEA, Mt. Olympus at 9,573 feet is the highest mountain in Greece. Mt. Olympus played an important role in Greek religion, myth, and literature. The Greeks believed that the mountain reached the sky and that it was the home of their 12 major gods and goddesses. These deities* were also called the Olympians, for the mountaintop on which they resided. Mt. Olympus may have been regarded as the home of the gods because early Greek immigrants originated from the region, or because the mountain was the farthest point known to the prehistoric Greeks. Homer's epic poem the *Odyssey* describes the mansion of the gods as a place that is unaffected by wind or rain and is always in brilliant sunshine—a place where "the blithe gods live all their days in bliss."

Mt. Olympus is the largest of a chain of mountains which form a boundary in northeastern Greece between the regions of Thessaly and MACEDONIA. In ancient times, these mountains served as a natural barrier to protect Greece from invasions from the north. Potential invaders had either to make their way through the narrow pass of Tempe in the east or to scale the high mountain passes in the west. (*See also* **Divinities; Geography and Geology, Mediterranean; Myths, Greek.**)

---

## OMENS

In the cultural traditions of the ancient Greeks and Romans, an omen was a predictor of a future event—good or bad. A sneeze, a dream, a stumble, a lightning strike, the appearance of a comet, and the flight patterns of birds were regarded as omens. The ancients believed that omens were sent by the gods and that they should be taken seriously. Major decisions and battles might be postponed if an omen indicated disaster ahead. When the Greek military commander XENOPHON felt an urge to sneeze while addressing his troops before a battle, everyone assumed that the gods were on their side. The Greeks regarded the sneeze as a sign of good luck.

In Greece the behavior of birds was especially important as an omen. Certain species of birds were believed to be messengers of the gods. For example, the eagle was associated with ZEUS, the falcon with APOLLO, and the owl with ATHENA. The direction from which birds appeared was also important. Anything coming from the right side was good; anything from the left meant danger. Omens had greater significance if the viewer was facing

See color plate 6, vol. 4.

* **seer** person who foresees future events; a prophet

* **entrails** internal organs, including the intestines

* **divination** art or practice of foretelling the future

north. The appearance of birds also signaled seasonal changes. In *Works and Days,* the Greek poet HESIOD advises farmers to "pay heed when you hear the voice of the crane, crying every year from the clouds on high: for she brings the sign to plow and shows forth the season of rainy winter."

Sacrifices were fraught with omens. A victim who approached the altar willingly was a positive sign, whereas an unwilling victim signaled disaster. Seers* examined the entrails* (especially the liver) of the sacrificed animal for omens too. The opinion of a seer was highly valued by military commanders, who were always on the lookout for an advantage in battle. Every army had a seer for this purpose. A good seer was a valuable asset to an army.

Simple objects were also used to predict the future. The ancient Greeks and Romans peered into bowls of water, drew lots, threw dice, and observed statues of the gods for signs of impending doom or good fortune.

The Romans regarded birds, lightning, and sacrificial victims as important omens. Like the Greeks, they also placed importance on a random word or phrase. When Rome's leaders were debating whether to abandon their city after its capture by the Gauls, it was the chance remark of a soldier marching his men through the FORUM that turned the tide of flight. The soldier had remarked casually, "We might as well stop here."

Not all the ancient peoples believed in omens. The followers of the philosopher EPICURUS expressed doubt, and the writer ARISTOPHANES poked fun at Athenians' belief in omens. In the late A.D. 300s, the emperor THEODO-SIUS forbade all forms of divination.* (*See also* **Augur; Divination; Oracles.**)

## ORACLES

* **shrine** place that is considered sacred because of its history or the relics it contains

* **divination** art or practice of foretelling the future

The term *oracle* had several meanings for the ancient Greeks and Romans. Oracles were divine responses to questions asked by human beings. Oracles were also the priests or priestesses through whom a god was believed to speak. Finally, oracles were the places—usually shrines*—where such questions and responses were exchanged. For the Greeks, oracles were the most important form of divination*. Oracles (responses) usually gave comfort to believers seeking to know if the gods favored their actions. The Greeks and Romans both had many oracles (sites). The most famous oracle in ancient Greece was located at DELPHI. The oldest oracle in Greece was located at Dodona and honored the god ZEUS.

The responses given were generally ambiguous, leaving the questioner to figure out the meaning. A misinterpretation of the response was never the fault of the oracle. The ancients consulted oracles on every imaginable topic. For example, pilgrims could obtain advice about the underworld by consulting the oracle of Trophonius at Lebadea.

At the Delphic oracle, pilgrims asked questions of the Pythia, the name given to the high priestess of APOLLO. She then entered a trance during which the god spoke his answer through her. The words of the Pythia were then communicated to the questioner by the priests of the Pythia. Other gods, such as Gaia, DIONYSUS, and HERMES also had oracular shrines. Messages from the gods also came through dreams. The priest of the oracle acted as interpreter of the dream.

Oracles provided divine responses to questions posed by the ancient Greeks and Romans. Greece's Delphic Oracle was the most famous of these sites. People of all classes sought advice from it. Even mythical figures—such as Oedipus pictured in this relief—were said to have consulted the oracle for answers.

Like the Greeks, the Romans believed it was of the utmost importance to have the favor of the gods, and they consulted many of the Greek oracles. They also visited local shrines, such as the oracle of Calchas in Apulia. There pilgrims sacrificed a black ram, slept on its fleece, and received the answers to their inquiries in dreams. Oracles were also enshrined in groves of trees. The oracle of Faunus was located in two groves outside Rome. In addition to sacrificing a sheep, pilgrims to Faunus fasted, wore simple clothing, and touched a bough of the sacred beech tree before falling asleep in the grove and receiving a divine message in a dream. People from throughout the Italian peninsula visited this oracle.

As Romans settled in the eastern provinces*, they became believers in the Greek oracles. The oracles of Apollo at Didyma and Claros, in western Asia Minor, were two notable Greek shrines that the Romans visited. No matter where oracles were located, they were besieged with ordinary questions that changed little over the centuries: Will I lose my money? Am I to be divorced from my wife? Will I be reconciled with my son? (*See also* **Afterlife; Augur; Divinities; Omens; Ritual and Sacrifice.**)

* **province** overseas area controlled by Rome

# ORATORY

* **city-state** independent state consisting of a city and its surrounding territory

* **Roman Republic** Rome during the period from 509 B.C. to 31 B.C., when popular assemblies annually elected their governmental officials

* **rhetoric** art of using words effectively in speaking or writing

O ratory, or the art of public speaking, played a major role in political and public life in the ancient world. This was especially true in the city-state* of ATHENS during the 400s and 300s B.C. and in the Roman Republic*. During these periods, political leaders used oratory to convince their fellow citizens of the wisdom and appeal of their policies. Oratory became the principal reason for the study of rhetoric*, which remained central to the educational system of the Greeks and Romans for centuries.

In his handbook *Rhetoric,* the Greek philosopher* ARISTOTLE defined three types of oratory. Judicial oratory, which concerned past events, consisted of courtroom speeches. Because participants in legal disputes

# ORATORY

represented themselves in court, many people hired professional speechwriters to prepare their speeches. Deliberative oratory involved public discussion of the best course to take in the future. Orators attempted to sway voters or move people to action during debates held in front of the assembly of citizens. Epideictic oratory, or display speeches, provided opportunities for orators to show off their skills. Such speeches were often given either to praise or to blame someone. Funeral orations were a type of epideictic oratory.

Greek oratory flourished during the late 400s and the 300s B.C. The great orators of this period were considered models of oratorical skill, and Hellenistic* scholars preserved many of their speeches. The earliest of these speechmakers was Lysias. He was known for his simple, direct style and for the way he used language to make the speaker appear likable and persuasive because the speech was written for a particular defendant to deliver for himself. The great orator DEMOSTHENES developed a grand, impressive style. In speeches such as the *Philippics* and *Olynthiacs* to the Athenian assembly, Demosthenes attempted to alert his fellow Athenian citizens to the threat of PHILIP II of Macedonia. He appealed to his listeners' sense of history and to their own nobility. Another great orator, Aeschines, delivered speeches that favored vivid descriptions rather than logic. Aeschines was Demosthenes' political enemy, and the rivalry between the two men came to a head in 336 B.C. Aeschines brought a suit against a man named Ctesiphon for illegally proposing to award a crown to Demosthenes for his service to Athens. When the case came to trial six years later, Demosthenes made a brilliant speech, titled *On the Crown,* in support of Ctesiphon, and Aeschines was overwhelmingly defeated. Aeschines left Athens and settled in Rhodes.

The education of upper-class Romans, which emphasized the study of rhetoric, was designed to produce skilled orators who could deliver speeches in the law courts, before the people, and in the Roman Senate. Students of rhetoric and oratory learned how to select appropriate subjects for their speeches and how to influence their listeners by appealing to their sense of logic and to their emotions. Students of oratory also learned various styles of speechmaking, which ranged from plain to grand. They used memory devices to help them remember points they wished to make in long speeches. Finally, they studied techniques for delivering effective speeches, including gestures and dramatic uses of the voice.

Orators also learned the five parts of a judicial speech. The beginning of a speech was the prologue, which was designed to win the goodwill of the audience. During the narrative, the orator presented the essential facts of the case. The speaker expressed his own point of view of the facts in the confirmation, and he attempted to demolish his opponent's opinions or point of view in the refutation. Finally, during the epilogue, the speaker delivered his conclusion, usually by rousing the emotions of the audience.

Beginning in the 100s B.C., Roman orators practiced their skills by delivering declamations. Declamations were speeches on selected topics. Those drawn from history and mythology were called *suasoriae;* those from complicated legal situations were called *controversiae.* One famous *suasoria* concerned the question of whether, during the Trojan War, AGAMEMNON should sacrifice his daughter IPHIGENIA to gain favorable winds for his ships. An example of a *controversia* is the following: The law says that a woman who has been raped has the choice of marrying the man or having him killed. A man is found guilty of raping two women in one night. One woman decides for death; the other decides for marriage. The speaker argues one side of the case or the other.

During the Roman Empire, oratory lost its importance as a political tool because the emperors held virtually absolute power. Instead, declamations became a form of popular entertainment. Declamations by great orators became social occasions, sometimes attended even by the emperor. Although oratory had lost its political force, people continued to study the great political speeches of Demosthenes and other famous orators as models of the power of language. (*See also* **Education and Rhetoric, Greek; Education and Rhetoric, Roman.**)

## ORESTEIA

See *Aeschylus.*

## ORESTES

In Greek mythology, Orestes was the son of CLYTEMNESTRA and AGAMEMNON, king of MYCENAE and Argos and commander of the allied Greek forces in the Trojan War. According to Homer's epic poem the *Odyssey,* Orestes killed his mother's lover, Aegisthus, who had murdered Agamemnon. Homer implies that Orestes killed Clytemnestra as well. Several Greek playwrights, including AESCHYLUS, SOPHOCLES, and EURIPIDES wrote versions of the story. These were most likely based on a work by the playwright Stesichorus titled *Oresteia,* which has been lost.

In each of the surviving plays, Orestes, following his father's murder, is taken in by Strophius (the king of Phocis and Agamemnon's brother-in-law). Orestes is raised along with Strophius's son, Pylades. A strong friendship develops between the two young men. Several years elapse, and the fully grown Orestes must decide what to do about his father's murder. He consults the oracle* at DELPHI and is instructed to avenge the murder. Accompanied by Pylades, Orestes returns home, where Aegisthus has reigned during his absence. He is met by his sister, ELECTRA, whom Aegisthus has married to a peasant in order to degrade her. Electra agrees to support her brother and assists in the killing of Aegisthus and maybe even in that of their mother.

In the versions by Homer and Sophocles, Orestes' actions are completely justified, even honorable, and they gain him great respect. Aeschylus and Euripides, on the other hand, report that Orestes was tormented by the FURIES for his deeds. The Furies were spirits who punished wrongdoers. In these versions of the tale, Orestes is driven mad by the Furies until he agrees to stand trial at Athens for the killings. The vote of the Athenian jury is evenly split between guilt and innocence, but Orestes is finally acquitted when ATHENA casts the deciding vote in his favor. (*See also* **Drama, Greek; Literature, Greek; Myths, Greek.**)

* oracle priest or priestess through whom a god is believed to speak; also the location (such as a shrine) where such utterances are made

## ORPHEUS AND EURYDICE

Orpheus and Eurydice are the main characters in one of the most famous ancient love stories. The son of APOLLO and the Muse Calliope, Orpheus was the finest singer and musician in Greek mythology. His music was so magnificent that it had the power to tame wild beasts and make rocks and trees move. According to legend, Orpheus accompanied Jason and the Argonauts on their voyage to capture the GOLDEN FLEECE. Orpheus's singing and playing of the lyre (a harplike instrument) calmed the stormy seas and saved the Argonauts by drowning out the voices of the SIRENS, whose songs often lured sailors to their death on treacherous rocks.

On his return to Thrace after saving Jason and his men, Orpheus married his beloved Eurydice. However, shortly after their wedding, Eurydice was fatally bitten by a snake while she tried to escape from an unwanted admirer. Orpheus was so overcome with grief that he stopped singing and playing his lyre. Eventually, he decided to go to the underworld* to find Eurydice. Orpheus's beautiful music persuaded the ferryman, Charon, to ferry him across the River Styx to the entrance of the underworld. With his song, he also charmed Cerberus, the three-headed dog who guarded the gates to the underworld. Having gained admittance to the land of the dead, Orpheus was able to charm HADES and PERSEPHONE, rulers of the underworld, into allowing him to take Eurydice back to earth. There was, however, one condition—namely, that he must lead her out of the underworld without looking back until he reached the surface. But just as their journey was almost completed, Orpheus had an irresistible urge to turn around and look at his wife's beautiful face. As soon as he did so, she vanished back into the underworld. Orpheus tried to return, but this time he was not allowed to pass.

In his misery, Orpheus hid himself away from everyone. The maenads, female worshipers of the god DIONYSUS, were angry at his refusal to share their company. They found him and tore him to pieces, leaving only his head intact. The head—still singing—floated down a river and out to the Aegean Sea, finally landing on the island of Lesbos. The people of Lesbos buried it and established a shrine to honor Orpheus. They were rewarded by the Muses with the gift of lyric poetry.

* **underworld** kingdom of the dead; also called Hades

After rescuing Jason and the Argonauts from disaster at sea, Orpheus returned to Thrace, where he married his beloved Eurydice. He is shown here playing for the Thracians.

# PEOPLE

## PLATE 1

In all respects, Gaius Julius Caesar was one of the most striking figures of the ancient world. A general, statesman, orator, writer, and the first "caesar"—a title that became the official designation of the Roman emperors—he was assassinated by his own followers in 44 B.C.

## PLATE 2
Called the Father of Medicine, Hippocrates is credited with helping to free medicine from the superstitious beliefs of his time. The medical writings attributed to him were probably written by his students and followers.

## PLATE 3
The man and his wife, shown in this fresco portrait, were probably members of the Roman aristocracy and patrons of the arts.

## PLATE 4

In this detail from a mosaic, young women hold palm branches as a sign of victory. Greek girls and young women competed in footraces, but there is no evidence to suggest that they competed in other athletic events.

## PLATE 5

Agrippina, the granddaughter of the emperor Augustus, married Germanicus and bore him nine children. Admired by many after she accompanied her husband on a military campaign, she lost favor with the imperial court of Tiberius and committed suicide after her two sons were murdered.

## PLATE 6
The wife of the emperor Claudius, Messalina is shown here holding her son Britannicus. She and her lover Gaius Silius were put to death for plotting against Claudius.

## PLATE 7
The formidable Scipio Africanus, at right, was the hero of the Second Punic War against the Carthaginian general Hannibal. Scipio's mastery of military tactics and strategy is still admired.

## PLATE 8
Sophocles and Aristophanes, represented in this double bust, were among the greatest dramatists of all time. Sophocles is remembered for his tragedies, Aristophanes for his comedies.

## PLATE 9
The emperor Hadrian is shown here. The gorgon on his breastplate, like the one Athena had on her shield, was intended to ward off evil and disaster.

## PLATE 10

Alexander the Great is depicted on his horse (at the left) in the midst of the Battle of Issus—his second major battle against the Persians.

## PLATE 11

As a student of Socrates and the teacher of Aristotle, Plato has had an influence on Western thought that continues to the present. His writings on education, politics, and the human soul still have relevance to modern readers and scholars.

## PLATE 12

Sappho, shown here, was one of the greatest lyric poets of antiquity. Most of Sappho's work was destroyed by early Christians who disapproved of the passionate descriptions of love in her poems.

## PLATE 13

The emperor Marcus Aurelius is represented in this equestrian statue. His reign was marked by almost constant warfare. He is probably best remembered for his writings, which reveal his sensitive and thoughtful nature.

## PLATE 14
This head of the playwright Menander is a Roman marble copy of a Greek bronze original. Menander's deep understanding of human nature was greatly admired by the Greeks, and his plays were widely imitated by the Romans.

## PLATE 15
Under the leadership of Pericles, shown here, Athens became the center of a mighty empire. Despite his aristocratic origins, Pericles favored increased participation in government by the middle and lower classes. His years as head of state were marked by great advances in philosophy and the arts.

Orpheus became the central figure of a mystery cult, Orphism, established around 600 B.C., and many poems and ORACLES were attributed to him. The legend of Orpheus has been a popular theme for artists, musicians, and poets through the ages. (*See also* **Cults; Myths, Greek.**)

## OSTIA

* **archaeologist** scientist who studies past human cultures, usually by excavating ruins

See map in Italy (vol. 2).

* **sack** to rob a captured city

* **silt** fine particles of earth and sand carried by moving water

Ostia was a port city on the west coast of Italy at the mouth of the TIBER RIVER. As the port for the city of Rome, which lay 16 miles away, Ostia played an important role in the history of Roman trade, communications, and military campaigns.

According to Roman tradition, King Ancus Marcius founded Ostia in the 600s B.C. Archaeologists* have discovered no trace of this early settlement, although they have found a fort at the site that was built about 400 B.C. During the PUNIC WARS against Carthage, Rome greatly increased the size of its navy, which was based at Ostia. After Rome defeated Carthage in 146 B.C., the size of the Roman fleet declined, and Ostia became the commercial and trade center for Rome. The port received grain shipments from Egypt and other places to feed Rome's growing population. Large ships, unable to sail up the Tiber River to Rome, unloaded grain at Ostia, where it was transferred to smaller vessels and transported upriver to the city.

During a civil war in 87 B.C., the Roman politician Gaius MARIUS captured and sacked* the port. Twenty years later, pirates raided Ostia and destroyed the Roman fleet. Even so, the emperors CLAUDIUS and TRAJAN improved and expanded the port's HARBORS. These improvements provided protection against storms and helped prevent the buildup of silt* that was carried downstream by the Tiber. During the A.D. 300s, the power of the Roman Empire declined, and Ostia's commercial importance lessened. The VISIGOTHS, a northern tribe, sacked the port in A.D. 408. By the A.D. 800s, Ostia was completely abandoned.

Archaeological excavations at Ostia reveal that the port city had apartment buildings four stories high, a theater, public baths, shops, bakeries, large public warehouses for storing grain, and various commercial and religious buildings. (*See also* **Houses; Naval Power, Roman; Trade, Roman.**)

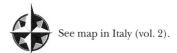

## OSTRACISM

* **agora** in Greece, the public square or marketplace

* **quorum** number of members of an organization who must be present for the group to conduct business

Ostracism was a method of banishment that was used in ATHENS during the 400s B.C. In a special election, Athenian citizens could vote to exile a person from the city for ten years. Other Greek states, including MILETUS, SYRACUSE, and Argos, also had some form of ostracism.

Once a year, the assembly of citizens in Athens voted on whether to hold an ostracism. If the assembly voted in favor, a special election was held in the agora* under the supervision of city officials. A quorum* of 6,000 was required for the ostracism to proceed. Each voter wrote the name of the person he wanted to exile on a piece of pottery, called an *ostrakon*. After the votes were cast, the pottery pieces were counted. According to most historical evidence, the man whose name appeared on the greatest number of *ostraka* was ostracized. (An alternative view is that a total of 6,000 votes against one individual was required to ostracize.) A banished citizen had to leave Athens within ten days and was not allowed to return for ten years. However, he could retain his CITIZENSHIP and property, and he could return to Athens at the end of his exile and live without any disgrace or further penalty.

Ostracisms were often held for political reasons. In some cases, Athenians ostracized prominent statesmen, such as Thucydides (the son of Melesias, not the historian) and Cimon, as a way of rejecting the policies for which they stood. However, Athenians could also vote to ostracize a person they simply disliked. The Greek biographer PLUTARCH relates the story of a man who wanted to ostracize the widely admired statesman Aristides, simply because he was tired of hearing people refer to him as "Aristides, the Just." More than 10,000 *ostraka* from the 400s B.C. have been found in Athens. Many bear the names of people who were actually ostracized.

It is not certain when ostracism started. Some scholars believe CLEISTHENES introduced some form of ostracism in 508–7 B.C., although the first actual ostracism did not take place until 20 years later. Ostracisms were held in three successive years beginning in 487 B.C. Since two of the three ostracized men were related to a former Athenian tyrant* and the third had ties to the PERSIAN EMPIRE, it is believed that the three exiled men were unpopular because they favored the Persians and wanted to restore the tyranny. Hyperbolus, the last Athenian to be ostracized, was exiled in 417 B.C. (*See also* **Democracy, Greek; Tyrants, Greek.**)

* **tyrant** absolute ruler

# OSTROGOTHS

* **province** overseas area controlled by Rome

See map in Visigoths (vol. 4).

* **sack** to rob a captured city

* **Byzantine** referring to the Eastern Christian Empire that was based in Constantinople

The Ostrogoths, or East Goths, are a branch of the people known as Goths. By the fourth century A.D., the Goths had become two distinct groups—the Ostrogoths and the Visigoths (West Goths). Both groups originated in Scandinavia and migrated south through Russia to the Black Sea.

The Goths first raided the Roman empire in the A.D. 200s. They invaded Greece, ASIA MINOR, and Rome's provinces* along the Danube River. Under the military leadership of the emperors Gallienus, Claudius II, and Aurelian, the Romans stopped these raids before the Goths could penetrate too deeply into the empire. At about this time, the distinction between the Ostrogoths and Visigoths was beginning to be made. The Ostrogoths settled between the Dnieper and Don rivers in eastern Europe.

Around A.D. 370, the HUNS, a tribe from central Asia, overran the Ostrogoths and drove the Visigoths across the Danube River into the Roman empire. Under the leadership of ALARIC, the Visigoths invaded ITALY and sacked* Rome. Eventually, the Visigoths established a kingdom in Gaul (present-day France) that extended into Spain.

In the late A.D. 400s, the Ostrogoths united under the leadership of Theodoric, invaded Italy, and established a kingdom there. Theodoric upheld the principles of Roman law, making them binding on Ostrogoths as well as on Romans. Under his rule, Italy experienced a period of peace and prosperity that it had not known for many years. Theodoric united all Goths into one kingdom, but this unified state fell apart soon after his death.

During the A.D. 500s, the Byzantine* emperor JUSTINIAN waged war against the Ostrogoths in SICILY and Italy. After 20 years of intense fighting, the Byzantines virtually wiped out the Ostrogoths and destroyed their kingdom. (*See also* **Barbarians; Migrations, Late Roman; Rome, History of.**)

## OVID

43 B.C.–A.D. 18
ROMAN POET

* **rhetoric** art of using words effectively in speaking or writing

* **philosophy** study of ideas, including science

* **Roman Republic** Rome during the period from 509 B.C. to 31 B.C., when popular assemblies annually elected their governmental officials

* **adultery** sexual intercourse by a married person with someone other than his or her spouse

Ovid was one of the greatest Roman poets and a leading figure in Roman society until the emperor Augustus banished him in A.D. 8. Traditional Roman values included military duty, hard work, and civic service. Before Ovid, love had been considered a kind of destructive illness that threatened one's personality. Ovid turned those ideas upside down as he celebrated love in his poetry as the more important and positive force in human nature.

**OVID'S LIFE AND TIMES.** Publius Ovidius Naso (Ovid) was born in 43 B.C. in the town of Sulmo, about 100 miles east of Rome. He received the standard education for a person of his class, studying rhetoric* in Rome as he prepared for a career in public service. After his formal training, Ovid, like most educated young men, studied philosophy* in Athens and toured the lands of the eastern Mediterranean before returning to Rome. He held several minor government offices, a career he soon abandoned to spend his time visiting booksellers' shops and becoming acquainted with the leading poets of his day. His career as a poet began when he was about 20 years old. Augustus had just begun his reign as emperor.

At that time, Rome was emerging from almost 100 years of civil war that transformed the serious, public-minded society of the Roman Republic* into the pleasure-seeking society of the Roman Empire. Ovid drew inspiration from the bustling urban life of Rome and became well known as a poetic spokesman for the younger, and more sexually liberated, element of society. His identification with this group was at odds with Augustus's view that increasing sexual liberation threatened the family and the fabric of society. Ovid published his *Amores* (Loves) in about 16 B.C. and *Ars amatoria* (Art of Love) about 17 years later. By A.D. 8 he was a prominent poet. Then suddenly in that same year, Augustus banished him from Rome to the remote town of Tomis on the Black Sea, where he remained until his death 10 years later. The cause of Ovid's banishment remains mysterious, but some scholars wonder whether it was connected with Augustus's banishment, in the same year, of his granddaughter Julia, who he discovered was committing adultery*. Augustus's disapproval of Ovid's *Ars amatoria,* combined with some minor court intrigue or knowledge of Julia's behavior on the part of Ovid, may have led Augustus to his actions. Ovid himself wrote that he had been banished because of "a poem and an error."

**AMORES.** Ovid's first great work was *Amores,* a collection of love poems in which he claims for the poet and lover the same traditional Roman values associated with military and civic life: duty, bravery, perseverance, and toughness. He portrayed love and romance as tasks that required as much effort, skill, and daring as making a military conquest or ruling an empire. The main character of *Amores* is the poet-lover-conqueror who combines the virtues of the old Rome with the attitudes of the new in a witty, original, and somewhat subversive way.

In a second edition of *Amores,* published about 3 B.C., a more mature Ovid shows the negative side of the main character. Because the character's goal is the pursuit of pleasure as an end in itself, he becomes a victim of the emptiness of a life dedicated to shallow "good times." For Ovid, love's true purpose is to uplift a person and allow him to achieve true humanity, not merely the satisfaction of his desires. This theme is developed more fully in his later works, *Ars amatoria* and *Remedia amoris* (The Cure of Love), in which he writes about how to fall *out* of love.

* **didactic** intended to instruct

ARS AMATORIA. A didactic* poem in three books, *Ars amatoria* advises young men on the art of courtship. It is similar to *Amores* in that it satirizes the civic virtues of the old Rome. In *Ars amatoria,* new Rome is about the pursuit of pleasure, especially sex, and Ovid plays the Professor of Love to his students, the young people of Rome. He details the many ways to take advantage of women, including a parody* of a victory parade through Rome, in which Ovid turns a glorification of Roman military virtues into a lesson on how to impress and seduce women.

* **parody** work that imitates another for comic effect or ridicule

In another section of the poem, Ovid sets out to give women guidance on successful lovemaking. He advises them to become the kind of sex objects that men want, thus facilitating the men's efforts at seduction.

* **epic** long poem about legendary or historical heroes, written in a grand style
* **classical** relating to the civilization of ancient Greece and Rome
* **mortal** human being; one who eventually will die

METAMORPHOSES. Ovid's greatest work, the *Metamorphoses* (Transformations), was written as a kind of playful epic* in which the heroic vision of the world, as in Homer's epic poems the *Iliad* and the *Odyssey,* is transformed. The *Metamorphoses* begins with the formation of the world after Chaos and comes down to the present and to the emperor Augustus. However, Ovid rejects the classical virtues and values of the ancient world by creating an epic that uses central characters who are not gods and heroes but frail and flawed human beings. The *Metamorphoses* has many stories rather than just one. The traditional epic themes of glory and honor are replaced by the triumph of the human soul searching for the meaning of love and truth.

The *Metamorphoses* draws from many classical* sources to show gods in conflict with mortals*. The stories typically end with the transformation, or metamorphosis, of the human being into another form. One of the final metamorphoses is Julius Caesar being changed into a comet in the heavens. These transformations usually occur as a character's punishment for opposing the divine will of the gods. But instead of glorifying the classical gods, as in the epics of Homer, some of Ovid's tales show them as callous, self-absorbed, and vengeful. The last books of Ovid's *Metamorphoses* (there are a total of 15) contain many Roman myths as well as Roman historical references. These have provided us with a fascinating source of information about Roman folklore and tradition.

## THE STORY OF MYRRHA

In the *Metamorphoses,* Ovid tells the story of Myrrha, a young woman whose forbidden passion has led her to commit a desperate act. She begs the gods that she be allowed neither to live (and thus pollute the living) nor to die (and thus pollute the kingdoms of the dead).

An unnamed goddess answers her prayer by transforming her into a myrrh tree and changing her eternal tears into myrrh, a fragrance used in the rites of the mystery religions. In this transformation, the horrors and chaos of the heart are made new and beautiful. Ovid shows the vulnerability of human beings and their great need for love, as well as their capacity for strength, honesty, and goodness.

OVID'S LATER WORKS. The *Metamorphoses* was the last work Ovid completed before his banishment. In Tomis he continued working on the *Fasti* (Calendar), which he had started earlier. In this work, which remained unfinished, Ovid described and explained the religious festivals of Rome. He also wrote *Tristia* (Sorrows) and *Epistulae ex Ponto* (Letters from Pontus), poems in the form of letters to friends and relatives in Rome. All these works were motivated in part by Ovid's desire to persuade Augustus to allow him to return from his exile. None of the later works approach the quality of his previous ones, but they serve to show how important the vibrant life of Rome and its people were as inspirations for his writing. (*See also* **Civil Wars, Roman; Divinities; Education and Rhetoric, Roman; Epic, Greek; Epic, Roman; Homer; Literature, Roman; Love, the Idea of; Poetry, Roman; Social Life, Roman.**)

## PAESTUM

Paestum was a Roman city at the mouth of the Silarus River southeast of Naples on the western coast of ITALY. Around 600 B.C., Greek colonists from the city of Sybaris in southern Italy founded the city as Poseidonia. These colonists expanded the city and built several magnificent TEMPLES. About 400 B.C., the Lucanians, the native people who lived in the surrounding hills, captured the city. They controlled the city for more than a century, until 273 B.C., when the Romans established a colony at the site, which they called Paestum.

Paestum successfully resisted the Carthaginian general HANNIBAL, who invaded Italy during the PUNIC WARS. The city was allowed to issue its own bronze coins during the early Roman Empire. In A.D. 71, the emperor VESPASIAN established a new settlement at the site with a large group of retired sailors from the Roman fleet. Paestum began to decrease in importance as the Silarus River filled with silt*, and malaria made the area unhealthy. Eventually, Paestum was abandoned.

Today Paestum is a major archaeological* site. Impressive remains from the Greek, Lucanian, and Roman periods have been uncovered, including an important group of Doric* temples. One of these temples, the Temple of Poseidon, is one of the best-preserved religious buildings from the ancient Greek world. Temples and shrines dedicated to ZEUS, HERA, and ATHENA have survived at the site. Paestum also has painted tombs of the Lucanian people and the city walls, public baths, forum*, senate house, and amphitheater* of the Romans. (*See also* **Archaeology of Ancient Sites; Architecture, Greek; Architecture, Roman; Colonies, Greek; Colonies, Roman; Construction Materials and Techniques; Peoples of Ancient Greece and Rome.**)

* **silt** fine particles of earth and sand carried by moving water

* **archaeological** referring to the study of past human cultures, usually by excavating ruins

* **Doric** relating to the oldest and simplest style of Greek architecture

* **forum** in ancient Rome, the public square or marketplace, often used for public assemblies and judicial proceedings

* **amphitheater** oval or round structure with rows of seats rising gradually from a stage or central open space

## PAINTING

See *Art, Greek; Art, Roman.*

## PALACES, IMPERIAL ROMAN

Imperial* palaces were a series of structures built for the early Roman emperors. These palaces included large areas for public functions and also served as the living quarters for the emperor and his family. The English word *palace* comes from Palatine Hill, the prominent hill in Rome on which most imperial palaces were constructed.

The imperial palaces of Rome, such as the one shown here, were known for their spaciousness and opulence. They not only housed the emperor and his family but also served as convenient locations for large public functions.

* **imperial** pertaining to an emperor or empire

See color plate 7, vol. 2.

* **basilica** in Roman times, a large rectangular building used as a court of law or public meeting place

The palace of the emperor TIBERIUS, built on Palatine Hill, was the first major construction project that used concrete faced with brick. This material was sturdy and resistant to fire, making it well suited to large building projects. An enclosed rectangular structure, the palace was two or more stories high. Another palace belonging to Tiberius, built on the island of Capri, had a similar construction.

The emperor NERO is famous for his Domus Aurea (Golden House), an extravagant palace built in Rome after a disastrous fire in A.D. 64. Adopting the style of an elegant country estate, Nero created a great private park that covered a large section of the center of the city. The main residence overlooked an artificial lake. Unfinished at Nero's death, most of the Golden House was later demolished, and the COLOSSEUM was built over part of the site. The Baths of Trajan also later included portions of the palace.

The last and greatest of the imperial palaces was built for the emperor DOMITIAN. Built into the southern side of Palatine Hill, Domitian's palace was divided into clearly defined official and private quarters, and included a basilica* and a private box for the emperor to view the events in the CIRCUS MAXIMUS. (*See also* **Architecture, Roman; Construction Materials and Techniques.**)

PAN

* **nymph** in classical mythology, one of the lesser goddesses of nature

Pan was the Greek god of shepherds, sheep, goats, and pastures. He was represented in art and literature as having the horns, ears, and legs of a goat. Like the god APOLLO, Pan was also a musician, and he played an instrument called the syrinx (also known as panpipes). According to myth, Pan chased the nymph* Syrinx, who escaped from him by becoming a bed of reeds, which Pan then made into his panpipes. Panpipes were played by shepherds as dance music for nymphs and satyrs (woodland deities).

Greek mythology included many different stories regarding Pan's parents and birth. He was generally believed to be the son of the god HERMES, but sometimes ZEUS, Apollo, and other gods were said to be his father. His mother was thought to be Penelope, Callisto, Hybris, or even a goat. When his mother saw that her newborn baby had little horns on his head and the legs of a goat, she abandoned him, and Pan was raised by nymphs.

Pan was sometimes a frightening god, and the word *panic* comes from his name. He became very angry if his sleep was disturbed, and he had the power to cause sudden terror in an enemy. It was believed that he came to the aid of Athens during the PERSIAN WARS, when he caused the Persians to panic and flee during the Battle of MARATHON. According to a story by the Greek historian HERODOTUS, an Athenian messenger reported that he heard Pan's voice asking him why the Athenians did not worship him, since he had helped them so often. After their victory at Marathon, the Athenians built a shrine to Pan that can still be seen today in a cave on the ACROPOLIS in Athens. (*See also* **Art, Greek; Divinities; Music and Musical Instruments; Myths, Greek; Ritual and Sacrifice.**)

Pan is the god of shepherds and pastures and is responsible for the fertility of the herds. Although lively and amorous, he was also fear-inspiring.

# PANDORA

* **mortal** human being; one who eventually will die

In Greek mythology, Pandora (whose name means "all gifts") was the first woman, created by ZEUS to punish mortal* men and their helper, PROMETHEUS. According to legend, only the gods knew the secret of fire, and they kept that secret hidden from the human race. Prometheus, however, tricked Zeus and brought the secret of fire to mortals.

Enraged by Prometheus's treachery, Zeus ordered Hephaestus, blacksmith of the gods, to create a woman out of clay. ATHENA gave Pandora life; APHRODITE made her irresistible to men; and HERMES taught her cunning and trickery. The gods then gave Pandora a sealed jar containing all the evils that would eventually befall human beings. The only good thing inside the box was Hope, buried at the very bottom. Pandora was then given as a bride to Prometheus's foolish brother, Epimetheus. (The literal meaning of the name *Prometheus* is "forethought," and the meaning of *Epimetheus* is "afterthought.") Although he had been warned by Prometheus never to accept a gift from Zeus, Epimetheus accepted Pandora as his wife.

Once settled among the mortals, Pandora was overcome by her curiosity regarding the contents of the jar. She opened it and unintentionally released all the evils it contained—War, Disease, Suffering, Sorrow, and so on—into the world. She put the lid back on as quickly as she could, but it was too late. Only Hope remained, trapped inside and crying to be let out in order to relieve the world of the evils that had escaped. Until this time, mortals had lived a life free from work and worry. Now they had to labor and suffer to earn a living.

In a variation of the tale, the jar actually belonged to Prometheus, and it contained all the good gifts that he had won for mortals and was keeping in storage for them. Pandora found the jar and, driven by curiosity, opened it. In doing so, she released all the gifts, which flew away and were forever lost. Only Hope, slower than the rest, remained inside.

The expression "opening Pandora's box" has become a warning that curiosity can lead to trouble and misfortune. (*See also* **Divinities**; **Fables**; **Myths, Greek.**)

## PANTHEON

* **portico** roof supported by columns, forming a porch or covered walkway
* **granite** hard rock consisting of grains from other rocks and formed by solidification from a molten state

The Pantheon is a magnificent temple dedicated to all the gods and commemorating Augustus's victory over Mark Antony at Actium. A special feature is the "eye" at the top of its dome, that lets in rays of light as the sun moves across the dome.

The Pantheon, or "temple of all the gods," was erected in Rome under the emperor HADRIAN, who ruled from A.D. 118 to 138. An earlier Pantheon, built between 27 and 25 B.C. by the Roman general Marcus Agrippa, stood on the same location but was destroyed by fire in A.D. 80. The Pantheon erected by Hadrian has been dated by the stamps on its bricks to the decade A.D. 118 to 128. It represents a complete redesign of the original and is one of the best preserved and most famous buildings of antiquity.

The Pantheon features a magnificent Greek-style portico*, or porch, of red and gray granite* columns, 40 feet high, in the ornate Corinthian

* **facade** front of a building; also, any side of a building that is given special architectural treatment

order. Some people think that the number of columns chosen for the facade* (eight) is an intentional reference to the most famous Greek temple of antiquity, the Parthenon of Athens. Others note that without the columns, the massive porch would have effectively hidden the rest of the building that lies behind it. Upon crossing the threshold of large bronze double doors at the back of the porch, one enters a vast rotunda—a cylindrical interior space, with floors and walls covered with multicolored marble. This space is perfectly proportioned: its diameter and height both equal 142 feet, while the dome that covers the space appears as a perfect hemisphere. The concrete dome, the biggest in the world until the twentieth century, is testimony to Roman engineering skill. Recent studies of the building have shown that it cracked, although it did not collapse. Clearly, the Pantheon demonstrates how Roman engineers pushed their materials to the breaking point in the pursuit of an awe-inspiring interior space.

* **vault** arched ceiling or roof

* **celestial** relating to the heavens

The most striking feature of the Pantheon is the circular opening, or *oculus* (meaning "eye" in Latin), at the top of the dome. This oculus, some 30 feet across, supplies the only source of light for the building and allows a sun disk to travel across the vault* of the dome, just as the sun itself travels across the heavens. The careful orchestration of engineering, luxurious imported marble, and celestial* symbolism has led some to view the Pantheon as a symbol of the power and might of Rome. (*See also* **Architecture, Roman; Columns; Construction Materials and Techniques.**)

## PAPYRUS

See *Books and Manuscripts.*

## PARALLEL LIVES

The Greek writer Plutarch wrote a series of biographies of famous men of the ancient world entitled *Parallel Lives*. The title reflects the organization of the work—the lives of two individuals (in one case two sets of people), one Greek and one Roman, are presented side by side for comparison. In all, Plutarch compares 23 pairs, comprising 46 lives. The title also refers to Plutarch's purpose in writing *Parallel Lives*. Plutarch set out to examine the lives of people who shared certain personal characteristics that made them outstanding in their fields. He wanted to gain a better understanding of those qualities.

Plutarch's Life and Influences. Plutarch was born about A.D. 40 into a wealthy family in Chaeronea, a city in central Greece whose turbulent history may well have had an influence on him. It was at Chaeronea that Philip II and his son Alexander the Great decisively defeated the Greeks in 338 B.C. and that the Roman general Sulla defeated the Greek king Mithradates 250 years later. Plutarch must have been aware of these events and of the parallels between the Greek and Roman civilizations.

As a young man, Plutarch served as a diplomat, representing his city in dealings with the local Roman authorities. He later traveled to Italy to represent his province*. There he made friends with several influential

* **province** overseas area controlled by Rome

See color plate 1, vol. 3.

Romans. Plutarch's exposure to the world of politics and power and his keen interest in history and human nature came together in *Parallel Lives*. In Plutarch's view, the Greeks and Romans had equal status and therefore were good subjects for comparative studies. He also believed that extraordinary situations brought out the special qualities that made certain people great. Therefore, the subjects he chose were primarily rulers, generals, and politicians. He included such important pairs of men as Alexander the Great and Julius CAESAR, DEMOSTHENES and CICERO, and Demetrius and Mark Antony.

**PLUTARCH'S PURPOSE AND METHOD.** Plutarch wanted not only to examine character in *Parallel Lives* but also to hold up his subjects as exemplary, or deserving of imitation. He believed that people were naturally drawn toward excellence and that by providing examples of men of outstanding character, his readers would want to emulate them. Because the main goal of *Parallel Lives* was to examine character, Plutarch was less concerned with presenting all the historical facts of a person's life than he was with concentrating on the events that shaped and revealed his subject's character. For example, in his biography of the Roman general POMPEY, Plutarch wrote that he would spend little time discussing his hero's early life in order to focus instead on "the great matters and those that show his character best."

One serious drawback to this approach is that Plutarch had a tendency to downplay the shortcomings of his subjects. He often blamed their less-than-admirable behavior on the petty plots or schemes of others. He also tended to omit events that contradicted his assessment of a subject's character, despite the fact that those incidents were well known or widely reported by other sources. Plutarch believed that character was the result of temperament, natural ability, and training, and that, once determined, one's character was fixed for life. Actions that were "out of character" for an individual were explained as being caused by circumstances. However, Plutarch was not simply a cheerleader for his subjects, and his aim was not to present false portraits of them. Indeed, not all men presented in *Parallel Lives* are examples of virtue. Plutarch included men whose characters showed great flaws as well because, as he noted, "great natures produce great vices as they do great virtues." Again, his goal was to give moral instruction to his readers by providing examples, and he felt that was best achieved by focusing more on "the beautiful things" in a man's life than on his "faults and blemishes."

*Parallel Lives* has long been the most popular of Plutarch's works, largely because it is written for people who read history for pleasure rather than for the specialist. Plutarch's ability to mix "the useful and the pleasant," as well as his interest in the psychological makeup of his subjects, makes *Parallel Lives* as compelling to modern readers as it was to its original audience. (*See also* **Literature, Greek.**)

## PARMENIDES

See *Philosophy, Greek and Hellenistic.*

# PARTHENON

See map in Agora (vol. 1).

The Parthenon is probably the best-known and one of the most beautiful TEMPLES of ancient Greece. It stands on the highest part of the ACROPOLIS in ATHENS and was dedicated to ATHENA, the goddess of war and the protector of Athens. The name of this magnificent structure comes from the word *parthenos,* meaning "virgin"—a reference to the goddess.

HISTORY AND CONSTRUCTION.   The Parthenon was begun in 447 B.C., during the time of the great Athenian statesman PERICLES. It was one of many impressive public buildings constructed during this period. The location of the Parthenon was the site of an earlier temple that had been started in 490 B.C., shortly after the Greek victory over the Persians at the Battle of MARATHON. Construction on the earlier structure was abandoned at the beginning of the second Persian War in 480 B.C. The work that had been completed was destroyed by the Persians when they captured the city. The new temple, begun by Pericles, used the foundation and platform that remained from the earlier structure and possibly some of the MARBLE elements that had been prepared for it as well.

Like all Greek temples, the Parthenon was intended as a place of worship. As such, it was designed to house a statue of Athena that worshipers could honor. The Parthenon also served as treasury for the Delian League, a political alliance of Greek city-states that was led by Athens.

ARCHITECTURAL DESIGN.   The Parthenon was designed by the architects Ictinus and Callicrates and is considered the most perfect example of the Doric style of Greek architecture. Its floor measures 228 feet by 101 feet. The structure has 8 COLUMNS at each end and 17 columns on each side. The interior room, or *cella,* is divided into two parts. The larger eastern portion housed the statue of Athena, and the smaller western portion served as

Standing on the Acropolis—the highest point in Athens—to honor the goddess Athena, the Parthenon remains a strong testimony to the architectural skill of the Greeks. The temple was built during the reign of Pericles, a time known as the Golden Age of Greece.

the treasury. Two double rows of Doric columns supported the roof of the eastern section, a design that some have suggested was intended to provide support for a second-story gallery from which visitors could view the statue. The western section featured four narrower but taller columns that were designed in the more elaborate Ionic style.

Because Doric architecture is known for its plain straight lines and very regular patterns, it is surprising to find so few straight structural elements in the Parthenon. The steps are slightly curved to match the curve of the terrain, as is the entablature—the horizontal beam that rests on top of the outside columns. The columns themselves are not completely vertical; they tilt slightly inward and are not evenly spaced, with the columns at the corners being slightly closer together. Many theories have been proposed to explain these deviations from the true vertical and horizontal. One theory maintains that they resulted from the purely functional consideration that a slightly curved structure would help deal with problems of drainage and settling. Another theory suggests that the deviations were used to correct optical illusions that distort perfectly vertical profiles. Others have suggested that such refinements were intended to place the building in greater harmony with its surroundings. Whatever the true reason, the effect is the same—a building of extraordinary beauty and grace.

SCULPTURE AND DECORATION. The Parthenon was seen by its designers not merely as an impressive building but also as a great work of art. The famous Greek sculptor PHIDIAS designed all the sculpture and statuary in the temple, including the gold and ivory statue of Athena that stood 40 feet high. The statue no longer survives, although it seems to have remained intact as late as the A.D. 100s. The only description of it comes from the Greek writer and traveler PAUSANIAS and a few small replicas of the statue that differ somewhat in detail. The Parthenon's outside frieze—the decorated band of marble just below the roof—contained carvings of combat between mythical figures, gods, giants, and AMAZONS. The frieze of battle scenes ran along all four sides of the building, but the variety of poses and attitudes of the figures added interest to this single subject.

An ingenious interior frieze around the *cella* shows a procession of Athenian citizens and is designed to create the impression of the passage of time. The figures in the procession are posed in such a way that, depending on the portion of the frieze being viewed, time and motion seem to speed up or slow down. The frieze was seen from below in a light that was reflected from a colored surface, and that made the plain walls more attractive by emphasizing the contrast of light and shadow in the carved figures on the frieze. The subject of the procession seems to be the procession that took place every four years during the All-Athenian Festival. The citizens of Athens gathered in the AGORA, or marketplace, and carried a robe for the statue of Athena to the Acropolis.

The most impressive of the statues from the Parthenon are the great marble sculptures in the pediments—the triangular spaces at each end of the temple that were hollowed out to hold carved figures. The sculpture on the east pediment told the story of Athena's birth, as she sprang fully grown from the head of ZEUS. The west pediment depicted the battle

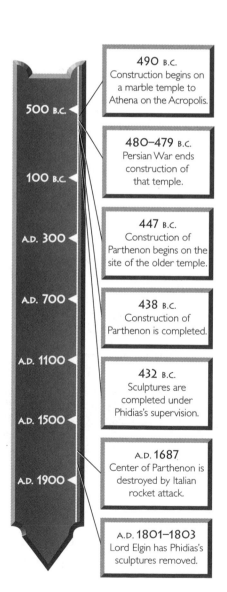

500 B.C.

**490 B.C.**
Construction begins on a marble temple to Athena on the Acropolis.

**480–479 B.C.**
Persian War ends construction of that temple.

100 B.C.

**447 B.C.**
Construction of Parthenon begins on the site of the older temple.

A.D. 300

A.D. 700

**438 B.C.**
Construction of Parthenon is completed.

A.D. 1100

**432 B.C.**
Sculptures are completed under Phidias's supervision.

A.D. 1500

**A.D. 1687**
Center of Parthenon is destroyed by Italian rocket attack.

A.D. 1900

**A.D. 1801–1803**
Lord Elgin has Phidias's sculptures removed.

## PAINTING THE TOWN

Many ancient buildings, including the Parthenon, were originally not white but painted—often in very bright colors. In the Parthenon, the colors provided a background against which the sculptures could be seen more easily and served to make the form of the building stand out against the bright Mediterranean sky. The colors also ensured that the different parts of the Parthenon were clearly distinguished from one another. As with so many ancient buildings that were once brightly colored, nothing remains of this aspect of the original temple.

* **archaeological** referring to the study of past human cultures, usually by excavating ruins

* **classical** in Greek history, refers to the period of great political and cultural achievement from about 500 B.C. to 323 B.C.

between Athena and POSEIDON, god of the sea, for control over ATTICA, the region in which Athens is located. The greatness of the sculptures lies in their naturalness, a quality that reflects Phidias's profound knowledge of the human form. Greek sculpture before Phidias generally showed the ideal form and did not reflect the natural movement and expression of the subject. Phidias's sculptures are enlivened by the way he captured the tension in the muscles, the sense of movement, and the emotions of the figures. The larger-than-life sculptures were removed from the Parthenon in the early 1800s by Lord Elgin, the British ambassador to the Ottoman Empire, which controlled Athens at that time. The sculptures, now known as the Elgin Marbles, are on display at the British Museum in London.

LATER HISTORY.    Throughout its history, the Parthenon served many functions in addition to its original use as a temple. It was converted into a Christian church dedicated to the Virgin Mary and later into a Turkish mosque. Until A.D. 1687, the original building was still largely intact, although the roof had been replaced. In that year, it was being used by the Turks as an ammunition dump in their war against Italy. A direct hit from an Italian rocket caused an explosion that destroyed the center of the building. During the late 1800s and early 1900s, some of the columns were reconstructed, but that work has recently been dismantled, and current preservation efforts concentrate on restoring and protecting those original portions of the building that still stand.

Although much of the original temple is gone, the Parthenon is probably the most carefully studied and measured building in the world. Archaeological* research has revealed much about the artistry and craftsmanship that went into the creation of this remarkable structure. Moreover, some 2,500 years later, the world still acknowledges the Parthenon as a masterpiece of classical* Greek art. (*See also* **Architecture, Greek; Art, Greek; Columns; Construction Materials and Techniques; Crafts and Craftsmanship; Festivals and Feasts, Greek; Persian Wars; Sculpture, Greek.**)

## PATRICIANS

* **Roman Republic** Rome during the period from 509 B.C. to 31 B.C., when popular assemblies annually elected their governmental officials

* **plebeian** member of the general body of Roman citizens, as distinct from the upper class

* **aristocratic** referring to people of the highest social class

* **clan** group of people descended from a common ancestor or united by a common interest

The patricians were a privileged class of Roman citizens who exercised great political and religious power, especially during the monarchy and the Roman Republic*. Patrician status was obtained only by birth, and for a brief time in the fifth century B.C., patricians were forbidden by law to marry plebeians*.

According to tradition, the patricians were descendants of the *patres,* or fathers, chosen by Rome's founder and first king, Romulus, to form the first Senate. However, some sources indicate that not all the patricians were originally from Rome but also included members of aristocratic* clans* (such as the Claudii) who came to Rome from outside. Still others suggest that the kings of Rome would occasionally raise certain men to patrician rank. Whatever their true origin, by the time of the republic in the late 500s B.C., the patricians had become a hereditary social class. It is certain that, throughout the monarchy and early republic,

This statue shows a Roman patrician proudly holding the busts of his ancestors. Citizens with ties to the aristocracy or to the original founders of Rome were set apart in a privileged class that held the political and religious power in Rome.

* **consul**  one of two chief governmental officials of Rome, chosen annually and serving for a year

* **praetor**  Roman official, just below the consul in rank, in charge of judicial proceedings and of governing overseas provinces

* **augur**  Roman official who read omens and foretold events

* **censor**  Roman official who conducted the census, assigned state contracts for public projects (such as building roads), and supervised public morality

patricians controlled all the important priesthoods, although the nature of their political power is not as clear. Under the law of the Twelve Tables, drawn up between 451 B.C. and 450 B.C., the number of patricians was effectively restricted by forbidding patricians to marry outside their class. It is likely, however, that the law merely made official a practice that had been well established for quite some time. The law was repealed in 445 B.C.

Despite the legends about their origins and status, not all members of the Senate were patricians. During the early days of the Roman Republic, most MAGISTRATES—government officials, such as consuls* and praetors*—were patricians, and some offices, such as that of augur*, were restricted by law to patricians. By the 400s B.C., patricians had developed a monopoly on the magistracies. During the 300s B.C., the class of ordinary citizens, the PLEBEIANS, succeeded in breaking the hold the patricians had on those positions and on the priesthoods as well. However, the patricians continued to occupy high offices in greater proportion to their numbers than the rest of the population. Until 172 B.C., one of the two consuls who shared the highest authority was always a patrician, and about half of all priestly positions were held by patricians. Some priesthoods remained patrician by law, with no possibility of a plebeian occupying them.

The fact that the patrician class was an aristocracy based on birth ultimately led to a decline in the number of patrician clans, from about 50 in the 400s B.C. to only 14 by the time of the Roman Empire in 31 B.C. Julius CAESAR and the emperor AUGUSTUS were granted the power to create new patricians, and later emperors used their power as censor* to elevate other citizens to patrician status. New patricians created in this manner could pass this status on to their descendants. Even so, the hereditary class of patricians seems to have disappeared by the A.D. 200s. The emperor CONSTANTINE revived the title of *patricius* in the early A.D. 300s, but it was given to individuals as an honor in recognition of service to the empire and did not carry the privileges or the hereditary status that the original term implied. (*See also* **Augur; Class Structure, Roman; Consul; Government, Roman; Law, Roman; Praetor; Priesthood, Roman.**)

## PATRONAGE

The term *patronage* refers to the widespread practice in the ancient world by which wealthy or powerful men, known as patrons, provided financial support and opportunities to men of lesser social standing or to clients, who in turn owed service and loyalty to the patron. This system, most fully developed in the Roman world, took several forms, including social, political, and artistic patronage.

**SOCIAL AND POLITICAL PATRONAGE.**  Social patronage usually involved an economic relationship between patron and client, like the tenant-farming arrangement that existed between many wealthy Roman landowners and those who worked on their large estates. A peasant might be granted a plot of land on which he and his family were allowed to live, grow crops, and raise livestock. In return, he was required to provide his patron with either a portion of the produce from his plot or a specified period of labor each year. Most free agricultural workers in ancient Rome were bound by this type of arrangement.

Patronage also existed between former slaves, or freedmen, and their previous owners, who were known as patrons. Roman law carefully defined the relationship of dependence between the freedman, who owed his patron respect as well as financial and political support. In return, the patron would defend the freedman's interests—for example, in legal cases. The freedman also had to promise to provide his patron with a stated number of days each year when he would work or perform services for him or his family—for example, as a hairdresser, craftsman, or teacher of his children.

Political patronage concerned power and political influence rather than money or economic issues. Such patronage usually developed between two members of the ruling elite who came from different social classes. For example, a local magistrate* might enter into such a relationship with a senator or other high-ranking governmental official in Rome. The magistrate would enlist local support for the official, including gathering large groups of supporters when the patron senator visited or mustering soldiers for a military campaign in exchange for increased political influence in Rome. During the Roman Empire (beginning in 31 B.C.), many provincial* citizens established such relationships to gain seats for themselves in the Roman Senate. A wealthy and powerful local magnate* might act as both a patron to those lower down and a client of those higher up on the political and social ladder. In both directions, there could be many degrees or levels of patronage.

**ARTISTIC PATRONAGE.** Artistic patronage was common in both Greece and Rome. Because there was no mass audience able to pay for literature or art, patronage was the primary means of support for most artists and writers. Wealthy patrons engaged artists and writers to produce artworks and entertainments for their pleasure and amusement. Many great public monuments were created as a result of state patronage, especially in democratic Athens during the reign of Pericles and in Rome during the Roman Empire. Artists received gifts, financial rewards, and favors—such as official government positions—for their services to their patrons. Most writers showed their gratitude by composing works that praised their patrons or celebrated a patron's achievements. In the first century B.C., the Roman poet HORACE was supported by Maecenas, a wealthy man and an adviser to the emperor Augustus. Maecenas furnished Horace with a country estate outside Rome so that the poet could devote himself to his art.

The system of patronage was an important part of the social fabric of ancient societies in which only a small percentage of the population controlled nearly all the wealth and power. Patronage gave ordinary people at least some influence in their dealings with the power structure and created a bond between classes that promoted stability. (*See also* **Agriculture, Greek; Agriculture, Roman; Class Structure, Greek; Class Structure, Roman; Labor; Land: Ownership, Reform, and Use; Working Class.**)

* **magistrate** governmental official in ancient Greece and Rome

* **provincial** referring to a province, an overseas area controlled by Rome

* **magnate** person of power or influence, often in a specific area

PAUL, ST.

See *Rome, History of: Christian Era.*

**BORN ca. A.D. 100**
**GREEK WRITER AND TRAVELER**

* **Archaic** in Greek history, refers to the period between 750 B.C. and 500 B.C.

* **classical** in Greek history, refers to the period of great political and cultural achievement from about 500 B.C. to 323 B.C.

* **archaeologist** scientist who studies past human cultures, usually by excavating ruins

Pausanias was a Greek writer best known for his *Description of Greece,* a ten-volume guide to the places he believed were worth seeing. He was born around A.D. 100 near the city of Smyrna in ASIA MINOR. *Description of Greece* was probably written about 50 years later.

Although Pausanias claimed to tell of "all things Greek," *Description of Greece* was actually limited to the area of central Greece that included the cities of ATHENS, CORINTH, and DELPHI. Pausanias explored the geography, culture, history, legends, and religion of the regions he visited. He was mainly concerned with the monuments and art of the Archaic* and classical* periods of Greece, and he showed little interest in monuments and artworks created after about 150 B.C. He did, however, offer many insights into the historical and religious significance of the objects he admired. *Description of Greece* shows that Pausanias had extensive knowledge of religious CULTS, as well as of local rituals and beliefs. In his work, he comments extensively on Greek myths and their local variations.

Although *Description of Greece* was written long after the periods in Greek history that comprise the book's focus, the accuracy of Pausanias's descriptions has been confirmed by modern archaeologists* and historians. For a work that was written almost 2,000 years ago, *Description of Greece* is still a valuable guide to the region, and it is the only source of information about many Greek statues and paintings that no longer exist. (*See also* **Transportation and Travel.**)

## PAX ROMANA

* **city-state** independent state consisting of a city and its surrounding territory

The Latin phrase *Pax Romana,* meaning "Roman peace," refers to the period of extraordinary peace and stability that existed in the Mediterranean world from the end of the reign of the Roman emperor AUGUSTUS in A.D. 14 to the death of the emperor Marcus AURELIUS in A.D. 180.

Beginning with the reign of TIBERIUS, the period of the *Pax Romana* included the reigns of such emperors as CLAUDIUS, NERO, TRAJAN, and HADRIAN. Before the *Pax Romana,* the Mediterranean region had been divided into hundreds of city-states*, territories, and kingdoms that often rose rapidly, enjoyed a brief moment of glory and achievement, and then collapsed as a result of internal unrest or foreign conquest. Under Augustus and his successors, however, the Roman Empire brought together the peoples of the Mediterranean under its leadership.

UNIFICATION OF THE MEDITERRANEAN.  The *Pax Romana* rested on Roman administrative ability and military supremacy. Although the Romans conquered lands as far away and as culturally diverse as BRITAIN, SPAIN, and EGYPT, they did not force the inhabitants to adopt Roman customs, and they allowed people from all parts of the empire to participate in the operations

Between A.D. 14 and A.D. 180, the Mediterranean world enjoyed a period of peace and stability that came to be known as the *Pax Romana.* The *Ara Pacis,* meaning "altar of peace," was built to commemorate the safe return of Augustus from Gaul and Spain and was an early indication of the great era of peace that followed.

\* **province** overseas area controlled by Rome

of government and in Roman social life. These lenient and tolerant policies, as well as the spread of Roman law, unified the empire and minimized ethnic and cultural differences that might otherwise have threatened its stability. Over time, with the exception of the JEWS and EGYPTIANS, who had strong cultural and religious traditions, people came to think of themselves not as Gauls or IBERIANS but as Romans.

Once the empire's frontiers had been firmly established, the Roman army ensured security in the provinces\* by strengthening trade and local industry. This led to widespread prosperity in which, for the first time in history, the average person could hope to share.

CULTURAL GROWTH DURING THE PAX ROMANA. Cultural activities abounded during the *Pax Romana.* Formal education increased, as more people learned to read and write, and many attended schools. Art, sculpture, and architecture thrived. Both the Colosseum and the Pantheon were built during this period. Literature flourished. Among the Greek writers of this period were PLUTARCH, PAUSANIAS, PTOLEMY, and GALEN of PERGAMUM. Latin authors of the period included SENECA, LUCAN, PLINY THE ELDER, JUVENAL, and MARTIAL. Libraries were built throughout the empire during this period. The *Pax Romana* in Roman history is sometimes likened to the cultural flowering that occurred in Greece in the fifth century B.C. during the Age of Pericles.

THE END OF THE PAX ROMANA. As prosperity grew, so did the size and power of the central government, especially the power of the emperor. Gradually, cities and towns began to lose their initiative and even their vitality. The frontiers that had once been manageable came under barbarian attack. When barbarian pressures from outside became great, the Roman armies that for years had done no serious fighting were unprepared and incapable of responding to raids and guerrilla-type warfare. With money and manpower directed toward maintaining frontier security, no new programs were initiated to renew the strength and vitality of the empire.

103

The rulers who followed Marcus Aurelius were unable to halt the economic and military decline that signaled the end of the great era of peace. (*See also* **Cities, Roman; Economy, Roman; Rome, History of; Trade, Roman.**)

## PEGASUS

* **immortal** living forever

* **hero** in mythology, a person of great strength or ability, often descended from a god

Pegasus was the immortal* winged horse of Greek mythology. The offspring of MEDUSA and the sea god POSEIDON, Pegasus became the magical steed of the mythical Corinthian hero* Bellerophon. Pegasus does not appear in Homer's *Iliad,* which includes the earliest surviving references to Bellerophon. However, the horse is mentioned in an ode by the Greek poet Pindar, who wrote in the 400s B.C.

Medusa was pregnant with Poseidon's child when the hero PERSEUS killed her by cutting off her head. Pegasus was born either from Medusa's head or from one of the drops of blood that fell from her body. The winged horse roamed the earth and flew through the air, wild and untamed. Occasionally he touched the ground, his hoofprint becoming a spring of water. The most famous of the springs believed to have been created by Pegasus was the Hippocrene spring on Mt. Helicon in central Greece, which was located near a grove of trees sacred to the MUSES, the goddesses of art, music, and literature.

One day, as Pegasus was drinking at a spring near the city of CORINTH, a young Corinthian man named Bellerophon approached him, carrying a golden bridle he had received from the goddess ATHENA. Pegasus allowed Bellerophon to place the bridle over his head, and from that time the winged horse allowed Bellerophon to ride him on land or in the sky. With the help of Pegasus, Bellerophon performed many heroic deeds. He slew the Chimaera, a fire-breathing monster with the head of a lion, the body of a goat, and the tail of a serpent, and he fought the AMAZONS, the legendary women warriors. Eventually, Bellerophon attempted to fly on Pegasus all the way to Mt. OLYMPUS, the home of the gods. This angered ZEUS, the ruler of the gods, who sent a fly to sting Pegasus. Pegasus threw Bellerophon off his back, and the fall disabled Bellerophon, who ended his days as a homeless wanderer. According to some versions of the story, Pegasus went on to carry Zeus's lightning and thunder.

Pegasus was a symbol of Corinth and appeared on that city's coins. Scenes from the adventures of Pegasus and Bellerophon were popular subjects for Greek vase paintings. To the Romans, Pegasus became a symbol of immortality, or eternal life. (*See also* **Myths, Greek; Myths, Roman.**)

## PELOPONNESIAN WAR

* **city-state** independent state consisting of a city and its surrounding territory

The Peloponnesian War was a long conflict in the late 400s B.C. between the Greek city-states* of SPARTA and ATHENS. In 431 B.C., Sparta attacked Athens, starting a war that eventually split the entire Greek world into two camps. Sparta and its allies, including CORINTH and THEBES, were known as the Peloponnesian League. Against them stood the Delian League, made up of Athens and its allies. The Greek historian THUCYDIDES wrote a detailed account of the causes of the war and its history through 411 B.C. The historian XENOPHON recorded the final years of the war, which lasted until 404 B.C. and ended with the defeat of Athens.

The Spartans started the war because they feared and resented the growing power of Athens. In the years before the war, the Athenians had built a powerful navy that could block the sea trade of any city with whom they had a dispute. The cities of the Peloponnese* were particularly concerned, since the Athenian navy was able to cut off their supply of wheat from SICILY, an island off the coast of ITALY. Athens had also extended its power over many other city-states in Greece and on the Asian coast, although some of these cities were growing restless under the agreement that bound them to Athens.

Although Athens had the finest navy in the Greek world, Sparta and its allies had the biggest and best armies. At the beginning of the war, Sparta invaded ATTICA (the region in which Athens is located) and destroyed the crops in an attempt to force Athens to surrender. Under the leadership of the statesman PERICLES, the people of Attica remained safe behind the city walls of Athens, while the navy protected ships carrying food and supplies to the port of Athens. Plague* broke out in Athens in 430 B.C., however, killing Pericles and causing great suffering inside the city.

Sparta attempted to seek peace in 425 B.C., after Athenian forces had trapped Spartan troops on the island of Sphacteria. However, the Athenians claimed the troops as prisoners of war and the conflict dragged on, with acts of cruelty, bravery, treachery, and good leadership on both sides. After a few more years of hardship, with no clear victories, the Athenian statesman Nicias arranged a peace treaty with Sparta in 421 B.C. The treaty failed, however, because several of Sparta's allies refused to accept its terms and continued the war against Athens. Diplomacy gave way to fighting, with each side trying to win smaller states over to its side. The Athenians attacked the

* **Peloponnese** peninsula forming the southern part of the mainland of Greece

See map in Greece, History of (vol. 2).

* **plague** highly contagious, widespread, and often fatal disease

This detail from a memorial stela in Attica shows an Athenian warrior killing a Spartan soldier during the Peloponnesian War. Lasting for over 25 years, the war finally ended with the surrender of Athens in 404 B.C.

Peloponnesian League in 418 B.C., but the Spartans won the battle at Mantinea. Two years later the Athenians, with brutal force, brought the island of Melos into their empire. Then in 415 B.C., Athens launched an expedition to gain control of Sicily and the city of SYRACUSE, which was Sparta's ally. The attack failed miserably, and during a two-year siege, Athens lost many men and numerous vessels.

Although the armies of the Peloponnesian League continued to ravage Attica, the final stages of the war involved much fighting at sea. The PERSIAN EMPIRE, eager to reclaim Asian cities that Athens had earlier freed from Persian rule, joined the conflict on Sparta's side. Athens won some impressive victories in this phase of the war. In 410 B.C., the Athenians, under the leadership of ALCIBIADES, crushed the Spartan navy and the Persian army. However, a brilliant admiral named Lysander then took charge of the Spartan navy, making it a force capable of defeating Athens at sea. Lysander's leadership, together with renewed support from Persia, enabled Sparta to capture the Athenian fleet and blockade* the city of Athens. After six months of starvation, the Athenians surrendered and the Peloponnesian War ended. (*See also* **Armies, Greek; Greece, History of; Wars and Warfare, Greek.**)

* **blockade** military means used to prevent the passage of enemy ships or troops into or out of a place

## PEOPLES OF ANCIENT GREECE AND ROME

* **archaeologist** scientist who studies past human cultures, usually by excavating ruins

The peoples identified as the ancient Greeks and Romans were distinct groups by the 700s B.C. Their ancestors had come to the Mediterranean region centuries earlier, during a period in which groups of people appeared, split apart, migrated, merged with other groups, and sometimes disappeared. Archaeologists* and historians are still attempting to untangle the complex web of prehistoric invasions, wars, migrations, and influences that gave rise to the ancient Greek and Roman cultures.

As the Greeks and Romans settled and became powerful, they encountered many other peoples. They traded with and fought against the inhabitants of Asia, Africa, and other parts of Europe. Greek and Roman historians and geographers left detailed accounts of many of these peoples. The Greeks considered themselves superior to all non-Greeks, referring to these others as BARBARIANS. The Romans felt equally superior to all who were not Roman.

Throughout the ancient period, people continued to migrate from one region to another, sometimes pushing out the former inhabitants and sometimes mixing with them. These migrations and mixtures shaped the population of Europe and the Mediterranean world during the Middle Ages.

* **dialect** form of speech characteristic of a region that differs from the standard language in pronunciation, vocabulary, and grammar

* **ethnic** relating to the national, religious, racial, or cultural origins of a large group of people

THE GREEKS. The first wave of Greeks came to Greece around 2000 B.C. or earlier. They evolved into the Mycenaeans, whose civilization flourished in southern Greece around the 1400s B.C. The second wave of migration to Greece came around 1200 B.C. from a people called the DORIANS. Scholars believe that all Greeks descended from a population that by about 1000 B.C. spoke a similar language. The Greeks called themselves Hellenes. Although there were many different states, tribes, and subgroups of Hellenes, all of them spoke dialects* of the same language, Greek.

Even when the Greeks were at war with each other, they shared a strong sense of ethnic* identity. The Greek historian HERODOTUS claimed

* **sacrifice** sacred offering made to a god or goddess, usually of an animal such as a sheep or goat

* **Peloponnese** peninsula forming the southern part of the mainland of Greece

* **city-state** independent state consisting of a city and its surrounding territory

Ancient Greece and Rome consisted of diverse groups of people from throughout the Mediterranean. Wars, invasions, and migrations forced these groups to move, mix, and blend with others. This map shows some of the many civilizations that existed in the ancient world.

that what set the Greeks apart from the peoples of the PERSIAN EMPIRE was that the Greeks were a single people. He wrote that the Greeks had "one blood, one language, common shrines and sacrifices* to the gods, and a shared way of life."

Although the Greeks considered themselves a single people, they recognized three large subgroups of Hellenes based on the dialects of different regions and on their own accounts of their early history. These groups were the Dorians, the IONIANS, and the Aeolians. The Dorians were believed to have come from the mountains of northwestern Greece. They settled in the Peloponnese* and on the island of CRETE. The Ionians occupied ATTICA, the region in which the city-state* of ATHENS was located, and settled on the southern islands of the AEGEAN SEA and on the coast of ASIA MINOR (present-day Turkey). The Aeolians lived in Thessaly, in the northern region of Greece, and on the northern Aegean islands. Many Greeks believed that the Dorians possessed the original, authentic Greek culture, with their patriotism, military strength, community spirit, and strong ties to traditional myths and beliefs.

Greece was bordered on the northeast by THRACE, on the north by MACEDONIA, and on the northwest by Illyria. Although the people of these regions shared some Greek ethnic characteristics, the Greeks did not consider the inhabitants of these regions to be Hellenes. The Macedonians,

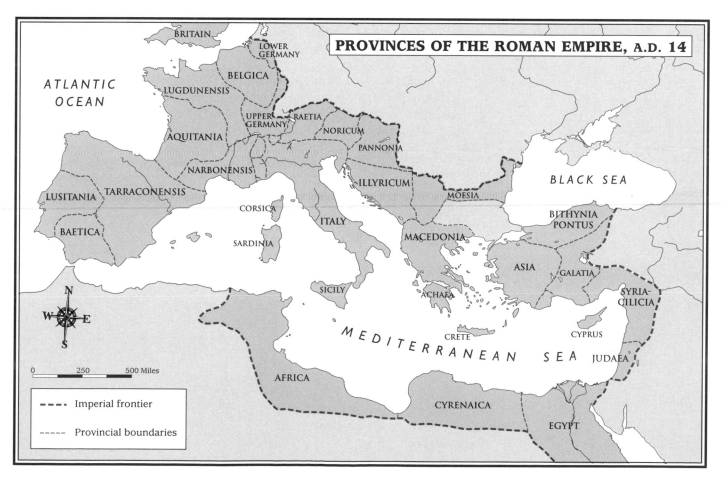

107

the Greeks' closest neighbors, eventually conquered Greece and adopted Greek culture, which they then spread into western Asia and Egypt as a result of the conquests of ALEXANDER THE GREAT in the late 300s B.C.

**THE ROMANS.** The Romans originated in LATIUM, a region in west-central ITALY inhabited by a people called the Latins. Rome, one of several cities built by the Latins, expanded and eventually dominated the rest of Latium. At the beginning of the Roman Republic\*, the Romans shared Italy with more than 40 other peoples. Greek colonies were located on the coasts of southern Italy, and the Samnites and the Lucanians lived in the mountainous interior of the south. The Sabines and the Umbrians inhabited the mountains of the north. The ETRUSCANS, the Romans' neighbors to the north, developed an advanced and influential culture long before the expansion of Rome. By the time of the late republic, Rome controlled all these peoples within Italy, and the Romans had also conquered other regions of the Mediterranean, including Greece, Asia Minor, North Africa, and much of Europe.

Originally a small city with a primarily Latin population, Rome became the capital of a vast empire that included dozens of very different groups of people. Even in the streets of their own city, Romans encountered people from many different regions and were exposed to foreign languages, religions, and customs. At the same time, Rome established colonies of Roman citizens throughout the empire. These colonies helped spread Roman language, culture, and traditions to other peoples of the Mediterranean region—a process known as Romanization.

**OTHER PEOPLES.** The Greeks and Romans were sturdy people of short to medium height. Although some had light hair and blue or gray eyes, most had dark hair and brown eyes. Their skin color ranged from light tan to fair. While the Greeks and Romans regarded these physical characteristics as the human norm, they did not generally classify foreign peoples by race, skin color, or physical features. They noticed ethnic differences more than racial ones. When describing foreign peoples, Greek and Roman writers focused on such features as names, marriage and burial rituals, religion, diet, sexual habits, hair and clothing styles, manner of swearing oaths, and other beliefs and customs.

In the 400s B.C., Herodotus recorded many details about the peoples known to the Greeks. Four centuries later, the Greek geographer STRABO, after much study in the great Library at ALEXANDRIA, summarized all available information about the known world and its peoples. Strabo's work and that of other historians, as well as ancient works of art, provide evidence as to how the Greeks and Romans perceived the other groups who inhabited their world.

The IBERIANS, who lived in far western Europe in present-day Spain, were known to the Greeks as early as the late 600s B.C. Roman writers described the Iberians as having dark skin and an abundance of curly hair. Modern historians believe that some of the people on the southern coast of Spain may have been descended from North Africans who migrated to Spain in prehistoric times. At the southeastern fringe of Europe (in the present-day Balkan

* **Roman Republic** Rome during the period from 509 B.C. to 31 B.C., when popular assemblies annually elected their governmental officials

See map in Languages and Dialects (vol. 2).

* **nomadic** referring to people who wander from place to place to find food and pasture

Peninsula) were the nomadic* Thracians. The Greek historian THUCYDIDES called the Thracians "the most bloodthirsty of barbarians." Several writers reported that the Thracians had blond or red hair, which they wore in knots on top of their heads, and blue or gray eyes.

The CELTS were a restless people who migrated into much of western Europe, including northern Italy, Spain, Thrace, Britain, and Ireland. The Celts' appearance seemed different from that of both the Greeks and the Romans. One ancient writer described them as "tall, with pale skin, rippling muscles, and hair which is not only naturally blond, but also bleached artificially to heighten their distinctive appearance." Strabo wrote that physical fitness was extremely important to the Celts. Young men who became fat or potbellied had to pay fines. Throughout the ancient world, the Celts were believed to have a warlike temper and to enjoy fighting. However, they were also said to lack stamina and often suffered from heat and thirst.

The GERMANS were "like the Celts, though larger and fiercer," wrote Strabo. The Germanic peoples probably originated in Scandinavia and northwestern Germany. They migrated south to the valley of the Rhine River, where they mingled with the Celts, and southeast to southern Russia and the shore of the Black Sea. To the Romans, the Germanic tribes were a constant menace along the northern borders of their empire. The Germanic tribes of OSTROGOTHS, VISIGOTHS, and VANDALS caused the decline of the Western Roman Empire in the A.D. 400s.

Although the ancient Greeks and Romans knew much about the SCYTHIANS, a nomadic tribe of southern Russia, they knew far less about other peoples of central and eastern Russia and central Asia. Among the most mysterious of these groups were the HUNS, battle-hardened nomads on horseback who emerged from the Black Sea region in the A.D. 300s to terrorize Europe.

The Greeks and Romans were familiar with many of the peoples who lived in Asia Minor and the Middle East. The Greeks and the Romans both engaged in trade, warfare, and conquest with the Syrians, PHOENICIANS, Babylonians, Persians, JEWS, and Arabs. The Greeks and Romans also knew a little about the Asian peoples who lived east of the Persians, in the lands that are now Afghanistan, Pakistan, and INDIA. The Romans had heard of China by the 100s B.C. because that land was the source of the silk that merchants were selling to the rich in cities throughout the Mediterranean region. Although Rome sent envoys* to China in A.D. 166 and A.D. 284, there was very little direct contact between the Roman world and eastern Asia.

* **envoy** person who represents a government abroad

The Greeks and Romans were familiar with the different ethnic and racial groups of EGYPT, Sudan, LIBYA, and northwestern AFRICA. About the rest of Africa the Greeks and Romans knew only what they heard from Egyptian and Arab sources. Although Greek writers as early as HOMER correctly described the Pygmies of the African interior as "black-skinned" and much smaller than other people, the Greeks and Romans had little real knowledge about Africa south of the Sahara desert. Their world centered on the Mediterranean Sea, which they regarded as the hub of the earth. (*See also* **Citizenship; Ethnic Groups; Greece, History of; Migrations, Early Greek; Migrations, Late Roman; Mycenae; Rome, History of.**)

## FANTASTIC PEOPLES

Many ancient writers reported accounts of strange and remarkable races of people who always lived somewhere just beyond the frontier of the known world. Herodotus reported that a race of one-eyed people lived in far northern Europe. One visitor to India reported hearing about a people whose ears were so large that they wrapped them around themselves when they slept. One race of people reportedly had dogs' ears and a single eye in their forehead, and another had feet that pointed backward. None of these fantastic peoples ever existed. They were nothing more than travelers' tall tales.

**PERGAMUM**

* **dynasty** succession of rulers from the same family or group

* **Hellenistic** referring to the Greek-influenced culture of the Mediterranean world during the three centuries after Alexander the Great, who died in 323 B.C.

* **frieze** in sculpture, a decorated band around a structure

* **Titan** one of a family of giants who ruled the earth before the Olympian gods

* **gladiator** in ancient Rome, slave or captive who participated in combats that were staged for public entertainment

* **tribute** payment made to a dominant power or local government

Pergamum in northwestern ASIA MINOR (present-day Turkey) became one of the most important cities of the ancient world. Pergamum's greatness was partly due to its favorable location. Sitting atop a ridge, Pergamum was naturally fortified. Just 15 miles from the AEGEAN SEA, it was close to a port. Pergamum also overlooked a rich farming valley.

Pergamum was the capital city of the Attalid dynasty*, which began in the middle 200s B.C. when Attalus I became king. Both Attalus and his successor strove to make Pergamum a magnificent and cultured city, and it soon ranked among the great Hellenistic* cities of Asia. Pergamum was a model of town planning, with impressive buildings and monuments constructed on terraces that lined the ridge. It had fortified barracks, a palace, TEMPLES, and a library that was second only to the great Library at ALEXANDRIA. The city also had the largest gymnasium ever built by the Greeks. Pergamum was especially noted for its sculptures, which significantly influenced art throughout the entire Greek world. One of the most famous is the Great Altar of Zeus, a frieze* depicting the victory of the gods over the Titans*.

Pergamum was famous for its medicinal waters and the hospital of ASCLEPIUS, the god of healing. Many people came to Pergamum for treatment, and the great Greek physician GALEN was born and raised there in the A.D. 100s. Galen began his career in the hospital of Asclepius as physician to the gladiators*.

The last Attalid king surrendered his kingdom to the Romans in 133 B.C., and Pergamum was declared a free city within the Roman empire. (It was not required to pay tribute* to Rome.) Pergamum continued to be an important center of culture, wealth, and healing. Although the city was attacked and partly destroyed by GOTHS around A.D. 250, Pergamum remained an important center of learning for many generations.

**PERICLES**

ca. 495–429 B.C.
ATHENIAN GENERAL AND
POLITICIAN

* **city-state** independent state consisting of a city and its surrounding territory

* **philosophy** study of ideas, including science

* **aristocratic** referring to people of the highest social class

Pericles was the leading statesman in the Greek city-state* of ATHENS for 30 years. Under his leadership, Athens strengthened its control over other city-states and became the center of a mighty empire. Pericles encouraged philosophy* and the arts in Athens. He changed the face of the city with a public building program that created the PARTHENON and other magnificent TEMPLES on the hilltop known as the ACROPOLIS. Pericles dominated the political, military, and cultural life of Athens for an entire generation. The historian THUCYDIDES reports that from 460 until 429 B.C., the government of Athens was "in name a democracy, but in fact the rule of the first man"—and that man was Pericles.

THE RISE OF PERICLES AND ATHENS. Pericles was born into a distinguished Athenian family. His father, Xanthippus, was involved in the politics of the city-state and commanded a Greek force during a battle of the PERSIAN WARS, and his mother came from a prominent aristocratic* family. The young Pericles received the best available education, with lessons from well-known musicians and philosophers. Throughout his life, Pericles remained deeply interested in the arts and in philosophy. One of his closest friends was the philosopher Anaxagoras. Some historians believe

As a great leader and statesman, Pericles guided Athens through major political and cultural changes. He is responsible for launching an ambitious public works program that created some of the city's most magnificent architectural structures.

* **orator** public speaker of great skill

### A WOMAN OF POWER

At a time when women had little say in public matters, Aspasia, Pericles' mistress, supposedly wielded great influence on Athenian political affairs. The comedies of the day ridiculed her power, accusing her of urging Pericles to attack the island of Samos, as well as blaming her for causing the Peloponnesian War.

* **tribute** payment made to a dominant power or local government

that the teachings of Anaxagoras provided Pericles with the calm, steady sense of purpose that he displayed in his public life, even in the face of severe setbacks and disappointments.

Pericles first appeared in Athenian politics around 463 B.C. as a prosecutor of the Athenian general Cimon. He soon became a follower of a democratic reformer named Ephialtes. When Ephialtes was killed a few years later, Pericles assumed the leadership of Athenian public life. A gifted orator*, Pericles quickly became the most popular and influential speaker in the citizen assembly, and he retained that influence until the end of his life. The citizens frequently elected Pericles to the post of *strategos*—one of ten generals in command of the Athenian forces. He held this post almost continuously from 443 B.C. until his death.

During Pericles' early years in power, Athens rose to its height of importance. Pericles pursued an aggressive foreign policy. He dispatched one navy to fight the Persians in Egypt, and other forces to fight against Phoenicia and Cyprus. At the same time, Athens made war on several states within Greece, capturing some major cities. The Athenians fought battles with the armies of their archenemy SPARTA and its allies. Pericles sometimes commanded troops in the field, leading a successful campaign in the Gulf of Corinth in 454 B.C.

Soon after that campaign, however, Pericles and Athens encountered several setbacks. The Persians won a victory in Egypt. Realizing that Athens could not defeat the PERSIAN EMPIRE, Pericles made peace with Persia. He then arranged a meeting in Athens of representatives from all Greek city-states to discuss rebuilding the temples destroyed by the Persians, but Sparta refused to participate, and the project fell through. Tensions mounted between Sparta and Athens. At the same time, the people of Boeotia revolted against Athenian rule. As Pericles tried to suppress the rebellion, Sparta invaded ATTICA, the region in which Athens is located. Pericles was forced to make a truce with Sparta (perhaps by bribing the Spartan king), and Athens failed to recapture some of the territories it had lost in the rebellion. In 445 B.C., Athens signed the Thirty Years' Peace with Sparta, giving up control of its conquered land on mainland Greece.

LATER YEARS OF PERICLES.    For many years, Athens had been the leader of the Delian League, an alliance of Greek city-states. Formed in 478 B.C., just after the Persian Wars, the League was originally intended to defend Greece against the Persian Empire. Pericles turned the League into an Athenian empire. He brought the other members of the League under Athenian rule, moved the League's treasury to Athens, used its funds to rebuild Athenian temples, and declared that the allied states must use Athenian coins, weights, and measures. Members who could not contribute ships to the League's defense (and therefore rank as equals with Athens) had to pay a tribute* and were reduced to a lower station.

Pericles tightened Athens's hold on its allies by establishing colonies in regions controlled by the allies. Athenian settlements were established at Brea and Amphipolis in the region of Thrace, and a settlement at Amisus on the south coast of the Black Sea helped to control the shipment of grain from Thrace and the Black Sea. These settlements of Athenian citizens generally occupied the most valuable or strategically important land in the subject state. The colonies, such as the one at Megara near the Gulf of Corinth, served as permanent military bases in states that were supposedly friendly but which might revolt at any moment. Athens acquired land for the colonies by force or as repayment of debts. Pericles was determined not to let Athens lose control of its allies or subject territories. When the island of Samos rebelled and attempted to leave the Delian League in 440 B.C., Pericles led a fleet against Samos and forced the city to surrender, tear down its walls, and repay the Athenians for their losses.

If Pericles was an imperial conqueror outside Athens, within the city walls he was a democratic reformer. He introduced the concept of paid civil service so that citizens who served on juries or public councils received a sum of money for each day of service. He also set up a fund to pay for theater admissions for poorer citizens. As the benefits of CITIZENSHIP grew, however, Pericles took steps to limit the number of people who could become citizens. In 451 B.C., he introduced a law that restricted Athenian citizenship to those people whose mother and father were both Athenian citizens.

During the 440s and 430s B.C., Pericles launched an ambitious and costly building program that crowned the Acropolis with the Parthenon and other temples. Pericles also supported literature and the arts, which he believed were essential to life in a democracy. Among his friends were the sculptor PHIDIAS and the playwright SOPHOCLES. Periclean Athens was a place of lively debate, intellectual inquiry, and artistic flowering. It was an era which some historians have called the GOLDEN AGE OF GREECE.

By the late 430s B.C., the prospect of war with Sparta loomed over Athens. Believing that war was inevitable, Pericles refused to compromise with Sparta and its allies or to yield to Spartan pressure. In 431 B.C., the long conflict known as the PELOPONNESIAN WAR broke out, pitting Sparta and its allies against Athens and its allies. Pericles' strategy was to bring Greek citizens from the countryside into Athens and to avoid battle on land, where the Spartans had superior forces. As long as the Athenian fleet was in full control of the Aegean Sea, Pericles believed, the empire could be held. The first year of the war brought such hardship to Athens that the people threw Pericles out of office. They soon restored him to power, however, perhaps believing that only his leadership could save them. By then, however, a deadly plague* was devastating Athens, and Pericles was one of the many who died. The war he had helped to start would be fought by his successors. (*See also* **Greece, History of.**)

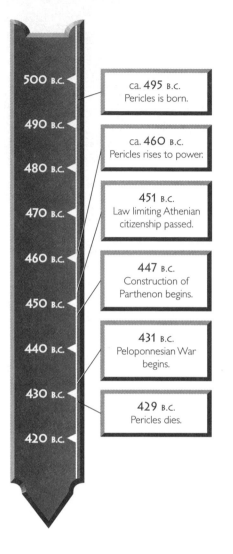

ca. **495** B.C.
Pericles is born.

ca. **460** B.C.
Pericles rises to power.

**451** B.C.
Law limiting Athenian citizenship passed.

**447** B.C.
Construction of Parthenon begins.

**431** B.C.
Peloponnesian War begins.

**429** B.C.
Pericles dies.

\* **plague** highly contagious, widespread, and often fatal disease

## PERSEPHONE

\* **underworld** kingdom of the dead; also called Hades

Persephone was the daughter of ZEUS, the king of the gods, and DEMETER, the goddess of grain. A grain goddess herself, Persephone was also the wife of HADES, the god of the underworld*, and thus the queen of the underworld. Greek women worshiped Persephone as the protector of marriage and children. The Romans called her Proserpina.

The most important myth about Persephone describes how Hades kidnapped her and brought her to the underworld to become his wife and queen. Because Persephone was exceptionally beautiful, her mother had kept her hidden on the island of Sicily for her protection. One day while Persephone was picking flowers in a field, Hades rose from the underworld in his chariot, seized her, and carried her off to his domain.

While Demeter searched for her daughter, she neglected her normal duties as the grain goddess. As a result, crops failed, and mortals would have starved had Zeus not eventually intervened. When Demeter finally discovered her daughter's whereabouts, she contrived to win her back. She persuaded Hades to agree to release Persephone on the condition that the girl had eaten nothing while in the underworld. But Hades had tricked Persephone into eating a few seeds from a pomegranate*, and so she was forced to stay. Demeter appealed to Zeus, who agreed to a compromise. Persephone had to live in the underworld as Hades' wife for four months of the year, but for the rest of the year she was allowed to return to live with her mother on earth.

The myth of Persephone was an important part of the ELEUSINIAN MYSTERIES, a Greek cult* in which worshipers believed that Persephone's return to the world symbolized the possibility of life after death. The myth of Persephone also symbolized the growth and the "rebirth" of plants each spring. (See also **Cults; Divinities; Myths, Greek.**)

* **pomegranate** thick-skinned, many-seeded berry about the size of an orange and with a tart flavor

* **cult** group bound together by devotion to a particular person, belief, or god

# PERSEUS AND ANDROMEDA

* **hero** in mythology, a person of great strength or ability, often descended from a god

* **Gorgon** any of the three snake-haired sisters in Greek mythology whose direct gaze turned an onlooker to stone

* **oracle** priest or priestess through whom a god is believed to speak; also the location (such as a shrine) where such utterances are made

Perseus, a hero* of Greek mythology, was the son of ZEUS. The best-known myth about Perseus recounts how he killed the snake-haired Gorgon* MEDUSA, and then claimed Andromeda for his bride after rescuing her from a sea monster.

Perseus's grandfather, Acrisius, had been warned by an oracle* that one day his own grandson would kill him. So, he had his daughter Danae shut away in a bronze chamber so that no man could touch her. Zeus, however, was able to reach Danae by changing himself into a shower of golden rain, which fell into her lap and impregnated her. After Perseus was born, Acrisius cast the baby and his mother out to sea. But Zeus protected them, and eventually they came safely ashore on the island of Seriphos. They lived happily on the island until Perseus was a young man. The king of Seriphos fell in love with Perseus's mother, and he attempted to remove Perseus from the scene by sending him to retrieve the head of Medusa. This was believed to be an exceedingly difficult task, because anyone who looked directly at the face of Medusa was instantly turned to stone.

The goddess ATHENA, who hated Medusa, came to Perseus's aid. She gave him a bronze shield with which to slay the monster and instructions on how to proceed. First, he had to visit the Graiae, three old hags who lived in the mountains of Africa and shared one eye and one tooth, which they passed around among them. They were sisters of the Gorgons and knew the mountain path that would lead to Medusa. Perseus outwitted the Graiae by seizing their eye and refusing to give it up until they told him where Medusa lived. Then, after he obtained the information, Perseus flung the eye into a lake, so that the Graiae could not warn Medusa that he was approaching. Next, some nymphs* gave Perseus gifts to aid him in his task—a bag in which to put Medusa's head and a cap which would make

* **nymph** in classical mythology, one of the lesser goddesses of nature

him invisible. The god HERMES provided him with a curved sword and a pair of winged sandals.

Thus armed, Perseus flew across the ocean to the shore where Medusa lived. As the monster lay sleeping, Perseus beheaded her with the sword, while safely watching her reflection in the bronze shield. Stuffing Medusa's head in the bag, Perseus put on the cap that rendered him invisible and escaped back across the ocean to Seriphos. According to one version of the myth, Perseus returned to Greece by way of the territory of the Titan* god Atlas, who, hearing that he was Zeus's son, tried to turn Perseus away by force. Perseus, in anger, held Medusa's head before him, and Atlas was turned into a vast mountain.

On his journey home, Perseus spotted Andromeda, who was tied to a rock and about to be devoured by a sea monster. Perseus killed the monster with his sword and saved Andromeda, who then became his wife. Perseus and Andromeda returned to Greece, where the old prophecy that Perseus would kill his grandfather eventually was fulfilled. In taking part in the games in Thessaly, Perseus threw a discus, accidentally hitting and killing Acrisius. At the end of their lives, Athena turned Perseus and Andromeda into constellations and placed them in the sky. (*See also* **Myths, Greek.**)

* **Titan** one of a family of giants who ruled the earth before the Olympian gods

# PERSIAN EMPIRE

* **dynasty** succession of rulers from the same family or group

## PERSIAN RELIGION

Before the time of Cyrus the Great, the Persians believed in many different gods of nature. Then, in the 500s B.C., a religious prophet named Zoroaster (also known as Zarathustra) appeared in their country. The prophet taught that there was just one supreme god, named Ahura Mazda, who was in constant conflict with the spirit of evil, called Ahriman. Zoroastrianism, the religion of the followers of Zoroaster, persisted long after the Persian Empire fell in the 300s B.C. The cult of the Magi arose from the priesthood of Zoroastrianism, and "Magicians" appeared at the royal courts of several nations and were generally welcomed by all.

The Persian Empire was founded in 550 B.C. by Cyrus II, known as Cyrus the Great. His reign marked the beginning of the Achaemenid dynasty*, which ruled the Persian Empire for more than 200 years. At its height, the empire extended from the west coast of ASIA MINOR to the border of INDIA. The empire was noted for its system of government, its religious and cultural tolerance, and its splendid PALACES. The empire ended in 330 B.C., when the last king of the Achaemenid dynasty was assassinated and the empire was taken over by the Macedonian king ALEXANDER THE GREAT.

**CYRUS THE GREAT.** The Persians originated in central Asia before settling in the region of present-day Iran. In 550 B.C., Cyrus II, the Persian king, conquered the large empire of the Medes, a neighboring and closely related people. This gave Cyrus control of the ancient kingdom of ASSYRIA and brought under his command a large army of both Persian and Median horsemen who were skilled with bow and arrow. With these mounted troops, Cyrus set out to conquer more lands and expand his empire.

Cyrus and his army first conquered the countries and cities on the seacoast of Asia Minor. Next, they captured the ancient city of Babylon without a fight, a victory that also brought Palestine into the empire. Cyrus and his army then pushed eastward, eventually expanding the empire all the way to India. The reign of Cyrus the Great ended in 530 B.C., when he was killed while fighting in the East. Cyrus was succeeded by his son, Cambyses, who added EGYPT to the empire.

**DARIUS THE GREAT.** In 522 B.C., Darius I, a relative of Cyrus, seized the throne from Cyrus's son. Darius the Great, as he was known, completed

* **tribute** payment made to a dominant power or local government

the system of government begun by Cyrus, a system in which the empire was organized into provinces, called satrapies. Each satrapy was ruled by a satrap, an official who was accountable to the king. The satrapies provided soldiers for the king's army, and the satraps paid tribute* to the king. Under this system, great wealth flowed into the empire's treasure houses, and the empire prospered. The Persians were a nomadic people, and it was customary for the king to travel throughout the year between the various capital cities of the empire. In this way, the king could be seen by all his people every year, and the royal court could avoid severe climatic conditions.

Darius also enacted and enforced strict laws and suppressed many revolts during his rule. In 499 B.C., several of the Greek-speaking cities of Asia Minor which were under Persian domination rebelled against Persia, marking the start of the PERSIAN WARS, which lasted another 20 years. After suppressing the revolt, Darius attempted to conquer ATHENS. However,

Aggressive rulers and successful military campaigns helped the Persians build a mighty empire. The empire was unable to withstand an invasion by Alexander the Great around 330 B.C., however.

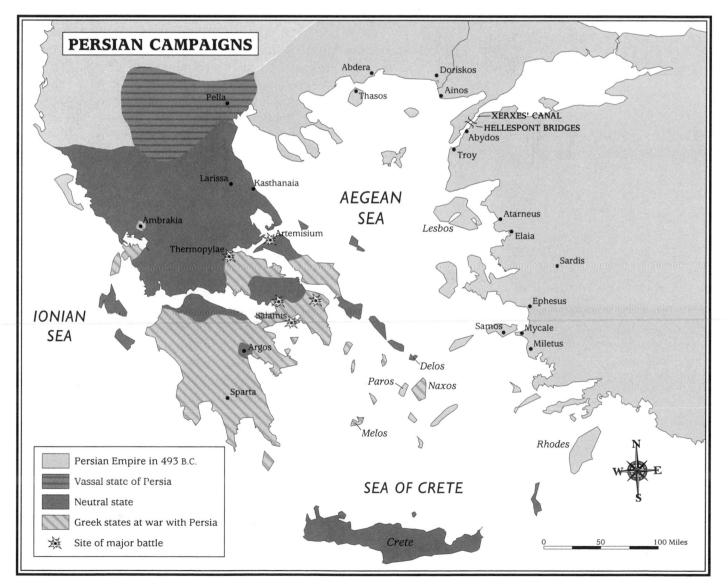

**PERSIAN CAMPAIGNS**

Abdera
Thasos
Doriskos
Ainos
XERXES' CANAL
HELLESPONT BRIDGES
Abydos
Troy
Pella
Larissa
Kasthanaia
AEGEAN SEA
Atarneus
Lesbos
Elaia
Ambrakia
Artemisium
Sardis
Thermopylae
Ephesus
IONIAN SEA
Salamis
Samos
Mycale
Miletus
Argos
Delos
Paros
Naxos
Sparta
Melos
Rhodes
SEA OF CRETE
Crete

Persian Empire in 493 B.C.
Vassal state of Persia
Neutral state
Greek states at war with Persia
Site of major battle

0      50      100 Miles

Darius was defeated at the famous Battle of MARATHON in 490 B.C., and his reign ended with his death in 486 B.C.

**DECLINE AND FALL OF THE EMPIRE.**   After the death of Darius, his son XERXES ruled until 465 B.C. Xerxes was a cruel but weak king who was also defeated by the Greeks in the Persian Wars. During Xerxes' reign, the Persian Empire declined. Although the empire continued for more than a century, it grew weaker as it constantly faced conspiracies, assassinations, and revolts by the people who were burdened with heavy taxes. Alexander the Great defeated King Darius III and the Persian army in 330 B.C. Darius was subsequently assassinated by one of his own followers. Although Alexander retained the Persian system of government until his own death in 323 B.C., Darius's defeat marked the end of the Achaemenid dynasty and the Persian Empire. (*See also* **Croesus; Greece, History of; Herodotus.**)

# PERSIAN WARS

* **city-state** independent state consisting of a city and its surrounding territory

The Persian Wars were a 20-year conflict in the early 400s B.C. in which the kings of the vast and powerful PERSIAN EMPIRE attempted to conquer Greece. The small, independent city-states* of Greece united to resist these attacks and remain free of Persian control. The story of the Persian Wars was told by the Greek historian HERODOTUS.

In 499 B.C., Greek cities along the western seacoast of ASIA MINOR, with support from ATHENS, revolted against Darius, the king of Persia. After suppressing the revolt, Darius decided to conquer Athens and extend his empire. In 492 B.C., he assembled a great military force and sent 600 ships across the AEGEAN SEA to attack Greece. However, the attack came to a sudden halt when a storm wrecked half the fleet on the rocks off the Greek coast.

Two years later, in 490 B.C., Darius dispatched an even stronger fleet that crossed the Aegean safely. Persian troops landed on the plain of MARATHON, about 25 miles from Athens. As they began to move toward Athens, a small army of Athenian troops and soldiers from the city-state of Plataea attacked the Persians, charging as they approached. The Greek troops killed more than 6,000 Persian soldiers and lost fewer than 200 of their own men. After the loss at Marathon, the Persian fleet returned to Asia.

Darius died in 486 B.C. before he could launch another major attack against Greece. However, his son XERXES, who succeeded him, continued the war. In 480 B.C., Xerxes set out with a huge army and navy to attack Greece. First, he built a canal for his ships through the rocks that had destroyed Darius's fleet. He also built a bridge of ships held together by cables. Then, for seven days and nights, his soldiers marched across the bridge to the Greek mainland. It has been said that Xerxes "marched his army over the sea" and "sailed his fleet through the land." Xerxes himself led the troops toward Athens.

On the way to Athens, Xerxes and his men had to cross the narrow mountain pass of THERMOPYLAE, which was held by a small force of Greek soldiers under LEONIDAS, a king of SPARTA. For two days, the Greeks held the pass. Then, on the third day, Xerxes' troops found another way through the mountains and circled back to attack Leonidas from behind. Knowing that he was defeated, Leonidas dismissed all his men except for the few hundred Spartans. Leonidas himself was soon killed, but the remaining Spartan soldiers continued to fight bravely until the last man died.

Although Xerxes and his troops took the pass and invaded mainland Greece, the Spartan stand at Thermopylae is still remembered as one of the most valiant battles in history. It delayed Xerxes for three days, during which time the Persian fleet was caught in a storm and many ships were lost. The Athenian general THEMISTOCLES tricked the Persian navy into entering the narrow strait off the island of Salamis. The Greek fleet, which was waiting for them, rammed and destroyed or captured many of the Persian ships. The remaining Persian ships fled for home, while Xerxes and his troops retreated by land.

In 479 B.C., the Persian army was defeated by a combined Spartan and Athenian force at Plataea. In the same year, the Persian fleet was defeated off the coast of Asia Minor at Mycale. With these two defeats, the Persian Wars—and the threat of Persian domination of Greece—ended. (*See also* **Armies, Greek; Greece, History of; Naval Power, Greek; Wars and Warfare, Greek.**)

# PERSIUS

## A.D. 34–62
## ROMAN SATIRIST

* **satire** literary technique that uses wit and sarcasm to expose or ridicule vice and folly

* **philosopher** scholar or thinker concerned with the study of ideas, including science

* **Stoicism** philosophy that emphasized control over one's thoughts and emotions

### NEGATIVITY IN PERSIUS'S SATIRE

Although satire is negative by nature, Horace and other Roman satirists did not just criticize what they were satirizing but also suggested positive alternatives. Persius, in contrast, focused almost totally upon the negative in his writings. He left it up to the reader to figure out any positive alternatives. For example, in his first satire, Persius criticized the verse of other poets. From the negative comments, the reader was left to deduce what Persius considered to be good poetry.

One of the most notable Roman poets of his time, Aulus Persius Flaccus wrote nothing but satires*. Because Persius believed that the form of a poem was as important as the message it conveyed, he labored long and hard over his work. Only 660 lines of his verse survive in his six *Satires,* but they are considered to be among the most brilliant poetry ever written in Latin. They are also among the most difficult to understand because they are extremely complex.

Born into a wealthy family, Persius was raised on an estate in the Italian countryside near present-day Florence. His father died when Persius was a small child, and he was sent to Rome at the age of 12 to study. Persius studied with the philosopher* Cornutus, who became a father figure and adviser to the young man, as well as his tutor. Persius died when he was only 28, and it was Cornutus who then published Persius's poems.

Persius did not write about the social and political issues of his time. Instead, he focused on what he believed was the general moral corruption of humanity as a whole. Although HORACE and other satirical poets addressed similar topics, Persius took a far more extreme, intolerant, and moralistic stand. He harshly criticized the corruption of his time and place, and he scorned the majority of people for not living up to the ideals of Stoicism*, which he greatly admired. Like other Stoics, Persius believed that people should lead rational, ordered lives and resist the temptations of the senses.

Unlike other Roman satirists, Persius did not attempt to soften his criticism in any way. He was more concerned with expressing his views honestly than in being popular with his readers. In fact, he hoped to offend the majority of his readers. Persius believed that the truth hurts, and he reasoned that the poetic techniques used to express the truth should "hurt" as well. Thus, he wrote harsh, abusive poems filled with ugly, disgusting, or obscene images. Although Persius himself was said to be gentle and modest by nature, many of his poems are hostile, unpleasant, and rude. He used offensive language to scandalize the audience with both its sound and its content.

In his poetry, Persius referred to many other works of literature, most of which are little known. While some scholars praise Persius's writing for the intellectual brilliance reflected in his use of literary references, others criticize his work because the references render his work almost incomprehensible. (*See also* **Juvenal; Poetry, Roman; Satire; Stoicism.**)

## PETRONIUS

DIED A.D. 66
ROMAN NOVELIST

* **consul** one of two chief governmental officials of Rome, chosen annually and serving for a year

Titus (or Gaius) Petronius is believed to be the author of the *Satyricon,* an early novel written in Latin. Some scholars consider the *Satyricon* one of the most brilliant and original pieces of Roman literature ever written. In addition to fragments of the *Satyricon,* some poems believed to have been written by Petronius also survive.

The author of the *Satyricon* was considered the "arbiter of elegance," or the authority on proper behavior and good taste, at the court of the emperor NERO. Because of this reputation, he is usually referred to as Petronius Arbiter. Petronius also served as consul*. He took his own life in A.D. 66 after being implicated in a conspiracy against the emperor.

Although no one knows how many books were in the complete *Satyricon*—perhaps as many as 24—only parts of two volumes of the work survive. If there had been as many as 24, the novel might have run several thousand pages. The surviving fragments describe the adventures of a shady character named Encolpius, who also narrates the story, and a boy called Giton, as they travel through southern Italy. The longest, best-known fragment describes an extravagant and ostentatious dinner party given by Trimalchio, a rich and uncouth former slave.

* **philosophical** referring to the study of ideas, including science

The *Satyricon* belongs to a class of literature known in ancient times as Menippean satire—a blend of prose and poetry, philosophical* views, and realism—that was invented by the Greek philosopher Menippus in the 200s B.C. As a Menippean satire, Petronius's novel includes both narrative and verse. For example, at his dinner party Trimalchio recites a short poem on death, a major theme of the novel:

> Nothing but bones, that's what we are,
> Death hustles us humans away.
> Today we're here and tomorrow we're not,
> So live and drink while you may.

* **parody** work that imitates another for comic effect or ridicule

* **epic** long poem about legendary or historical heroes, written in a grand style

* **satirist** writer who uses wit and sarcasm to expose or ridicule vice and folly

* **verse** writing that has a systematically arranged and measured rhythm, or meter, such as a poem

* **prose** writing without meter or rhyme, as distinguished from poetry

Petronius believed that intellectual pleasures were superior to those of the senses. He intended his novel to be a critical portrayal of the crass pursuit of sensual pleasures that characterized real-life Roman society during the time he was writing. Petronius may also have meant the novel to be a parody* of HOMER's great epic* poem the *Odyssey.* The wanderings of the narrator, Encolpius, can be seen as a low-class, comic version of the travels of ODYSSEUS, the hero of the *Odyssey.*

While other Roman satirists*, such as HORACE and PERSIUS, wrote in verse*, Petronius combined satire and comedy in narrative prose*.

Petronius's *Satyricon* is also unusual for its time for the degree to which it uses common speech. In fact, more common Latin and slang are known from the fragments of the *Satyricon* than from any other single source. (*See also* **Languages and Dialects; Literature, Roman; Novel, Greek and Roman;** *Odyssey;* **Satire.**)

## PHAEDRUS

See *Fables.*

## PHAETHON

* **nymph** in classical mythology, one of the lesser goddesses of nature

According to Greek mythology, Phaethon was the son of Helios, the sun god. He received permission to drive the chariot that carried the sun across the sky. But he was too young to manage the horses, and he came too close to the earth. ZEUS killed him with a thunderbolt to save the world from fire.

Phaethon's mother was the nymph* Clymene. When Clymene married Merops, the king of Egypt, Phaethon discovered that Helios was his real father. Seeking his father, Phaethon arrived at Helios's palace in the east just as the sun was rising. Delighted by the visit, Helios told the boy that he would grant him any wish. Phaethon replied that he wanted to drive the sun-chariot across the sky for one day. Although surprised by the request, Helios granted it.

After the four strong horses were attached to the chariot, Helios instructed his son and presented him with the reins. Once in the sky, however, Phaethon was too small to control the horses. They galloped out of control across the sky, leaving a fiery streak that became the Milky Way. According to the myth, the horses then approached the earth, causing a drought and blackening the skins of the people of Africa.

When Zeus saw how much destruction Phaethon was causing, he struck him with a thunderbolt that knocked him out of the chariot. His flaming body fell into the Eridanus River (present-day Po River). His sisters, who were nymphs, stood on the banks of the river and wept in sorrow for their loss. They turned into poplar trees, which are still common along the banks of the Po River. According to some versions of the myth, Zeus then flooded the earth to cool it after Phaethon's fiery ride. The Roman poet OVID told a version of the story in the *Metamorphoses.* (*See also* **Divinities;** *Metamorphoses;* **Myths, Greek.**)

## PHIDIAS

ca. 490–ca. 430 B.C.
GREEK SCULPTOR

Phidias, an Athenian sculptor, was one of the most famous artists in the ancient world. In addition to creating numerous impressive sculptures of gods and goddesses, Phidias oversaw the sculptural decoration of the stone buildings on the Athenian ACROPOLIS. The only known surviving examples of his work are the marble statues of the PARTHENON, known as the Elgin marbles, which were carved either by Phidias himself or by other sculptors following his designs.

# PHIDIAS

Phidias supervised the sculptural decoration of the Parthenon. Artemis, Apollo, and Poseidon are shown here in a detail from the frieze on that magnificent temple.

See
color plate 10,
vol. 2.

* **patron** special guardian, protector, or supporter

Phidias's early works included a group of bronze statues at DELPHI that celebrated the Battle of Marathon, and a 30-foot tall bronze statue of ATHENA, the patron* goddess of ATHENS, on the Acropolis. He also created a statue of Athena on the Greek island of Lemnos in the AEGEAN SEA. Although these works were impressive, Phidias was best known for his later statues of Athena at the Parthenon at Athens and of ZEUS, the king of the gods, at the temple of Zeus at OLYMPIA. Both statues were made of gold and ivory covering a wooden frame, and both were decorated with precious metals, glass, and paint. The statue of Zeus, the larger of the two, was considered one of the Seven Wonders of the Ancient World.

The statue of Athena at the Parthenon is known from descriptions of the original and from a number of copies. The original statue was nearly 40 feet high and covered in nearly a ton of gold. Begun in 447 B.C., it took nearly ten years to complete. Athena held a figure of Nike, the Greek goddess of victory, in her right hand and a spear and shield in her left hand. Her shield was covered inside and out with AMAZONS and giants. The snake-haired monster MEDUSA adorned her breastplate, and several other mythological creatures decorated her helmet.

The statue of Zeus at Olympia was probably completed around 430 B.C. Although the original no longer exists, vase paintings and coins that depict the statue indicate that Zeus was seated on a lavishly decorated throne, holding a figure of Nike in his right hand and a staff in his left. Amazons adorned his footstool.

Because of Phidias's versatility as an artist, the Athenian statesman PERICLES placed Phidias in charge of the artistic program on the Acropolis in the early 440s B.C. Phidias oversaw the sculptural decoration of the magnificent temple of the Parthenon, as well as other religious and civic structures. Because of Phidias's closeness to Pericles, Pericles' enemies accused Phidias of stealing precious materials that had been supplied for one of his statues. Rather than face imprisonment, Phidias fled to Olympia. While in exile, he created his statue of Zeus. His workshop in Olympia has been discovered, as have his tools and molds. A drinking cup inscribed with his name has even been found at the workshop.

Not long after he completed the statue of Zeus, Phidias died or was killed while still in exile. His students continued to dominate Athenian sculpture for another generation. Phidias's work was also the chief influence on later Hellenistic* and Roman sculpture. (*See also* **Architecture, Greek; Sculpture, Greek.**)

* **Hellenistic** referring to the Greek-influenced culture of the Mediterranean world during the three centuries after Alexander the Great, who died in 323 B.C.

## PHILIP II

### 382–336 B.C.
### KING OF MACEDONIA

* **annex** to add a territory to an existing state
* **city-state** independent state consisting of a city and its surrounding territory

Father of the formidable Alexander the Great, Philip II was a powerful leader in his own right. During his reign, strife-ridden Macedonia became a strong empire. Philip's ambition paved the way for his son's future conquests.

Philip II was one of several kings named Philip who ruled the ancient kingdom of MACEDONIA, which lay north of Greece. During his reign, Philip converted Macedonia from a minor strife-torn state into a great military and economic power. He was also the father of one of the best-known leaders of the ancient world, ALEXANDER THE GREAT.

Before Philip came to power, Macedonia was frequently torn apart by civil war and foreign interference. The low point came in 359 B.C., when Philip's brother, who was then king, died in battle while attempting to defend the kingdom from Illyrian invaders from the northwest. Upon taking the throne at his brother's death, Philip made his first priority the defense of Macedonia against several hostile powers. However, he needed time to build up and train a large army. Therefore, he quickly fought a minor battle against the Athenians, who were supporting a rival Macedonian leader, and made peace with other hostile forces to prevent them from attacking Macedonia, at least for a while.

Philip created a powerful professional army, which he trained well. He provided his soldiers with a new weapon—a heavy spear about 18 feet long called a *sarisa*. In 358 B.C., he led his troops to a victory against the Illyrians, and he used that victory to pull together the previously independent states of northern Macedonia and to annex* them. Philip invited their nobles to join his court and recruited their commoners for his army, thereby increasing his power.

Philip soon turned his army against Athens and other Greek city-states*, gaining more land, soldiers, wealth, and power with each victory. In 356 B.C., Philip occupied Crenides, a settlement in THRACE, and renamed it Philippi after himself. Nearby gold mines yielded great wealth, which helped him pay his large army and influence politicians in southern Greece. In 352 B.C., Philip's victory at the Battle of Crocus Field won him the Thessaly region of eastern Greece, which was noted for its great wealth and fine cavalry.

From the beginning of his rule, Philip had shown a genius for compromise and strategy, skills that he used in 348 B.C. to capture the northeastern Greek city of Olynthus, a traditional enemy of Macedonia. He enslaved the population of Olynthus and took over its land. This conquest convinced the people of Athens to seek peace with Macedonia, and in 346 B.C., an alliance was signed.

Philip expanded his kingdom further after 346 B.C., adding more territory in the regions of Illyria and Thrace to the north and in Thessaly to the south. In 338 B.C., he attacked Athens and the powerful Greek city-state of THEBES, which were now united against him. In the Battle of Chaeronea, Philip destroyed Thebes as a military power and became the undisputed master of the Greek world. The next year, Philip declared war against the PERSIAN EMPIRE. In 336 B.C., the same year he launched the first attack against the Persians, Philip was assassinated. At his death, Macedonia was a military and economic power, but the kingdom was almost as internally divided as it had been when he became king. (*See also* **Armies, Greek; Greece, History of; Wars and Warfare, Greek.**)

# PHILOSOPHY, GREEK AND HELLENISTIC

* **Hellenistic** referring to the Greek-influenced culture of the Mediterranean world during the three centuries after Alexander the Great, who died in 323 B.C.

The word *philosophy* comes from the Greek words *philo* (which means loving) and *sophia* (which means wisdom). A philosopher is a seeker of wisdom, and philosophy is the study of ideas, including moral, religious, and scientific ideas. The ancient Greeks gave more than a name to this branch of study. They also created some of the most important early philosophical works and ideas. Early Greek philosophy influenced Hellenistic* scholars, who carried on the Greek tradition in various parts of the Mediterranean world after 300 B.C.

The Greeks developed several branches of philosophy. One is ethics, the study of moral principles or values. Ethics is especially concerned with the specific moral choices an individual makes in his or her relationship with others. Metaphysics asks questions about the nature of reality and the meaning of existence. Logic, a third branch of philosophy, is the science of reasoning. Logicians study methods of expressing ideas and facts and then linking them together. A fourth branch of philosophy is natural philosophy, the study of nature and the physical world. In modern times, natural philosophy has evolved into various sciences, such as biology and physics.

Over hundreds of years, Greek and Hellenistic philosophers laid the foundations of all these branches of philosophy. They shaped the thinking of people throughout the ancient world, and their influence was long lasting. Even after the end of the Greek and Roman eras, the writings of Greek philosophers were the starting point for much of the literary, intellectual, and scientific activity of the Western world.

EARLY PHILOSOPHERS. The earliest known Greek philosophers were concerned with natural philosophy and metaphysics. In particular, they were interested in cosmology, the study of the nature of the universe. They wanted to understand how the universe and the world around them originated, what they were made of, and what forces or elements were operating in them.

Thinkers in Miletus, a Greek city on the west coast of ASIA MINOR, attempted to answer these questions in the 500s B.C. The first was THALES, who is sometimes called the father of philosophy. Although Thales left no written records, later writers reported that he believed that all things were made of the same basic element—water. Anaximander and Anaximenes, the next generation of philosophers in Miletus, also thought that everything in the universe came from one original substance. However, they recognized that whatever that original substance was, it must undergo many changes to appear as the great variety of things that exist in the natural world. Their inquiries were directed toward questions that would today be part of physics and chemistry.

Another early philosopher was the mathematician PYTHAGORAS, whose followers kept his teachings alive for centuries. The Pythagoreans not only developed some basic principles of mathematics and astronomy, but they also believed that numbers had mystical* and spiritual meanings. One influential Pythagorean idea was that the soul lived forever. After death, the soul was reincarnated, or reborn in a new body. Pythagoreanism shaped the thinking of Empedocles, who was active in the late 400s B.C. Empedocles believed that all living things were connected. He urged his fellow Greeks to stop making sacrifices* of animals, although such sacrifices were central to many religious rituals*. Empedocles also taught that everything in the universe is made from four elements—earth, air, water, and fire.

HERACLITUS of Ephesus and Parmenides of Elea were active around 500 B.C. Only brief, obscure statements remain of Heraclitus's writings, such as "the way up and down is one and the same." He warned people not to trust their senses, which can be fooled. His main contribution to philosophy was the idea that everything in the universe is constantly changing and flowing. Nothing is fixed, even if it appears solid. Parmenides inquired into the origin of the universe, asking how it could come into being from nothingness. He decided that the universe did not have a beginning but must have always existed.

Anaxagoras, who lived in the 400s B.C., was interested in natural philosophy. He considered such topics as the qualities of physical matter and the causes of growth and movement. Unlike Heraclitus, Anaxagoras believed that the senses were reliable sources of knowledge. Another philosopher interested in matter was DEMOCRITUS, who worked in the late 400s B.C. He developed the first atomic theory of matter, claiming that everything in the universe was made of tiny particles, called atoms, that moved about in empty space.

THE ATHENIAN PHILOSOPHERS.    Beginning in the mid-400s B.C., Athens became the center of Greek philosophy. About this time, philosophical thinkers shifted their interest from cosmology to human affairs. They concerned themselves with such issues as moral behavior, the relationship between the individual and society, and the nature of wisdom. Philosophy attempted to define and educate good leaders and citizens. RHETORIC, or the art of using words effectively in writing and speaking, became an important part of education. A number of learned men, called SOPHISTS, taught rhetoric and the various branches of philosophy in Athens.

SOCRATES, one of the key figures in the history of Greek philosophy, attacked the Sophists for claiming to know what moral virtue was and for claiming to be able to teach it. How could they have true understanding, Socrates asked, when each Sophist defined virtue differently? PLATO, a student of Socrates and one of the most influential of the Greek philosophers, also criticized the Sophists. According to Plato, the Sophists lacked firm moral values. Although they taught their pupils how to win arguments, Plato reasoned that they did not impart real knowledge and that they explained the workings of the universe in mechanical or physical terms, without moral meaning.

Although Socrates left no writings of his own, most scholars believe that many of his ideas are reflected in the works of Plato. One of Socrates' most

* **mystical**  referring to the belief that divine truths or direct knowledge of God can be experienced through meditation and contemplation as much as through logical thought

* **sacrifice**  sacred offering made to a god or goddess, usually of an animal such as a sheep or goat

* **ritual**  regularly followed routine, especially religious

Greek and Hellenistic philosophers, such as the one shown here, laid the foundations of several branches of learning, including mathematics, logic, ethics, politics, and natural science. In addition to being great thinkers, many ancient philosophers were also great teachers.

important contributions to philosophy was his method of teaching, which is called dialectic (or the Socratic method). Dialectic takes the form of a conversation or a series of questions and answers. Instead of simply stating his own opinions, Socrates questioned the opinions and ideas of others, trying to expose false thinking and make people discover the truth on their own.

Plato raised metaphysical and ethical questions that have continued to attract the attention of philosophers ever since. He also established the Academy, a school in Athens that survived for centuries after his death. Many scientists and philosophers of the ancient world received their training there.

Plato's best-known pupil, ARISTOTLE, determined that the highest goal of human life—the activity that produced the greatest happiness—was the use of reason in the study of philosophy. In using the gift of reason to seek what is good, humans came closest to the divine. Aristotle, who taught the young ALEXANDER THE GREAT, founded a school in Athens called the Lyceum. His philosophy and school of teaching became known as peripatetic (which means "walking around" in Greek), because Aristotle taught while walking around with his students. Aristotle's boundless curiosity led him into nearly every branch of philosophy and science. He wrote volumes on biology, logic, ethics, poetry, politics, and many other subjects. His writings were studied by later philosophers during the Hellenistic period in Greece and in Rome. During the Middle Ages, Aristotle's works were highly esteemed by many Christian and Arabic scholars. St. Thomas Aquinas, one of the greatest philosophers of the period, called Aristotle simply "the philosopher."

HELLENISTIC PHILOSOPHERS.    In the late 300s B.C., Alexander the Great conquered much of the known world. His conquests initiated a period known as the Hellenistic era, when Greek culture mingled with other cultures of the eastern Mediterranean. Although Athens remained the chief center of philosophical activity, the Egyptian city of ALEXANDRIA and other Hellenistic cities also produced important Hellenistic philosophers.

Hellenistic philosophy took a new direction. The spirit of speculation and inquiry gave way to the search for peace of mind, comfort, security, and happiness. Rival schools of philosophy competed for attention, each offering to show followers the way to "the good life." At the same time, the sciences of geography, medicine, and astronomy flourished as researchers looked for practical results that could be applied to everyday life. Science and philosophy were beginning to have separate identities.

EPICURUS founded one of the three main schools of Hellenistic philosophy. His basic idea was that all living creatures seek pleasure and that people can be guided to what is good by seeking in moderation what is pleasurable—and especially by avoiding pain and anxiety. To the Epicureans, human happiness had nothing to do with the gods. Instead, every person had the power to ensure a happy inner life by arranging pleasant circumstances—by living a life of moderation, displaying wisdom, caution, and courage, and through the joys of friendship. A person forced to endure difficult circumstances could achieve happiness by concentrating on pleasant memories.

The chief rival of Epicureanism was STOICISM, a school founded by Zeno of Citium around 280 B.C. While the Epicureans identified good with pleasure, the Stoics identified good with virtue or excellence. The Stoics

See color plate 11, vol. 3.

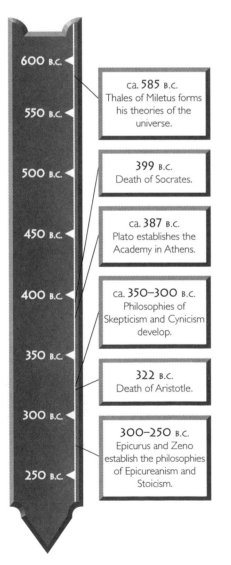

600 B.C.

ca. 585 B.C.
Thales of Miletus forms his theories of the universe.

550 B.C.

500 B.C.

399 B.C.
Death of Socrates.

450 B.C.

ca. 387 B.C.
Plato establishes the Academy in Athens.

400 B.C.

ca. 350–300 B.C.
Philosophies of Skepticism and Cynicism develop.

350 B.C.

322 B.C.
Death of Aristotle.

300 B.C.

300–250 B.C.
Epicurus and Zeno establish the philosophies of Epicureanism and Stoicism.

250 B.C.

developed a complex theory of matter, space, and time, but their ideas about physics were less influential than their moral teachings. According to the Stoics, people could achieve wisdom only by eliminating all emotions, passions, and affections. The Stoics believed that by observing nature, people could arrive at universal laws and principles that all reasonable beings should follow in their dealings with one another. The various versions of Stoicism that arose in the last two centuries B.C. had a profound influence on Roman thinkers.

The third major school of Hellenistic philosophy, SKEPTICISM, arose during the 300s B.C. and took many forms. Instead of putting forward ideas or beliefs, the skeptics used negative or critical arguments to attack other positions. They claimed that because so many different schools and philosophers had failed to agree on universal truths, such truths did not exist. Because no underlying realities can be known, there is no basis for a system of beliefs. The only thing of which a skeptic can be sure is the evidence of the senses. For example, a skeptic might say that honey *tastes* sweet *to him,* but he would not go so far as to say that it *is* sweet.

A final approach to philosophy, too simple and disjointed to be called a school or a system, was that of the CYNICS. Their goal was to be self-sufficient, free of ties to family, community, or society. They saw themselves as reformers whose mission was to point out dishonesty and vice in others—a mission that made them universally unpopular. Their philosophy originated in the 300s B.C., and Cynics were numerous during the Hellenistic and Roman eras. (*See also* **Astronomy and Astrology; Mathematics, Greek; Medicine, Greek; Philosophy, Roman; Science.**)

## PHILOSOPHY VS. POETRY

Greek and Hellenistic thinkers were deeply concerned about the relationship between philosophy and poetry. About 380 B.C., Plato referred to "a long-standing quarrel between philosophy and poetry" concerning which field offered greater knowledge and understanding. Yet some philosophers were also poets. Parmenides and Empedocles, for example, set forth their philosophical ideas in poems. Aristotle argued that philosophical writing was superior to poetry, but he admired poetry as an art form that appealed to the emotions as well as to reason. The Stoics, on the other hand, believed that the only good poems were educational poems.

# PHILOSOPHY, ROMAN

* **philosophy** study of ideas, including science

As they did with many intellectual pursuits, the Romans learned philosophy* from the Greeks. Beginning in the 100s B.C., Greek philosophers visited Rome and lectured widely. By about 100 B.C., Greek philosophy was well established among upper-class Romans, who commonly traveled to Greece to study. By 50 B.C., the first Roman philosophers had translated the works of selected Greek philosophers into Latin and had begun to create philosophical literature of their own.

LUCRETIUS. LUCRETIUS was one of the founders of Roman philosophy. Around 50 B.C., he composed *On the Nature of Things,* which was a lengthy poem that attempted to explain the teachings of the Greek philosopher EPICURUS. Lucretius's goal was to free the Roman people from the two great fears that haunted human existence—the fear of the gods and the fear of death—by providing a scientific explanation for events in the natural world.

As a follower of Epicurus, Lucretius believed that the gods did not affect human lives or events. Therefore, Lucretius argued, humans alone were responsible for their own happiness. He attempted to show that worlds were created and destroyed merely as a result of physical processes, without any divine plan. Lucretius also claimed that physical processes accounted for many other events that were often explained by the action of the gods. The

See color plate 13, vol. 3.

* **rhetoric** art of using words effectively in speaking or writing

* **ethics** branch of philosophy that deals with moral conduct, duty, and judgment

* **dialogue** text presenting an exchange of ideas between people

* **Stoicism** philosophy that emphasized control over one's thoughts and emotions

* **prose** writing without meter or rhyme, as distinguished from poetry

## POLITICS AND PHILOSOPHY IN ANCIENT ROME

In ancient Rome, politics played an important role in most aspects of life, including philosophy. The Roman philosopher Seneca provides a good example. Seneca was a prominent politician who was exiled for eight years during the emperor Claudius's reign. Some historians believe that Seneca's writings in praise of poverty and the simple life were attempts to console himself. After his return from exile, Seneca became a tutor and then a major adviser to the young emperor Nero. However, he soon fell out of favor with Nero and was charged with conspiracy. As punishment, Nero forced Seneca to commit suicide.

world, he believed, consisted of only two things: atoms and empty space. Besides atoms and void, nothing else existed. Hence, all events and objects could be explained in purely physical or material terms.

**CICERO.** A prominent statesman, Marcus Tullius CICERO studied Greek philosophy as a youth and remained interested in philosophy throughout his life. He began writing philosophy somewhat late in life. He composed most of his philosophical works during a period of less than two years—following the death of his daughter in about 45 B.C. Apparently Cicero wrote philosophy as a way to forget his great sorrow.

Cicero attempted to make philosophy attractive to Romans by combining it with rhetoric*. He translated Greek works on ethics* that had relevance to Roman life into understandable and often stimulating dialogues*. As a follower of STOICISM*, Cicero believed that the laws of any society must be based on the universal law of nature, which he saw as the rationality that existed in nature. His strong beliefs were already apparent in his first philosophical work, *De Republica,* in which Cicero described his ideal vision of the future of Rome.

**SENECA.** Like Cicero, SENECA was a prominent statesman who wrote Stoic philosophy in Latin rhetorical prose*. He had a wonderful gift for summing up his thoughts in short, memorable phrases. Like Lucretius, Seneca's goal was to help people overcome fears by explaining natural phenomena in scientific terms. Unlike Lucretius, however, Seneca believed that the gods controlled everything that happened in the world.

In his writings, Seneca emphasized human relationships, and he called for mutual love and forgiveness. He believed that clemency, or mercy, was the most desirable human quality. More than any other ancient philosopher, Seneca insisted that slaves were human beings who should be treated with the same respect given to others.

**MARCUS AURELIUS.** All Roman philosophy was based on Greek models, and after Seneca, Roman philosophers used Greek, rather than Latin, to express their ideas. One of the best known of these later Roman philosophers was Marcus AURELIUS, who was emperor of Rome in the late A.D. 100s.

Marcus Aurelius had read and admired Greek Stoic philosophers, especially the work of EPICTETUS. He wrote his own personal reflections regarding this work in the form of a diary, the first in Western literature. He supported the Stoic view that the world is governed by God, and that humans should accept whatever lot God assigns them. Unlike earlier Roman philosophers, Marcus Aurelius did not cite examples from Roman history or recognize a distinctly Roman use for philosophy. Rather, he regarded himself as a citizen of the world, and he used philosophy as something that transcended national boundaries.

**NEOPLATONISM.** During the A.D. 200s, the most important development in Roman philosophy was Neoplatonism, which revived the philosophy of PLATO, the great Greek philosopher of the 300s B.C. The philosopher PLOTINUS, who founded Neoplatonism, came to Rome in A.D. 244 from Alexandria in

Egypt. Neoplatonists believed that the world and everything in it flowed from a great being, with whom each person's soul was reunited after death. A carefully thought-out system of philosophy, Neoplatonism also had a strong mystical* component. Neoplatonism greatly influenced CHRISTIANITY, which was gaining widespread popularity during this period. After Plotinus, the center of philosophy shifted away from Rome to the East, and pagan* Roman philosophy came to an end. (*See also* **Education and Rhetoric, Roman; Philosophy, Greek and Hellenistic.**)

* **mystical** referring to the belief that divine truths or direct knowledge of God can be experienced through meditation and contemplation as much as through logical thought

* **pagan** referring to a belief in more than one god; non-Christian

# PHOENICIANS

The Phoenicians were a people who lived along the eastern coast of the Mediterranean Sea. As the principal seafarers in the eastern Mediterranean as early as the 700s B.C., they established trading posts and settlements as far away as Spain and the Red Sea and explored the coasts of Africa. The Phoenician colony of CARTHAGE developed into a powerful city that rivaled Rome in the western Mediterranean until the Roman victory in the PUNIC WARS.

According to the Greek historian HERODOTUS, the Phoenicians migrated to the Mediterranean coast from a region near the Persian Gulf around 2700 B.C. Archaeological traces of the Phoenician presence in Lebanon have been dated to as early as 3000 B.C. The history of the Phoenicians has always been closely connected to the sea. By the 900s B.C., they had replaced the Greek Mycenaean civilization as the principal traders in the eastern Mediterranean. With their advanced shipbuilding and navigation skills, the Phoenicians conducted an extensive international trade in metals, TEXTILES, purple dye, crafts, and food.

The important Phoenician cities were Sidon, Tyre, and Byblos, with Tyre becoming the leading Phoenician port in about 700 B.C. The Phoenicians established trading posts and settlements in many places along the Mediterranean, including Spain, North Africa, and Egypt. Carthage in North Africa was the largest and most famous of their settlements. The spread of these settlements left traces of Phoenician art, crafts, religion, and inscriptions* throughout the Mediterranean.

From the beginning of their expansion, the Phoenicians had contact with the Greeks. During the 700s B.C., the Greeks adopted the Phoenician alphabet and modified it for their own language. However, it was not until after the PERSIAN WARS in the early 400s B.C. that Greek culture began to substantially influence that of the Phoenicians. That influence rapidly increased after ALEXANDER THE GREAT conquered the Phoenicians in about 330 B.C. Tyre, the only Phoenician city that resisted Alexander, was eventually captured after a long siege*. After Alexander's death, the Ptolemaic and Seleucid dynasties fought over the land of the Phoenicians until the Seleucid kingdom under Antiochus III gained control in 200 B.C. After Phoenician territory came under Roman rule in the 60s B.C., the area became part of the province* of Syria. Under the later Roman Empire, the Romans created a separate province of Phoenice with its capital at Berytus (present-day Beirut). (*See also* **Alphabets and Writing; Inscriptions; Trade, Greek.**)

* **inscription** letters or words carved into a surface as a lasting record

* **siege** long and persistent effort to force a surrender by surrounding a fortress with armed troops, cutting it off from aid

* **province** overseas area controlled by Rome

## RED PHOENICIANS?

The Greeks called the seafaring people who lived in Tyre, Sidon, and other cities along the eastern Mediterranean coast Phoinikes (Phoenicians). There are several theories about what this name meant. One is that the name came from the Greek word for red, which may have been a reference to the Phoenicians' reddish complexion or to the purple dye they produced and exported. Other scholars think the name *Phoenician* derives from Egyptian words for Asiatic or woodcutters.

## PINDAR

### 518–438 B.C.
### GREEK POET

* **city-state** independent state consisting of a city and its surrounding territory

* **aristocratic** referring to people of the highest social class

* **Panhellenic** referring to all of Greece or to all Greek people

* **patron** special guardian, protector, or supporter

The ancient Greeks considered Pindar to be one of their greatest poets. Although he lived and worked in a time of war and rivalry among the Greek city-states*, his talent and fame made him a celebrity throughout the Greek world and protected him from the worst of the conflict. Pindar wrote choral lyrics, which were poems sung by choruses, with accompanying music and dance. The composer of choral lyrics created all elements of the performance—words, music, and dance. By the time Pindar wrote his poetry, the choral lyric was becoming a traditional art form. Pindar brought that tradition to its highest point.

THE POET FROM BOEOTIA. Pindar was born in a village near the city of THEBES, in a part of Greece called Boeotia. Although he later traveled widely and lived in other places, he was always known as a Boeotian. Pindar spent much of his life in Thebes. For several centuries after his death, a building in Thebes was identified as "Pindar's house." According to legend, when ALEXANDER THE GREAT invaded and destroyed Thebes, he ordered his soldiers not to burn the house where the great poet had once lived.

Little is known about Pindar's life or his family background. He probably came from an aristocratic* family, since the ideas and values that he expressed in his poems were those of the traditional rural nobility of his time. Pindar received his education and musical training in ATHENS, an important center of artistic activity in the late 500s and 400s B.C. According to accounts of his life that were written over a century after his death, Pindar married and had two daughters and a son. He may have spent some time at DELPHI, a city important to the Greeks as a religious center and the host of one of the four great Panhellenic* festivals.

The earliest of Pindar's surviving poems is dated from 498 B.C. Although Pindar was only about 20 years old at the time, the poem is the work of a skilled and confident poet. He soon became established as a successful composer of choral lyrics. As a professional poet, Pindar had clients from all over the Greek world. Some of his clients were kings or rulers. Others were wealthy or aristocratic patrons* of the arts who hired Pindar to write choral lyrics for particular occasions, such as a festival, wedding, or the funeral of an important person.

One of Pindar's clients was Hieron, the ruler of the Greek colony of SYRACUSE on the island of SICILY. Hieron commissioned several poems from Pindar, and some versions of Pindar's life say that the poet lived in Syracuse for several years in the 470s B.C. as Hieron's guest. The city of Athens also commissioned several poems from Pindar. In one of them, Pindar praises the beauties of "violet-crowned" Athens. According to legend, the Athenians were so pleased with the lyric that they rewarded Pindar with the very handsome sum of 10,000 drachmas. When Thebes and Athens went to war in the 450s and 440s B.C., Pindar's fellow Thebans made him pay a fine as punishment for his earlier praise of Athens. Some of Pindar's later poems express his loyalty to Thebes and his pride in being Boeotian. Scholars have suggested that in these poems Pindar was assuring the people of Boeotia that, although he had won fame in other regions, he was still one of them. He shared their determination to remain independent of Athens, which had already tried once to conquer Boeotia.

Pindar's last dated poem was composed in 446 B.C., although he may have continued to write until his death. More than 100 years after Pindar's death, scholars at the Library of ALEXANDRIA collected his lyrics into 17 books. The poems fell into many categories, including hymns, funeral songs, songs to accompany processions or parades, songs of praise, and victory odes*. Of all Pindar's poems, only 44 victory odes survive to the present day. More accurately, only the words survive—the music and the dancing that accompanied them have been lost.

**THE VICTORY ODES.**   Pindar wrote his victory odes, also called epinician odes, to honor winners at the Greek games. Athletes and musicians from all over the Greek world competed for glory at these events. The four largest competitions were the Pythian, Nemean, Isthmian, and OLYMPIC GAMES, each held every two or four years. Because Pindar composed odes for the victors of all four of the major games, his surviving poems are grouped into four volumes—*Pythian, Nemean, Isthmian,* and *Olympian.*

A victory in one of these games brought glory not just to the person who won the prize but also to the city in which the winner lived. Since the rulers, governments, or citizens' committees of those cities commissioned Pindar to write the victory ode, each poem celebrated a city's history, achievements, and beauties, as well as a particular individual's talents and efforts.

Most victory odes contain certain similar elements. The poet described the winner and the nature of the event he won. Next, the poem might mention other victors in the winner's family or in the city's history. The poet would probably also refer to gods, heroes*, and other mythological or legendary figures who had some connection with either the event or the athlete's home city.

One distinctive feature of Pindar's odes is their solemn, religious tone. Pindar's victory odes contain expressions of great gratitude and awe toward the gods. They reflect the poet's deep attachment to the traditional religious beliefs and legends of the ancient Greeks:

> The race of the gods is one thing, that of men,
>   quite another.
> We both get our breath from Earth, our common mother.
> Yet the powers of the two races are wholly
>   different, so that one of them is nothing—
> while the bronze heaven of the gods stays secure forever.
> (*Nemean* 6.1–4)

The odes also reveal that Pindar admired those willing to struggle, suffer, and sacrifice in a noble cause. A victor was touched by the gods, and he shared their glory. Pindar spent little time describing the athlete's training, performance, or victory. To him, these details were unimportant. What mattered was that the athlete's struggle made him a noble, heroic figure, worthy of comparison to the kings and heroes of legend:

> But we can become something *like* the immortal
>   gods
> through greatness—greatness of mind or greatness
>   of body—
> though we don't know from day to day, or night to

* **ode** lyric poem often addressed to a person or an object

* **hero** in mythology, a person of great strength or ability, often descended from a god

**IMITATING THE MASTER**

The Roman poet Horace warned that anyone who tried to copy Pindar was doomed to fall in failure like the Greek mythological figure Icarus. Icarus had fallen on wax wings into the sea when he had dared to fly too close to the sun.

Despite Horace's warning, European poets many hundreds of years later continued to admire, and to some degree imitate, the structure and imagery of Pindar's odes. John Milton's *On the Morning of Christ's Nativity,* John Dryden's *Alexander's Feast* and *Ode for St. Cecilia's Day,* and Thomas Gray's *Progress of Poesy* all reflect the influence of the Greek master on English poetry of the 1600s and 1700s.

night, what course
fate has drawn for us to run our race.
(*Nemean* 6.5–8)

(*See also* **Games, Greek; Literature, Greek; Poetry, Greek and Hellenistic.**)

# PIRACY

## ROUGH JUSTICE

Piracy was such a difficult problem in the Mediterranean that the Romans imposed the maximum penalty to stop it. Under Roman law, a captured pirate was to be crucified, beheaded, or thrown to wild animals. The law recommended that the punishment be inflicted in public and that the body be displayed on a cross or post "so that the sight will deter others from the same crimes."

Sometimes angry people did not bother to wait for the law. When they caught a pirate, they either beat their captive to death or burned him alive.

---

* **hero** in mythology, a person of great strength or ability, often descended from a god

* **epic** long poem about legendary or historical heroes, written in a grand style

* **plunder** to steal property by force, usually after a conquest

* **sack** to rob a captured city

* **classical** in Greek history, refers to the period of great political and cultural achievement from about 500 B.C. to 323 B.C.

* **Hellenistic** referring to the Greek-influenced culture of the Mediterranean world during the three centuries after Alexander the Great, who died in 323 B.C.

* **inscription** letters or words carved into a surface as a lasting record

* **booty** riches or property gained through conquest

* **aristocrat** person of the highest social class

Piracy, or robbery on the sea, was widespread throughout the ancient world. Pirates were a constant threat to travelers and traders and to the safety of coastal communities. Although the naval power of ATHENS, RHODES, and the Roman Empire solved the problem of piracy for short periods of time, piracy continued to cause hardships during most of ancient Greek and Roman history.

The earliest references to piracy are found in the poems of HOMER. In ancient times, piracy brought no shame to those who practiced it. Although the heroes* in Homer's epics* are never referred to as pirates, they often acted as such, raiding and plundering* coastal towns. In the *Odyssey,* after ODYSSEUS and his men left Troy to return home, they sacked* a city in THRACE. There they "killed the men and, taking the women and plenty of cattle and goods, divided them up." According to the Greek historian THUCYDIDES, early Greeks and non-Greeks engaged in piracy and the sacking of towns. "This was a lifelong pursuit for them," he wrote, "one that had not as yet received any stigma but was even considered an honorable profession." Widespread piracy forced the people who lived on islands and along the coasts of the mainland to build their homes either a safe distance from the sea or on defensible sites next to the sea.

During the classical* period of Greek history, piracy came to be viewed as dishonorable. Athens, with its powerful navy, succeeded in keeping the AEGEAN SEA relatively free of pirates. However, with the outbreak of the PELOPONNESIAN WAR and Athens's defeat in 404 B.C., piracy revived. During the 300s B.C., the Athenians were eventually able to reestablish a naval base in the Adriatic Sea to protect their trading ships from raids by Illyrian pirates who operated along the coast.

Attacks on ships in the eastern Mediterranean during the Hellenistic* period are mentioned only occasionally in ancient sources. The main threats of piracy continued to be raids on coastal towns and settlements. Numerous inscriptions* from islands in the Aegean Sea and from coastal communities record incidents of raiding by pirates in search of booty* and prisoners to be ransomed or sold into SLAVERY. The kidnapping of young aristocrats* by pirates became a common subject of Greek and Roman literature.

The island state of Rhodes succeeded in keeping the eastern Mediterranean Sea free of pirates during the late 200s and early 100s B.C. Rhodes did not have the heavy ships that required hundreds of rowers, common in the navies of the large Hellenistic kingdoms. Instead, the navy of Rhodes used squadrons of lighter and faster ships that could more easily chase and capture pirate ships. However, the growing power of the Roman Empire ended the wealth and independence of Rhodes. With the decline of the Rhodian navy, piracy revived and even flourished.

The Romans before about 30 B.C. made little attempt to check piracy in the western Mediterranean. Although the Romans strengthened their fleet during the PUNIC WARS of the 200s and 100s B.C., the new fleet declined after Rome's victory over CARTHAGE in 146 B.C. By the first century B.C., pirates roamed the Mediterranean at will, raiding ships and coastal communities and kidnapping and holding wealthy Romans for ransom. Pirates even plundered the Roman port of OSTIA, which was only 16 miles from Rome. When piracy threatened the Roman grain supply, officials finally took steps to eliminate the problem. In 67 B.C., the Roman general POMPEY successfully rid the Mediterranean of pirates, but the Roman civil wars that followed soon afterward left the region in disarray and enabled piracy to return. AUGUSTUS, the first Roman emperor, built a permanent Roman fleet that finally halted piracy in the region. However, when the Roman Empire began to break apart during the A.D. 400s, piracy once again became a major problem for the peoples of the Mediterranean. (*See also* **Naval Power, Greek; Naval Power, Roman; Ships and Shipbuilding; Trade, Greek; Trade, Roman.**)

# PLATO

## 428–348 B.C.
## GREEK PHILOSOPHER

* **philosopher** scholar or thinker concerned with the study of ideas, including science

* **dialogue** text presenting an exchange of ideas between people

* **ethics** branch of philosophy that deals with moral conduct, duty, and judgment

* **metaphysics** branch of philosophy concerned with the fundamental nature of reality

### PLATO'S ACADEMY

Plato founded the Academy for the systematic study of philosophy and the sciences. The school soon became famous as a center of learning. All the leading mathematicians of the 300s B.C. were pupils of Plato. Rulers and citizen assemblies from many cities turned to the legal experts of the Academy for advice on kingship or for help in writing laws and constitutions. The Academy existed until A.D. 529, when the emperor Justinian closed it because it was not a Christian institution.

Plato was one of the most important philosophers* in history. A pupil of SOCRATES, he was the teacher of another great philosopher, ARISTOTLE. Plato's writings, consisting almost entirely of dialogues*, analyze a variety of philosophical issues including questions of ethics* and metaphysics*. His complex and thought-provoking work has served as a starting point for many philosophers who succeeded him. Plato founded a school, known as the Academy, that remained an important training ground for philosophers and scientists for centuries after his death. Some historians consider the Academy the world's first university.

PLATO'S LIFE.   Few details are known about Plato's life. Both of his parents came from high-ranking, distinguished Athenian families. Plato grew up in an educated and cultured setting, with family connections to some of the most powerful figures in Athens. He may have studied with a philosopher named Cratylus, but the major influence on his life and thought came from Socrates, a longtime associate of Plato's mother's family. Plato probably was introduced to the older philosopher at an early age, and the two became close friends.

Although urged by his relatives to enter politics, Plato decided instead to devote his life to philosophy. Unlike Socrates, Plato did not believe that he had a duty to marry and raise a family of sons to swell the ranks of Athenian citizenry. After Socrates died, Plato left Athens and spent 12 years traveling. In Italy and Sicily, he met the followers of the mathematician and philosopher PYTHAGORAS and learned of their belief that dreams and visions pointed the way to spiritual truth.

Around 387 B.C., Plato returned to Athens and founded the Academy with the intention of training future statesmen and politicians. He supervised the Academy until his death 40 years later. According to some sources, Plato was invited to Syracuse in Sicily in the 360s B.C. to train Dionysius II, the young man who had inherited the throne. Plato made two trips to Syracuse, but Dionysius resisted his teacher. Plato died in Athens and supposedly was buried in the Academy.

# PLATO

One of the great ancient philosophers, Plato created thought-provoking works that are still read and discussed today. His Academy—founded to explore issues such as ethics and metaphysics—is considered by many to be the first university.

THE DIALOGUES.    Plato left a record of his thought in a collection of writings called dialogues. Between 25 and 30 of the surviving dialogues are genuine works of Plato. These documents are in the form of conversations, almost like plays or stories, in which characters discuss philosophical issues by asking and answering questions. They test each other's arguments and explore the strengths and weaknesses of opposing points of view. This method, which is sometimes called dialectic, reveals one of Plato's fundamental beliefs. For Plato, the value of philosophy lay not in telling people what to think or how to act but in making them question, ponder, and eventually recognize the truth for themselves.

Plato himself does not participate in the dialogues. Instead, Socrates appears as the main character in most of Plato's writings. This is especially true in Plato's earlier dialogues, such as the *Apology,* which relates Socrates' speech in his own defense at his trial. Unlike many philosophers, Plato never wrote a systematic explanation of his views. For these reasons, it is sometimes difficult to know whether a particular concept originated with Plato or with Socrates. Understanding Plato's philosophy requires a careful analysis of the content of the dialogues.

In the dialogues, Plato raised a series of important questions and then showed how a thoughtful person might set about answering them. Some of those questions concern ethics. Plato often portrays Socrates exposing the ignorance of people who claimed to know what was right and true. For example, in a dialogue called *Euthyphro,* Socrates meets a man who claims to be a religious expert. By the end of the dialogue, Socrates has shown that Euthyphro cannot even define what piety, or religious devotion, truly means.

Other philosophical questions deal with metaphysics. Plato was always concerned with the question of how the truth can be perceived. He believed that wisdom meant understanding the eternal truths or realities of the universe. One of Plato's most important concepts was that these truths, or realities, exist as ideals that he called Forms. We perceive something as cold, for example, because it embodies something of the quality or Form of absolute coldness.

Plato maintained that people had souls that did not die when the body died. The philosopher's primary goal was to care for the soul, which would be reborn over and over again into new bodies until it achieved ultimate wisdom. The true philosopher did not fear death, which was simply the separation of the soul from its prison in the body. In his dialogue *Timaeus,* Plato presented his belief that the universe was created by a well-meaning god. Although evil existed, the universe was ultimately a place of goodness and order.

The *Republic* and the *Laws* are long dialogues that express Plato's political ideas. Plato wrote in the *Republic* that states would not be well governed until kings became philosophers or philosophers became kings. He outlined the appropriate education for such a philosopher-king and also described the structure of the ideal state. Because Plato believed that the human soul had three parts—reason, emotion, and appetite (desire)—he believed that the state, too, should have three parts—rulers, the rulers' helpers or guardians, and producers. Rulers were to the state what reason was to the soul—the part that knew what was best for all operated according to this expert judgment. When a soul was governed by reason, it was in a state of harmony. A state governed by reasonable philosopher-kings would also be in a state of harmony, which Plato equated with justice.

PLATO'S INFLUENCE.   Plato's influence on Western thought began during his lifetime and has continued to the present. Through his Academy, Plato influenced philosophers, politicians, writers, and scientists throughout the Greek world. He also influenced many Roman thinkers, especially the great Roman orator* CICERO. In the A.D. 200s, the Greek philosopher PLOTINUS combined Plato's philosophy with Eastern mysticism* to form a new system of philosophy known as Neoplatonism.

After Plato's writings were translated into Latin in the late 1400s, European philosophers studied Platonic ideas. Although Plato had lived centuries before the founding of CHRISTIANITY, Renaissance* scholars believed that his philosophy did not clash with Christian beliefs. Interest in Plato increased during the 1800s. Some modern thinkers admire his ideas about education and about the human soul. Others, however, have pointed out that the ideal society and state that Plato described in the *Republic* and the *Laws* is really a dictatorship. (*See also* **Philosophy, Greek and Hellenistic; Philosophy, Roman.**)

* **orator** public speaker of great skill

* **mysticism** belief that divine truths or direct knowledge of God can be experienced through faith, spiritual insight, and intuition

* **Renaissance** period of the rebirth of interest in classical art, literature, and learning that occurred in Europe from the late 1300s through the 1500s

## PLAUTUS

### 254–184 B.C.
### ROMAN PLAYWRIGHT

Titus Maccius Plautus, an author of comic plays, was one of the most accomplished and popular of Roman writers. He was also the author of the earliest Latin literary works that have survived in complete form to the present day. Although Plautus's plays are important and entertaining as literature, they also provide valuable information about the Latin language as it was spoken around 200 B.C.

Almost nothing is known for certain about Plautus's life. It is believed that he was born in a part of Italy north of Rome called Umbria. If this is true, he grew up speaking Umbrian, a language related to Latin. Yet Plautus later became so skilled in Latin that he is regarded as a master of puns, jokes, and wordplay in the language. His name itself was probably a joke of his own creation. In Umbria, where people used only one name, he would have been called simply Titus. But Romans generally used three names, and Plautus apparently created the Roman-sounding name Titus Maccius Plautus, which means something like "Titus the clown." Plautus supposedly began writing plays while working in a mill for a living. Nothing is known about his later years or his death.

Although Plautus was said to have written more than 100 plays, only 21 survive. They are closely modeled on the works of MENANDER and other Greek playwrights who wrote in a style called New Comedy, which flourished in Athens during the late 300s B.C. Plautus adapted the plots of the Greek originals, giving the characters Roman names and rewriting the plays to suit Roman audiences. Because the Greek originals are now lost, it is difficult to determine how much of Plautus's plays is a faithful rendering of the Greek plays and how much is his original invention.

New Comedy relied on plot devices such as secret love affairs, misunderstandings, disguises and mistaken identities, and reunions of long-lost relatives. New Comedy also featured many recognizable types, or stock characters, such as the clever slave and the bragging soldier, whose traits were often exaggerated. Plautus employed the story lines and stock characters of New Comedy. For example, his play *The Pot of Gold* features a miserly, suspicious old man and a pair of young lovers. In *Epidicus,* a clever slave outwits his master and wins his freedom. *The Two Menaechmuses* features identical twins, a traditional plot device for creating comic confusion.

Yet Plautus did more than simply translate and copy Greek plays. Although his plays are set in Greece, they have a Roman flavor. They frequently refer to Roman people, places, and events. They are also filled with sparkling wit. Plautus's humor contains so many puns and other examples of clever wordplay in Latin that it cannot fully be translated into any other language. Plautus altered his New Comedy models in other ways too. He added more music, and he gave some of the traditional stock characters more distinct individual personalities.

Roman acting companies continued to perform the comedies of Plautus for several centuries after his death, and Roman audiences continued to enjoy them. The plays were also popular in Europe between the 1400s and 1600s. Just as Plautus had borrowed his plots from the Greek playwrights, some European playwrights, such as William Shakespeare, borrowed their plot ideas from Plautus. In his *Comedy of Errors,* Shakespeare uses identical twins to create comic situations—a technique Plautus had employed centuries before. (*See also* **Drama, Greek; Drama, Roman; Terence.**)

# PLEBEIANS, ROMAN

* **patrician** member of the upper class who traced his ancestry to a senatorial family in the earliest days of the Roman Republic

* **Roman Republic** Rome during the period from 509 B.C. to 31 B.C., when popular assemblies annually elected their governmental officials

* **magistrate** government official in ancient Greece and Rome

* **patron** special guardian, protector, or supporter

Plebeians were all Roman citizens who were not patricians*. *Plebeian* referred to the mass of the Roman population—all those belonging to the lower classes of Roman society. At the beginning of the Roman Republic*, plebeians were excluded from all important positions in the government. After a centuries-long struggle, which was known as the Conflict of the Orders, plebeians largely attained political equality with patricians.

In 510 B.C., after overthrowing the last of their kings, the Roman patricians were firmly in control of the government. Only patricians could be members of the Roman Senate, and only patricians could become magistrates*. Patricians held all the priesthoods as well. Many plebeians, on the other hand, were poor and in debt to their patrician patrons*. During the early republic, Roman citizens could be enslaved or executed if they were unable to repay their debts.

In 494 B.C. scores of plebeians withdrew from Rome and assembled outside the boundaries of the city. This was the first of five secessions by the plebeians that occurred during the early years of the republic. They formed their own popular assembly and elected their own officials, called TRIBUNES, to protect their interests against the actions of the patricians. Because the withdrawal of large numbers of citizens weakened the army, the patricians relented. Eventually, they accepted the plebeian assembly as able to make laws binding on the plebeians and their tribunes as legitimate officials, thus creating a plebeian state within Rome.

See color plate 6, vol. 2.

The plebeians developed their own institutions that were completely separate from those of the patricians. They formed an assembly called the *concilium plebis,* which excluded all patricians. Decisions (called *plebiscita*) made by the *concilium plebis* were binding only on plebeians, although they could be applied to all Romans if they were also approved by the patricians. When this condition was removed at the end of the Conflict of the Orders, *plebiscita* became law for all the Roman people.

During the late Roman Republic, the *concilium plebis* became the main legislative body of the Roman government. However, AUGUSTUS, the first Roman emperor, removed all the legislative power of the *concilium plebis* and gave it to the Roman Senate.

The *concilium plebis* also elected the tribunes and the two plebeian aediles\*. Each year, the assembly elected ten tribunes to represent the interests of the plebeians. Although they were not magistrates of the Roman government, tribunes had considerable power. They helped any plebeian who was mistreated by the patricians, and they could block all legislation of the magistrates and decrees of the Roman Senate that they believed were not in the best interest of the plebeians.

Around 450 B.C., the plebeians demanded that the Roman rulers codify\* Roman laws so that they would apply to all citizens equally. Although the result, known as the Twelve Tables, was harsh and restrictive, it made the laws known to all and not subject to the arbitrary decisions of magistrates.

The plebeians' greatest success was the passage of the Licinian-Sextian laws of 367–366 B.C. For the first time, plebeians were allowed to hold the office of consul\*. In addition, laws were passed that limited the amount of public land that one person could hold, thereby reducing the amount of public land that wealthier citizens could legally own. By the end of the 300s B.C., plebeians could hold important governmental offices and state priesthoods, and imprisonment for debt had been abolished.

After the plebeians' final secession in 287 B.C., the Romans passed the Hortensian law, which validated legislation passed by the plebeian assembly and applied it to all Roman citizens, not just plebeians. After this time, plebeians and patricians had equal political and legal rights. Although this marked the end of the Conflict of the Orders, most political power remained in the hands of the wealthier noble families.

During the late Roman Republic, ambitious plebeian politicians became plebeian aediles and tribunes as a step on the path to higher office. Because tribunes could veto the acts of consuls and praetors\*, they were sometimes used by the Roman Senate to control other Roman magistrates. Some tribunes continued to act in the best interest of the plebeians. For example, the tribunes Tiberius and Gaius GRACCHUS attempted to use the office to distribute public lands to the poor and to provide free grain for the citizens of Rome. Because of reformers such as these, the dictator SULLA limited the powers of the tribunes in the 80s B.C., but this change lasted only about ten years. (*See also* **Aedile; Class Structure, Roman; Consul; Government, Roman; Law, Roman; Magistrates; Patricians, Roman; Patronage; Praetor; Rome, History of.**)

\* **aedile** Roman official in charge of maintaining public property inside the city, such as roads, temples, and markets

\* **codify** to arrange according to a system; to set down in writing

\* **consul** one of two chief governmental officials of Rome, chosen annually and serving for a year

\* **praetor** Roman official, just below the consul in rank, in charge of judicial proceedings and of governing overseas provinces

## PLINY THE ELDER

ca. A.D. 23–79
ROMAN ADMINISTRATOR
AND WRITER

* **procurator** Roman official who managed the financial, and sometimes administrative, affairs of a province as an agent of the emperor

* **patron** special guardian, protector, or supporter

* **rhetoric** art of using words effectively in speaking or writing

* **oratory** art of public speaking

aius Plinius Secundus, known as Pliny the Elder, was a Roman government official, writer, and scholar. He was the uncle and adoptive father of the Roman writer PLINY THE YOUNGER. Today, the elder Pliny is best known as the author of *Natural History,* a massive encyclopedia of information about many different subjects.

Pliny was born in Comum in Cisalpine GAUL (present-day northern Italy). He spent 12 years in the army, mostly in Germany where he served alongside the future emperor TITUS. Upon his return to Italy, Pliny practiced law. Under the emperor VESPASIAN, he became a procurator* in Gaul, Spain, and North Africa. He served as an adviser to Vespasian and Titus, and he became commander of the Roman fleet at the port of Misenum. He died during the eruption of Mt. VESUVIUS, which destroyed the cities of POMPEII and Herculaneum.

Pliny was a prolific writer, completing many books on a variety of topics. In addition to the biography of his patron*, Pomponius Secundus, Pliny wrote a 20-volume history of the Roman campaign against the Germans and a 31-volume history of his own time. Pliny produced works on rhetoric* and oratory*, and during his military service, he wrote an essay on spear-throwing for cavalrymen.

The only work of Pliny's that has survived is the 37-book *Natural History,* which he dedicated to Titus. The *Natural History* is a vast, wide-ranging collection of information about people, animals, plants, and minerals. It provides an important look at the state of scientific knowledge in the first century A.D. The importance of the work was quickly recognized. During the Middle Ages in Europe, Pliny's *Natural History* held a position of great authority and influence. It has been translated into several languages, including English in the early 1600s. (*See also* **Literature, Roman; Science.**)

## PLINY THE YOUNGER

ca. A.D. 61–ca. 112
ROMAN SENATOR AND WRITER

* **province** overseas area controlled by Rome

* **rhetoric** art of using words effectively in speaking or writing

* **legion** main unit of the Roman army, consisting of about 6,000 soldiers

* **praetor** Roman official, just below the consul in rank, in charge of judicial proceedings and of governing overseas provinces

* **consul** one of two chief governmental officials of Rome, chosen annually and serving for a year

Gaius Plinius Caecilius Secundus, known as Pliny the Younger, was the nephew and adopted son of PLINY THE ELDER. Although he was a Roman senator and the governor of a province*, he is mostly known for his collected letters, which provide an important source of information about Roman society in the first and second centuries A.D.

Pliny was born at Comum (the site of the modern city of Como) in northern Italy. After the death of his father, he was raised and adopted by his uncle. He studied rhetoric* in Rome before starting on a long and successful career as a government official. After serving for a year on the staff of a Syrian legion*, Pliny returned to Rome and worked on law cases in the civil courts. He skillfully practiced law for the rest of his life, specializing in cases that involved inheritance.

While still in his 20s, Pliny became a senator with the help of family friends. In the Senate, he successfully prosecuted several provincial governors charged with corruption. He ascended the *cursus honorum,* or Roman political ladder, serving as a praetor* and then as consul*. He served three times on the judicial council of the emperor TRAJAN, who appointed Pliny governor of the province of Bithynia, where he apparently died in A.D. 112.

Near the end of his life, Pliny published nine books of letters that he had written on a wide range of topics. Some of the letters commented on the political and social events of his time, while others offered advice to friends or discussed candidates for senatorial elections. Each letter is carefully composed and written in a formal and eloquent literary style.

Although Pliny wrote about daily events, he wanted to create something of more enduring interest: a picture of Roman life in all its aspects, as seen and experienced by a Roman official with a strong moral point of view. In his letters, he criticizes the cruelty of slave masters and the insensitivity of rich Romans who cared more about money than about people. But he was not a satirist. He does not give the names of those he criticizes and generally maintains a positive attitude. Pliny praises the work of the emperor Trajan, and he writes about the virtues of friends and acquaintances, the value of education, and literary life in Rome. Other letters discuss such matters as senatorial debates, trials, and elections. Pliny's *Letters* provide a valuable source of information about the Roman upper class as well as his own career.

Pliny also produced other kinds of writings. He published two volumes of his own poetry as well as a long speech called the *Panegyricus,* which is an expanded version of the speech he delivered in the Senate at the end of his year as consul. In the speech, Pliny praises the emperor Trajan as an example of the good emperor, comparing him favorably to the recently assassinated emperor DOMITIAN.

The tenth book of his letters contains the official correspondence between Pliny and Trajan while Pliny served as provincial governor in the province of Bithynia (now part of modern Turkey). The most famous of these letters discusses Pliny's difficulties in dealing with the Christians during his time as proconsul of the province. His letter sheds important light on the early history of Christianity and is one of the earliest statements we have about that religion from an outside source.

During much of the Middle Ages, Pliny and his uncle were believed to be the same person. However, in the 1300s, an Italian scholar established the distinction between the two men. Thereafter, they were distinguished by the titles of Younger and Elder. (*See also* **Letter Writing; Literature, Roman.**)

# PLOTINUS

### A.D. 205–269/70
### GREEK PHILOSOPHER

* **philosopher** scholar or thinker concerned with the study of ideas, including science

* **mystic** one who believes that divine truths or direct knowledge of God can be experienced through meditation and contemplation as much as through logical thought

* **Renaissance** period of the rebirth of interest in classical art, literature, and learning that occurred in Europe from the late 1300s through the 1500s

Plotinus was a Greek philosopher* who taught in both ALEXANDRIA and Rome. His teachings, which were later collected by one of his students, combined the ideas of PLATO and Eastern mystics* to create a new Greek philosophy called Neoplatonism. Some scholars consider him the greatest philosopher between the time of ARISTOTLE, in the 300s B.C., and the beginning of the Renaissance*.

Plotinus was born in Lycopolis, in Egypt. He began studying philosophy at the age of 27, spending 11 years in Alexandria teaching and studying under a famous teacher, Ammonius Sacas. Hoping to learn more about Eastern philosophy, Plotinus joined a military expedition against Persia. At about the age of 40, he settled in Rome, where he became the leader of an influential group of thinkers. He did not write anything until he was 50 years old, when he composed a series of philosophical essays that circulated among his students. One of his students, Porphyry, later collected the essays and arranged them by subject into six groups of nine books, called the *Enneads.*

* **ethics** branch of philosophy that deals with moral conduct, duty, and judgment

* **aesthetics** branch of philosophy concerned with the nature of beauty

* **cosmology** branch of philosophy that deals with the origin and structure of the universe

* **metaphysics** branch of philosophy concerned with the fundamental nature of reality

The essays cover the entire field of ancient philosophy with the exception of politics, which Plotinus chose not to write about. Plotinus covered ethics* and aesthetics* in the first of the six *Enneads,* physics and cosmology* in the next two, psychology in the fourth, and metaphysics* and logic in the last two. Because of his poor eyesight, Plotinus never revised his work. As a result, his essays often read as if he is thinking aloud or explaining a lesson to a student.

Through St. AUGUSTINE, who knew his work well, Plotinus's work influenced later generations of Christian thinkers. Plotinus also had a significant influence on the thinkers of the Renaissance. (*See also* **Philosophy, Greek and Hellenistic; Philosophy, Roman; Science.**)

## PLUTARCH

ca. A.D. 40–ca. 120
GREEK WRITER AND PHILOSOPHER

* **philosopher** scholar or thinker concerned with the study of ideas, including science

* **classic** serving as an outstanding example of its kind

* **magistrate** governmental official in ancient Greece and Rome

* **oracle** priest or priestess through whom a god is believed to speak; also the location (such as a shrine) where such utterances are made

* **dialogue** text presenting an exchange of ideas between people

Plutarch has been called "the prince of ancient biographers," and he is best remembered for the 46 great Greeks and Romans he profiled in his *Parallel Lives.* In his own time, however, Plutarch was better known as a philosopher*, and many of his writings concerned philosophical issues.

A remarkably productive writer, Plutarch wrote some 250 works, about a third of which survive. He has always been a very popular writer. His works were already considered classics* by A.D. 300, and they were used as textbooks in the 500s and 600s. During and after the Middle Ages, Plutarch's works served as a major source of information about the ancient world. Plutarch is still appreciated as a major thinker whose view of the ancient world merits respect and study.

PLUTARCH'S LIFE AND TIMES.    Plutarch was born to a wealthy family in the small town of Chaeronea in central Greece. He lived most of his life in his hometown, where he was active as a teacher and magistrate*. He completed his education in ATHENS, where he studied and was influenced by the writings of PLATO. Plutarch also traveled to Asia, EGYPT, and ITALY, and he lived for a time in Rome, where he lectured and taught.

Although he was Greek by birth, Plutarch's world was dominated by the Roman Empire. He believed that Greece and Rome could be partners, and he considered himself loyal to both. Plutarch served as an ambassador to Rome, a position for which he was ideally suited. He was a keen observer of human nature, and he had a charming and persuasive manner. With the help of influential friends, he obtained Roman citizenship.

Plutarch was a deeply religious man and believed devoutly in the gods of traditional Greek religion. He was a priest of the oracle* at DELPHI for the last 30 years of his life. He worked hard to revive the shrine to the god APOLLO. It was while he was a priest at Delphi that he wrote most of his works, including *Parallel Lives.*

RANGE OF SUBJECTS.    The bulk of Plutarch's work consists of dialogues* and essays covering a wide range of subjects that include philosophy, religion, literature, science, and prophecy (foretelling the future). Prophecy played an important role in Plutarch's religious beliefs. Plutarch often used the literary form of the dialogue. In these works, he discussed a variety of

issues, many involving social behavior, as in *On the Reasons for Roman Customs* and *On the Reasons for Greek Customs.*

Among the most popular of Plutarch's writings are the *Moralia,* or moral essays. These include "The Control of Anger," "Bashfulness," "Advice on Marriage," and "Rules for Politicians." He wrote these essays in a warm and sympathetic style that made them enjoyable to read.

BIOGRAPHIES.   *Parallel Lives* is considered to be Plutarch's greatest achievement and the work for which he is best known. In all but one of the 23 pairs of lives that survive, Plutarch compared two similar individuals—one Greek and one Roman. He believed that comparing two people with the same qualities helped the reader better understand the essence of those qualities. In his biographies, he wrote about men he admired, typically statesmen or generals, such as ALEXANDER THE GREAT and Julius CAESAR.

Plutarch never intended his biographies to be histories, although they have often been used as historical sources. He aimed for accuracy, but his research was sometimes incomplete, and his biographies were not always well balanced. Plutarch focused on the details and events in the subject's life that led to the development or revelation of admirable traits. In chronological order, he wrote about the individual's family background, education, turning points in public life, and later years. Because Plutarch wanted his biographies to be helpful to his readers as well as entertaining, he downplayed his subjects' faults and accentuated their good qualities to make them better models for behavior. (*See also* **Literature, Greek;** *Parallel Lives.*)

## POETRY, GREEK AND HELLENISTIC

* **hero** in mythology, a person of great strength or ability, often descended from a god

Aside from drama, ancient Greek poetry can be divided into epic poetry and lyric poetry. Epics are long, serious poems that tell a story. They are composed in a grand style and usually describe the deeds of heroes* or gods. The greatest Greek epic poems, the *Iliad* and the *Odyssey,* were composed by HOMER in the 700s B.C. The ancient Greeks considered the epic the highest form of literature.

Most lyric poems were sung, usually to the accompaniment of an instrument. They were often about love or other personal themes. Lyric poetry reached its peak during the 600s to the early 400s B.C., with the works of such great poets as SAPPHO and PINDAR. Greek lyric poetry is considered an important ancestor of much modern Western poetry.

### EPIC POETRY

Epic poetry had its roots in traditional, oral narrative verse, which told of the mighty exploits of war heroes. Homer composed his epics in the 700s B.C., and in the A.D. 400s the poet Nonnus wrote the last significant ancient Greek epic, the *Epic of Dionysus.*

HOMERIC EPIC.   Out of traditional narrative verse, Homer created his two great epics. In the *Iliad* and the *Odyssey,* he introduced several poetic techniques that were adopted by later epic poets. These techniques came to be the defining features of the Greek epic.

One of the most important features of Homeric epic was dactylic hexameter. In this verse line, one long syllable is followed either by two short ones or by a second long syllable, and this pattern is repeated six times in each verse. After Homer, virtually all epic poets wrote in dactylic hexameter. In addition, because Homer used the Ionic dialect* of the Greek language, Ionic was considered the only suitable dialect for the epic.

Homer used the technique of direct speech extensively. Even in sections of his work that are filled with action, about a third of the verses are written as the actual words of the characters. Dialogue makes Homer's narrative seem more vivid, and it reveals much about the characters and their motives. Modeling themselves after Homer, later epic poets also used direct speech. Other features of Homer's works that were adopted by later epic poets include invocations (prayers) to the Muse, dreams that foretell the future, visits to the underworld*, extended similes*, and gods that guide the course of action.

**DIDACTIC POETRY.** A type of poetry that was closely related to epic poetry was the didactic poetry of HESIOD, who wrote around the same time as Homer. Unlike Homer's epic poetry, which was intended to tell a story, Hesiod's didactic poetry taught a moral lesson or instructed the reader in some other way. In his poems *Works and Days* and *Theogony,* Hesiod provided advice to the workingman and explained how mythical heroes were related to the gods.

The idea that poetry was a means of teaching important truths influenced how the Greeks regarded all epic poetry and epic poets. Some Greeks considered Homer an authority on everything from medicine to military tactics, and they believed his poems had political authority. So influential was Homer's work in Greek culture that it has been called the "Bible of the Greeks."

**HELLENISTIC EPIC.** Epics continued to be written in the Homeric* style until the middle of the 400s B.C., when epic poets adopted more sophisticated literary techniques. Antimachus, one of the best-known poets of this time, was greatly respected, both as a scholar and as a poet. Because of his influence, technical skill and elegance of form became essential features of fine epic poetry.

The poet and critic CALLIMACHUS, who lived during the 200s B.C., criticized Antimachus's work and the epic in general. According to Callimachus, the epic was too long to be written with the care that was expected of literary works during the Hellenistic* age. In response to Callimachus's criticism, poets wrote short epic fragments, called epyllia, which remained popular for centuries.

The long Homeric epic did not completely fall out of fashion, and many epics were written during the Hellenistic age. This may have reflected an interest in distant places, which was especially great after the conquests of ALEXANDER THE GREAT. However, the audience for the epic had changed. While the Homeric epic had reached almost everyone, epics written in the Hellenistic age were intended for an educated audience, which was largely of men from the highest social classes.

* **dialect** form of speech characteristic of a region that differs from the standard language in pronunciation, vocabulary, and grammar

* **underworld** kingdom of the dead; also called Hades

* **simile** figure of speech that compares two unlike things; often introduced by the word *like* or *as*

* **Homeric** referring to the Greek poet Homer, the time in which he lived, or his works

* **Hellenistic** referring to the Greek-influenced culture of the Mediterranean world during the three centuries after Alexander the Great, who died in 323 B.C.

**BUCOLIC POETRY.** Around 275 B.C., THEOCRITUS invented a new form of poetry, called bucolic poetry. Like the epic, bucolic poetry was written in dactylic hexameter. Unlike the Homeric epic, however, bucolic poems were comparatively short. Moreover, this form did not feature heroes and gods in distant lands but focused instead on the common people in the Greek countryside. In Greek, the word *bucolic* means "pertaining to cowherds," and the style was called bucolic because the main character was often a herdsman. Greek poets continued to write bucolic poetry for another 200 years after Theocritus.

## LYRIC POETRY

Lyric poetry may actually be older than epic poetry because it arose from ancient folk and religious songs. It first appeared in written form during the 600s B.C. For the next 200 years, many of the best poets of Greece expressed themselves in lyric poetry. Such poetry remained important until the 400s B.C., when drama replaced the lyric as the most significant form of Greek literature.

There are three different forms of Greek lyric poetry. The lyric itself was sung to the accompaniment of a lyre*. Another type of lyric, the elegy, was not sung but spoken, often to the accompaniment of a flute. Iambic lyric, the third type of lyric, was spoken without accompaniment. Either an individual or a chorus performed Greek lyric poetry. Lyric that was performed by an individual is called monodic lyric, and lyric that was performed by a chorus is called choral lyric. Monodic and choral lyric differ in form and content, as well as in style of performance.

**MONODIC LYRIC.** A monodic lyric is a short poem that usually describes the personal experiences and feelings of the poet. Typically, it is written in the first person. The leading practitioners of the monodic lyric were Sappho and Alcaeus, both of whom wrote around 600 B.C., and Anacreon, who wrote around 500 B.C.

Although only fragments of Sappho's poetry have survived, she was without doubt the greatest of the monodic lyric poets. She had no equal in the eloquence, imagery, and metrical skill of her verse. She also wrote with great intensity and feeling, yet with delicacy. The only completely preserved poem of Sappho is her famous "Ode to Aphrodite." As is true of most of Sappho's poems, this ode* is about love.

Like Sappho, the poet Alcaeus also wrote about love. However, he also wrote on political topics and wrote several drinking songs. Only fragments of Alcaeus's work survive. Anacreon wrote poems that were less personal than those of Sappho or Alcaeus. His wit and wordplay distanced his poetry from his personal feelings. Several centuries later, this approach characterized Greek literature throughout the Hellenistic age.

**CHORAL LYRIC.** Longer and more complex than monodic lyric, choral lyric is less concerned with the personal experiences and feelings of the poet. Instead, it focuses on group values and attitudes and is often based on shared myths and common knowledge. The earliest known example of

* **lyre** stringed instrument similar to a small harp

* **ode** lyric poem often addressed to a person or an object

### SIMILES IN GREEK EPIC POETRY

Greek epic poets made great use of a literary device that came to be called a Homeric simile. More extensive than a simple comparison, a Homeric simile vividly describes a character or an event. For example, a hero in Homer's *Iliad* did not go to battle merely "like a lion," but

like a mountain-bred lion, who for a long time has been starved of meat, and his proud heart urges him to go for the flocks and get inside the well-built fold. And should he find the herdsmen there guarding their flock with spears and dogs, he has no thought to leave the fold without attacking but leaps in and seizes his prey or else is himself wounded among the foremost by a dart from some swift hand.

choral lyric is a poem by Alcman of Sparta that was written in the 600s B.C. Alcman's work is quite long and complex in its structure, suggesting that a long tradition of choral lyric already existed by that time. After Alcman, the length and complexity of choral lyric increased even more. Stesichorus, who wrote choral lyrics around 600 B.C., was the earliest Greek poet to come from the Greek colonies in Italy. The poet Simonides, who wrote around 500 B.C., may have been the first ancient Greek poet to charge fees for his work.

The final period of choral lyric lasted from 500 B.C. to 450 B.C., when Pindar and Bacchylides composed their victory odes. Pindar, the more brilliant poet of the two, composed victory odes for the OLYMPIC GAMES and the other great athletic contests of Greece. After Pindar, the writing of victory odes seems to have come to a halt, perhaps because his work was considered to be the high point of this literary form. (*See also* **Alphabets and Writing; Books and Manuscripts; Drama, Greek;** *Iliad;* **Languages and Dialects; Literacy; Literature, Greek;** *Odyssey.*)

## POETRY, ROMAN

* **epic** long poem about legendary or historical heroes, written in a grand style

* **elegiac** sad and mournful poem

* **lyric** poem expressing personal feelings, often similar in form to a song

* **satire** literary technique that uses wit and sarcasm to expose or ridicule vice and folly

* **narrative** a descriptive account of events; a story

* **hero** in mythology, a person of great strength or ability, often descended from a god

The ancient Romans wrote little, if any, poetry before about 250 B.C., and another hundred years passed before poetry was an acceptable literary form for people of high social standing. Like much of their culture and learning, Roman poetry arose from its Greek counterpart, and most Roman poets were greatly influenced by their Greek predecessors. Roman poetry also took the same general forms as Greek poetry. These forms included the epic*, the elegiac*, and the lyric*. In addition, the Romans established satire* as a literary form.

## EPIC POETRY

The earliest Roman poems were epics patterned after the works of the Greek poet HOMER, who composed the *Iliad* and the *Odyssey* in the 700s B.C. Like Homer's epics, the early Roman epics are long narratives* about heroes* and gods that retell important events of the past. Although epics continued to be written in Rome until about A.D. 100, the form underwent many changes. While some of these changes were the result of Greek influences, others were a reaction to political events that occurred in Rome.

EARLY ROMAN EPIC. The first Roman epic was a Latin translation of the *Odyssey* in about 250 B.C.—the work of a slave named Livius Andronicus. Around the same time, the poet Naevius wrote an epic about the first PUNIC WAR. The best-known early Roman epic poet, however, was Quintus Ennius.

* **dactylic hexameter** line of verse that consists of a stressed syllable followed by two unstressed syllables (such as in the word *passageway*), repeated six times

* **meter** in poetry, a pattern of stressed and unstressed syllables

Most Romans considered Ennius the greatest of all Roman poets, and he was called the "father of Latin literature." The *Annales,* written around 170 B.C., retold the story of the founding of Rome and its subsequent history. Ennius adapted the Latin language to dactylic hexameter*—the same meter* that Homer had used in his Greek epics. Ennius's work was greatly admired, in part because it was so heavily influenced by the highly respected Greek poetry. Ennius had many imitators, including the statesman

CICERO, who himself wrote three epics. However, Ennius had many critics as well, some of whom considered his verses very clumsy.

Around 60 B.C., the Neoterics, or "new poets," dominated the literary scene. The Neoterics, who included the poets CATULLUS, Calvus, and Cinna, were influenced primarily by the Greek poet CALLIMACHUS, who had criticized the epic almost 200 years earlier. Like Callimachus, the Neoterics believed that learning, sophistication, and conciseness were more important to good poetry than a lengthy narrative. Because of their influence, no respectable poet wrote an epic for another generation or more, and the best poets completely rejected the form. Instead, they wrote epyllia, or short epic fragments, a poetic form that had been introduced by the Hellenistic* poets.

AUGUSTAN EPIC.    The end of the Roman Republic* and the rise to power of the Roman emperor AUGUSTUS led to a return of the epic. Augustus considered himself the new founder of Rome, and he encouraged Roman poets to celebrate his life and achievements in epic poetry. Some poets, including HORACE, refused to write epics for Augustus, claiming that their talent and skill were no match for such a grand and important theme.

The poet VERGIL undertook the challenge, and he wrote the greatest of all Roman epics, the *Aeneid.* Like earlier Roman epics, the *Aeneid* was heavily influenced by Homer. Vergil not only used Homer's poetic form and techniques but also many of the same themes. The *Aeneid* was so good that no other Roman poet of Vergil's time tried to match it, although many lesser epics were written by later poets.

Vergil quickly achieved the same status in Rome that Homer had held in Greece. He was considered to be the greatest Latin epic poet and a genius of literature. In addition to the *Aeneid,* Vergil wrote ten poems called the *Bucolics,* or *Eclogues.* Like other bucolic poetry, Vergil's work is set in the countryside and the main characters are common folk. In this work, Vergil expressed the conflict between his private world of creativity and his public involvement in the outside world. The *Eclogues* was very popular and influenced many later poets. Vergil also wrote the *Georgics,* an instructional as well as philosophical poem about man's relationship with the land. *Georgics* is divided into four books, each on a specific topic: grain production, tending vines and orchards, raising livestock, and keeping bees.

Another important poet of this time was OVID, who is best known for his *Metamorphoses.* This work is epic in length (the poem begins with the world's creation and comes down to Ovid's day) but otherwise resembles the epic very little. Instead, it is a collection of short narrative poems about myths and legends of the ancient world. Many of the stories involve a character undergoing a change, or metamorphosis—such as going from human to animal form. Ovid was more influenced by Callimachus than by Homer.

RHETORICAL EPIC.    Beginning in the 30s B.C., Roman poets recited their work in public. Public recitals of poetry became widespread, and by the end of the A.D. 100s, literature and public speaking had become closely linked. As a result, poets adopted a style of writing that appealed to the public, and what most appealed to the public was concise, clever writing.

* **Hellenistic** referring to the Greek-influenced culture of the Mediterranean world during the three centuries after Alexander the Great, who died in 323 B.C.

* **Roman Republic** Rome during the period from 509 B.C. to 31 B.C., when popular assemblies annually elected their governmental officials

The best-known epic poet of this time period was LUCAN, who wrote his major work, the *Civil War,* around A.D. 62. Lucan's epic describes the conflict between Julius CAESAR and POMPEY, which had occurred about 100 years earlier. The work is full of vivid descriptions, memorable phrases, and many direct speeches, yet it falls short of the *Aeneid* as a poem. However, Lucan introduced one important innovation to the epic—there are no gods to intervene in the action of *Civil War.*

When the emperor VESPASIAN came to power around A.D. 70, he encouraged the writing of epics that were based on myth. Two epics from this period survive, the *Argonautica* of Valerius Flaccus and the *Thebaid* of STATIUS. Statius is often considered to have been the more influential poet of the two. His epic, which is about the quarrel between Eteocles and Polynices, sons of the Greek mythical character OEDIPUS, was well written and was still highly respected centuries later.

## ELEGIAC AND LYRIC POETRY

During the first century B.C., many Roman poets wrote elegies and lyrics. The Greeks first developed elegiac and lyric poetry, but the Roman versions were quite different from the Greek. Many outstanding poems were written during the 75 years that these two forms of poetry flourished in Rome.

* **pentameter** line of verse consisting of a specific pattern of stressed and unstressed syllables that together comprise five divisions, or "feet"

ELEGIAC POETRY.   Elegiac poetry is written in elegiac couplets—two successive lines of verse that form a unit—with the first line written in a meter of dactylic hexameter and the second line in pentameter*. Roman elegiac poetry is almost totally confined to the love elegy, a form created by Catullus around 60 B.C. In his love elegies, Catullus wrote about his own experiences with love and the problems that may arise when two people fall in love. Catullus's poetry inspired many later poets, who further explored love and relationships from their own perspective.

About a generation after Catullus, the poets PROPERTIUS and TIBULLUS wrote their love elegies. Although greatly influenced by Catullus, Propertius wrote poems that were longer and more worldly. He introduced the ideas of love as slavery and love as war, which appeared in European poetry for centuries afterward. These comparisons were an attempt to explain a sensation—love—in terms of things that were concrete and factual—and both slavery and war were facts of life in ancient Rome. Although Tibullus's poetic output was small, he is noted for his creation of the "stream of consciousness" technique. In this technique, the poet seems to describe his own thoughts and feelings as they occur.

Influenced by the increasing importance of public recitation of poetry, the love elegies of Ovid are witty and sophisticated. Ovid's works were so successful that all later elegists adopted his techniques. Ovid's later works, in particular his *Art of Love,* offended the moral ideals of the emperor Augustus. Partly because of this, Augustus banished Ovid from Rome. Because of Augustus's repressive actions and because this form of poetry was difficult to improve on after Ovid's witty treatment of it, the love elegy was abandoned by Roman poets.

**LYRIC POETRY.** Roman lyric poetry was characterized by the direct expression of emotions in a sophisticated style. The first Roman lyric poetry was written by Catullus, who was influenced by the great Greek lyric poet SAPPHO. The poet Horace carried on the lyric tradition in his *Odes,* but his poems differ from Catullus's in several ways. Whereas Catullus's poems are intensely personal, Horace's are cheerful and even humorous.

## SATIRE

* **orator** public speaker of great skill

The Romans developed satire as a literary form. The great orator* QUINITIL-IAN boasted: "Satire at least is a wholly Roman achievement." Gaius Lucilius became the first important figure in the development of verse satire. He made biting personal attacks on prominent people of his time, as well as attacks on the vices of Roman society as a whole. Lucilius successfully used the hexameter for his work, and this became the meter of choice for later satirists. His style—conversational and down-to-earth—was also copied by later satirists.

HORACE modestly claimed second place in the development of satire. In his *Satires* and *Epistles,* Horace provided a new standard of artistry for hexametric satire in language, rhythm, and tone. Unlike his predecessor Lucilius, Horace rarely singled out for criticism living people or individuals who could be identified.

PERSIUS was strongly influenced by the philosophy of STOICISM, which stressed self-knowledge and a freedom from base passions. Persius wrote satire of uncompromising harshness, often in a hostile and sometimes grossly obscene manner. His use of striking combinations of images gave his poetry a unique style that was very popular with Roman audiences of his day.

JUVENAL's poetry represented the culmination of the Roman satiric tradition. Juvenal wrote 16 satires, which differed from previous satires in one important respect: He adopted the voice of the indignant and disgusted observer who cannot help attacking, although sometimes with caution, the evils of the Roman world he lived in. Juvenal was the poet who most affected the prestige of satire in the eyes of later generations. (*See also* **Education and Rhetoric, Roman; Epigrams; Literature, Roman; Love; Martial; Oratory; Poetry, Greek and Hellenistic; Satire.**)

## POLIS

* **classical** in Greek history, refers to the period of great political and cultural achievement from about 500 B.C. to 323 B.C.

* **monarchy** nation ruled by a king or queen

* **Hellenistic** referring to the Greek-influenced culture of the Mediterranean world during the three centuries after Alexander the Great, who died in 323 B.C

The *polis,* also known as the city-state, was the dominant form of political and social organization during the classical* period of Greek history. City-states were fundamentally different from the monarchies* of the earlier Mycenaean period and of the later Hellenistic* age. Although some city-states, such as ATHENS, had tens of thousands of citizens, Greek city-states were notable for their small size and strong sense of community.

**FEATURES OF THE POLIS.** A polis consisted of an urban center and the surrounding territory, which the city controlled. Although natural features, such as mountains, set the boundaries of some city-states, many others bordered

* **agora** in ancient Greece, the public square or marketplace

* **patron** special guardian, protector, or supporter

* **sacrifice** sacred offering made to a god or goddess, usually of an animal such as a sheep or goat

* **oracle** priest or priestess through whom a god is believed to speak; also the location (such as a shrine) where such utterances are made

* **magistrate** governmental official in ancient Greece and Rome

* **aristocrat** person of the highest social class

on one another. Border wars were common but so were cooperation and agreements between city-states. Although each polis jealously guarded its independence, foreign threats and competition for trade led to the establishment of alliances and leagues. Religion, commerce, and athletic competitions, such as the OLYMPIC GAMES, helped create a common Greek culture.

The economy of a polis was based on the agriculture of the surrounding territory. The agora*, TEMPLES, and other sites served as the commercial, social, religious, and political centers of urban life. The Greeks defined the polis in terms of its citizens. However, citizens made up only a small part of the population of a polis because many foreign residents and slaves lived in the cities but were excluded from CITIZENSHIP. Adult male citizens controlled the political life of the polis; women had no political rights and were excluded from public life.

Common religious beliefs and practices created a strong bond among the citizenry. Each polis had a special patron* god or goddess who protected the city. Many feasts and festivals were held during the year in both the urban center and in the surrounding rural area. At these festivals, animals were sacrificed* to a god or goddess and the meat distributed to the participants. City-states also organized athletic, dance, and theater competitions.

Divine permission, usually obtained from the oracle* of APOLLO at DELPHI, was required before a new polis could be established. The founders of a new polis provided a sacred fire that was carried to the new city. Citizens of a polis paid great honor to their founder, who received a lavish public funeral when he died, as well as burial inside the city walls. A large tomb usually marked the founder's grave.

Greek city-states had many of the same institutions—magistrates* who were elected annually, a council of elders, and an assembly. Citizens participated in the assembly, the council, and the courts and in the election of magistrates. Respect for the law was an important feature of a polis. Citizens took pride in regulating their lives according to the laws of their community. Each polis kept a list of citizens who could be called on to defend the city's independence against external threats.

THE ATHENIAN POLIS. Athens and Sparta were the largest of the Greek city-states. Sparta eventually became a military dictatorship, and Athens a democracy, which implied an equality of participation in government activities. At the peak of its greatness, the Athenian polis had almost 200,000 inhabitants. While Athens had many of the same features as other Greek city-states, it developed distinctive features of its own. During the classical period, the Athenian polis was shaped by a series of reforms. In about 508–507 B.C., CLEISTHENES prevented Athenian aristocrats* from controlling the assembly by limiting citizenship. He also instituted the Council of 500, whose members were chosen by lot from male citizens 30 years of age or older.

Several years later, additional reforms were instituted. A board of ten generals was created to distribute military power more evenly. Members of the Council of 500 were required to swear an oath to act in accordance with the laws and in the best interest of the polis. They were to supervise the city magistrates. In addition, they swore not to take action on important matters "without a decision of the people in assembly." They also

## PHILOSOPHY AND THE POLIS

The great Greek philosophers Plato and Aristotle believed that the best place to live was in a polis. In his dialogue the *Republic,* Plato imagined an ideal state that was governed by a philosopher-king. Although different from any existing polis, Plato based his ideal state on the Greek polis. The concept of the city-state was even more fundamental to Aristotle. He began his great work in political philosophy by stating that "man is by nature an animal of the polis."

* **archon** in ancient Greece, the highest office of state

* **quorum** number of members of an organization who must be present for the group to conduct business

* **depose** to remove from high office

swore not to imprison any citizen except those charged with treason, revolution, or breaking their tax contracts.

In the early 400s B.C., Athenian lawmakers introduced the practice of OS-TRACISM. In an ostracism, the assembly voted to banish a citizen from the city for ten years. Ostracisms were relatively common at first, but after about 480 B.C., they occurred less frequently, and the practice ended in the late 400s B.C.

Perhaps the most extreme reform occurred in 487–486 B.C., when the method for choosing magistrates changed from direct election to selection by lot. As a result of this particular reform, magistrates no longer tended to be the leading citizens of the city. Instead, they were average citizens taking their turn at fulfilling their civic duty. Another reform came in 462–461 B.C., when Athens reduced the powers of the Areopagus, a legislative body and high court consisting of former archons*. The Areopagus also had been the traditional source of aristocratic power.

As a result of these reforms, the Athenian assembly became the supreme authority. Persuasive leaders could steer the assembly toward support for their programs. For example, with support from the assembly, THEMISTOCLES built up the port of Piraeus, turned Athens into a strong naval power, and led the Greeks to victory over the PERSIAN EMPIRE. Similarly, Cimon was able to expand the Athenian empire and increase the economic strength of the polis. While the assembly made leaders, it could also break them. Despite all he had accomplished for the polis, Cimon was ostracized by his fellow citizens.

The Athenian assembly met regularly on a hillside that overlooked the city. The assembly required a quorum* of at least 6,000 citizens, and it had the power to elect and depose* government officials. The agenda for each assembly meeting was prepared by the Council of 500. Assembly meetings lasted from dawn to midday, and votes were taken by a show of hands.

During the Hellenistic period, the polis was marked by increasing conflict between rich and poor. During the Roman Empire, the Greek polis continued a tradition of independence and competition, of civic pride and a sense of cultural superiority over the Romans. (*See also* **Democracy, Greek; Government, Greek; Greece, History of.**)

## POLYBIUS

ca. 205–ca. 125 B.C.
GREEK HISTORIAN

* **aristocrat** person of the highest social class

olybius was a Greek historian who wrote an impressive account of Rome's rise to a position of leadership in the Mediterranean world. Although only the first 5 books of his 40-book *Histories* exist in complete form, much of the rest of the work survives in collections of passages produced by later scholars.

Polybius was the son of Lycortas, a wealthy Greek aristocrat* who was active in an organization of Greek states called the Achaean League. Polybius himself worked for the league, attaining its second-highest position while he was still only in his 20s. After the Romans defeated the Greeks in 168 B.C., Polybius was one of 1,000 aristocrats who were deported to Italy.

Polybius spent most of the next 16 years in Rome, where he became friends with Scipio Aemilianus, the son of the Roman general who defeated Greece. Polybius traveled widely after his release from captivity, maintaining a close association with Scipio. He was with Scipio when the

Romans burned and destroyed CARTHAGE in 146 B.C., and he also helped the Romans organize Greece into a province* after the final defeat of the Greeks following the Achaean War. Polybius was more than 80 years old when he died, reportedly from falling off a horse.

The 40 books of the *Histories* cover the history of Rome from 220 B.C. and the beginning of the Second Punic War to the fall and destruction of Carthage and CORINTH in 146–145 B.C. Polybius was a careful researcher who used many sources for his work. These included documents, INSCRIPTIONS*, letters, public records from Rome and Greece, memoirs, and the works of other historians. Perhaps most important, he interviewed eyewitnesses of the events he described.

Polybius carefully organized his work in accordance with the Olympiads, which are the periods of time between the OLYMPIC GAMES that were held in Greece every four years. During each year within an Olympiad, Polybius described events in geographical order—from west to east. First, he recounted events in Italy, Sicily, Spain, and North Africa, then those in Greece and Macedonia, then Asia and Egypt. He treated books 1 and 2 differently. These two volumes introduce the work, describing Roman history from the First Punic War (264–241 B.C.) to 220 B.C. and providing background and explaining how Rome developed its aim for domination of the known world. The careful and consistent arrangement of his work has made it easier for later scholars to place the surviving excerpts from his work in the correct order.

Polybius believed that the writing of history had two main objectives—to train statesmen and to teach people how to face disaster. His work focuses mainly on political and military subjects, but it also includes analyses of economic, religious, and social institutions. In book 6, Polybius discusses Rome's army and constitution in detail. He describes Rome's government as a mixture of three basic forms—a monarchy*, an aristocracy (the Roman Senate), and a democracy (the assemblies). His description of the Roman government as a system of checks and balances influenced later political thinkers, including those who created the United States Constitution.

In addition to his *Histories,* Polybius wrote several other works, all of which have been lost. They included a tribute to a Greek statesman, a work on military tactics, a history of the Roman war in Numantia, and a treatise on regions near the equator. (*See also* **Achaea; Government, Roman; Greece, History of; Rome, History of.**)

POMPEII

ompeii was a coastal Roman city in Campania, a region in southwestern Italy. In A.D. 79, Mt. VESUVIUS erupted and buried the city under a thick blanket of volcanic ash. Because the buried city is so well preserved, Pompeii is probably the most spectacular and informative archaeological* site in the world.

According to the Greek writer STRABO, the first inhabitants of the region were the prehistoric people called Oscans. The Etruscans later took control of the small fishing and farming village when they expanded their control over Campania. Greek colonists in southern Italy also established

Pompeii and two other ancient cities were buried for centuries following the eruption of Mt. Vesuvius in A.D. 79. Statues, wall paintings, and other artworks were discovered when archaeologists began excavating the region in the 1700s. The House of the Faun was among the ruins they uncovered.

* **siege** long and persistent effort to force a surrender by surrounding a fortress with armed troops, cutting it off from aid

* **amphitheater** oval or round structure with rows of seats rising gradually from a stage or central open space

* **pumice** volcanic rock used to clean and polish materials

* **excavate** to uncover by digging

* **portico** roof supported by columns, forming a porch or covered walkway

* **gladiator** in ancient Rome, slave or captive who participated in combats that were staged for public entertainment

* **forum** in ancient Rome, the public square or marketplace, often used for public assemblies and judicial proceedings

* **colonnade** series of regularly spaced columns, usually supporting a roof

* **basilica** in Roman times, a large rectangular building used as a court of law or public meeting place

a trading settlement there. Some Greek buildings that have been found at the site date from before 500 B.C.

In the 400s B.C., migrating people from the interior of Italy, known as Samnites, took control of Pompeii. In the early 200s B.C., Rome defeated the Samnites, and Pompeii came under Roman control. During HANNIBAL's invasion of Italy (in the Second PUNIC WAR, 218–201 B.C.), Pompeii remained loyal to Rome. However, in the Social War, in which the Italian people rose up against the Romans, Pompeii sided with the rebels. The Roman general SULLA lay siege* to Pompeii and captured the city in 89 B.C.

As punishment for siding with the enemy, Sulla colonized Pompeii with a large number of his retired soldiers, a move that caused friction between the colonists and the longtime residents. During the reign of the emperor NERO, a riot between rival factions broke out in the amphitheater*, causing many deaths. In A.D. 62, only 17 years before the eruption of Mt. Vesuvius, an earthquake severely damaged the city.

In A.D. 79, Pompeii was suddenly destroyed by the eruption of Vesuvius. Together with the neighboring village of Herculaneum, Pompeii was buried under pumice*, volcanic ash, and eventually a layer of earth. At the time of the disaster, Pompeii had a population of about 25,000 people, most of whom seem to have escaped.

The site remained little known and largely unoccupied until it was rediscovered in the 1700s. Pompeii immediately became the subject of great interest and curiosity. Since then, the city has been heavily excavated*. About 80 percent of the area inside the city walls has now been uncovered and examined. Much of the recent work at the site has involved record keeping, preservation of the site, and analysis of what has already been excavated.

Archaeological studies have concluded that there were three main areas of public buildings inside the walls that surrounded the city. The first contained a Greek temple, a temple of Isis, a portico* that was converted into a school for gladiators*, and two theaters. In the second area, the city's large main forum* was flanked by two-story high colonnades*; a basilica*; temples of Jupiter, APOLLO, Venus, and the Genius of the Emperor; and five government buildings.

The oldest existing Roman amphitheater and a large sports area were located in the third area. The city had at least four public baths. At first, the city obtained its water from wells and cisterns*, but in later years an aqueduct* delivered water to the public baths and fountains and to some private homes.

Pompeii's most famous feature is its private houses. Although they varied in size and layout, most were built around a central reception hall, or atrium*, and had an interior colonnaded garden. Wall paintings decorated the interiors of the houses, and MOSAICS covered the floors. The artwork from Pompeii gives us a sense of what Roman houses looked like and how they were decorated. Many of the wall paintings were copies of important Greek works that have been lost. (*See also* **Archaeology of Ancient Sites; Architecture, Roman; Art, Roman; Etruscans.**)

## POMPEY

### 106–48 B.C.
### ROMAN GENERAL

Gnaeus Pompeius Magnus, or Pompey, was one of the most important Roman generals and statesmen of the late Roman Republic*. His military campaigns were so successful that his fellow Romans called him *magnus* (great) and compared him to ALEXANDER THE GREAT. Pompey extended Roman power in the East and cleared the MEDITERRANEAN SEA of pirates. His fame and popularity led to a fatal rivalry with another popular general, Julius CAESAR, for control of the Roman world. Pompey's defeat and death enabled Caesar to establish himself as dictator, or sole ruler, of Rome.

Pompey learned his military skills while serving under his father, another prominent Roman general. As a young man, Pompey led three legions* in SICILY and AFRICA in support of the Roman dictator SULLA. Despite his youth, he celebrated a triumph* in Rome. Recognizing Pompey's military talents, the Roman Senate gave him a special command, later sending him to Spain as a proconsul*. Upon his return from Spain, Pompey helped the general CRASSUS crush the massive slave uprising led by SPARTACUS. For this latter success, he celebrated a second triumph. In 70 B.C., Pompey and Crassus served as consuls*.

In 67 B.C., Pompey accepted a special command that involved finding a solution to one of Rome's most serious problems—PIRACY in the Mediterranean that threatened grain imports to Rome. He received virtually unlimited power to deal with this critical situation. Although the command was for three years, Pompey solved the problem in just three months. He commandeered ships from the navies of RHODES, Marseilles, and other Roman allies. He then divided the Mediterranean and its shoreline into 13 zones, assigning a commander and a fleet to each one. The fleets then attacked the pirate hideouts within their respective zones. At the same time, he headed 60 ships eastward from Gibraltar, driving pirates into the arms of waiting Roman fleets or back to the main pirate base at Cilicia in ASIA MINOR. Trapped pirate ships surrendered in large numbers. With his land forces, Pompey attacked the pirates who fled to their home base. In just three months, Pompey had freed the Mediterranean of pirates, a feat that no other naval commander had been able to accomplish before.

The following year, Pompey was assigned another special command, this time to direct the continuing war in the east against Mithradates, the king of Pontus. Pompey defeated Mithradates, forcing him over the

* **annex** to add a territory to an existing state

* **sovereignty** ultimate authority or rule

* **patrician** member of the upper class who traced his ancestry to a senatorial family in the earliest days of the Roman Republic

mountains to Crimea, where the king committed suicide. Pompey annexed* Syria, founded numerous colonies, doubled the revenues of the Roman treasury, and greatly expanded and strengthened the range of Roman sovereignty* in the east. The Romans considered Pompey's eastern campaigns his greatest accomplishment.

Upon his return to Rome in 62 B.C., Pompey celebrated his third and greatest triumph. He soon formed an alliance with Caesar and Crassus, called the First Triumvirate, and married Caesar's daughter Julia. However, Caesar's popular victories in the GALLIC WARS increased the rivalry between the two men, which intensified after the deaths of Julia and Crassus in the late 50s B.C. Patricians*, worried about Caesar's growing power, considered Pompey their best hope to stop him. When Caesar decided to fight for control of the Roman world, Pompey was placed in charge of government forces. The civil war reached its climax in 48 B.C., when Caesar defeated Pompey at Pharsalus in Greece. Although Pompey escaped to Egypt, he was shortly afterwards assassinated by local rulers hoping to earn Caesar's favor. (*See also* **Armies, Roman; Government, Roman; Triumvirates, Roman; Wars and Warfare, Roman.**)

## POPULATION

* **city-state** independent state consisting of a city and its surrounding territory

* **classical** in Greek history, refers to the period of great political and cultural achievement from about 500 B.C. to 323 B.C.

 See map in Migrations, Early Greek (vol. 3).

 See map in Migrations, Late Roman (vol. 3).

Estimates of the population of ancient Greece are very rough approximations. Population figures are scarce and incomplete, and most existing records involve taxes or military service, which applied only to adult male citizens. Statistics for women, children, foreign residents, and slaves—the people who made up a large portion of the population—simply do not exist. Even for ATHENS, which provided a more complete picture than any other city-state*, population figures are merely estimates.

Attica, the region in which Athens was located, may have had a population of more than 100,000 citizens during most of the classical* period. At the beginning of the PELOPONNESIAN WAR in 431 B.C., the population of Attica—including women, children, slaves, and foreigners—totaled more than 300,000 people. The city-state of Argos had about the same number of citizens, although fewer slaves and foreigners, and CORINTH had fewer than half that number. The Greek colonies on the island of SICILY may have had a population as high as 750,000 people.

Because all adult male Roman citizens were required to register for the census, more complete population figures are available for Rome. These figures suggest that there were about 120,000 adult male Roman citizens in the 400s B.C. This rose to about 300,000 two centuries later. As the Roman empire expanded, and certain conquered peoples received Roman CITIZENSHIP, the population increased accordingly. In 70 B.C., after citizenship was granted to all people of Italy south of the Po River, the figure reached 900,000.

A census of the empire conducted by the emperor AUGUSTUS in 28 B.C. put the figure at about 4 million citizens. In the first century A.D., the city of Rome had about a million inhabitants, and the total population of the Roman empire is estimated to have been more than 50 million people. (*See also* **Census, Roman; Greece, History of; Rome, History of.**)

# POSEIDON

* **deity** god or goddess

* **cult** group bound together by devotion to a particular person, belief, or god

* **trident** three-pronged spear, similar to a pitchfork

* **underworld** kingdom of the dead; also called Hades

* **nymph** in classical mythology, one of the lesser goddesses of nature

* **mortal** human being; one who eventually will die

Called Neptune by the Romans, the Greek god Poseidon reigned over the sea. He is shown here riding sea horses and brandishing his famous three-pronged spear called a trident.

In Greek mythology, Poseidon was the god of the sea as well as of earthquakes and horses. One of the oldest and most widely worshiped of the Greek deities*, he was associated with many cults*, and numerous shrines were erected in his honor throughout the ancient world. Poseidon was considered one of the most powerful and violent of the gods, and he was identified with sea storms, tidal waves, and other natural disasters. Greek art usually portrayed him as a bearded man with a fierce expression who held a trident*. The Romans also worshiped Poseidon, although they called him Neptune, the name of an ancient Italian water god.

Poseidon was one of the three sons of Cronos and Rhea, the king and queen of the Titans (the original race of gods who ruled the universe before the Olympian gods). Along with his brothers, ZEUS and HADES, Poseidon overthrew his parents and imprisoned the Titans in the region of the underworld* known as Tartarus. The brothers then divided the universe between them, with Zeus (who became the supreme ruler of the gods) receiving the sky, Poseidon the sea, and Hades the underworld. Poseidon had many children with goddesses, sea nymphs*, and mortal* women. Most of his children inherited his violent nature, and many of them were giants and

monsters. Several of Poseidon's offspring were horses, including the famous winged horse Pegasus, the offspring of his union with MEDUSA.

Poseidon figures prominently in the epic* poems of HOMER, the *Iliad* and the *Odyssey.* In the *Iliad,* he is a fierce enemy of the Trojans because they refused to pay him for the walls he had helped to build around the city of TROY. In the *Odyssey,* Poseidon attempts to destroy the Greek hero* ODYSSEUS, who blinded Poseidon's son Polyphemus, the CYCLOPS. Although Odysseus survives, Poseidon kills all his companions, and Odysseus's return home is delayed because of the hardships and disasters he suffers at the hands of Poseidon.

Although Poseidon was not associated with the official cults of any city, he was important in ATHENS because some myths considered him to be the father of the Athenian hero Theseus. Poseidon competed with ATHENA, the goddess of war and wisdom, to become the patron* of Athens. The contest, won by Athena, is depicted in the sculptures that decorate the PARTHENON, the great temple located on the ACROPOLIS in Athens. In Athens, Poseidon bore the additional name of Erechtheus, which was also the name of a legendary early king of the city. The ERECHTHEUM, another important temple on the Acropolis, supposedly contained the mark of Poseidon's trident, and the same family that provided the priestess for the cult of Athena also provided the priest of Poseidon Erechtheus. (*See also* **Cults; Divinities; Epic, Greek; Religion, Greek; Religion, Roman.**)

* **epic** long poem about legendary or historical heroes, written in a grand style

* **hero** in mythology, a person of great strength or ability, often descended from a god

* **patron** special guardian, protector, or supporter

# POSTAL SERVICE

* **Hellenistic** referring to the Greek-influenced culture of the Mediterranean world during the three centuries after Alexander the Great, who died in 323 B.C.

* **city-state** independent state consisting of a city and its surrounding territory

* **classical** in Greek history, refers to the period of great political and cultural achievement from about 500 B.C. to 323 B.C.

* **Roman Republic** Rome during the period from 509 B.C. to 31 B.C., when popular assemblies annually elected their governmental officials

Several kingdoms in the ancient world, such as ASSYRIA and the PERSIAN EMPIRE, developed and supported postal services. Riders on horseback delivered messages, transported goods for the state, and accompanied the rulers or other officials on their journeys. While the Hellenistic* kingdoms developed similar systems, the Greek city-states* never organized any coordinated postal service. During the classical* period, professional private couriers delivered messages.

The Roman Republic* also relied on private messengers, and the number of Roman messengers was much greater than that of the Greeks. The Roman emperor AUGUSTUS introduced a public postal service throughout the empire that was designed specifically to serve the government. Under this system, cities and towns were responsible for providing their own animals, vehicles, and supplies to support the service in their area. Since this quickly became one of the most unpopular forms of government intrusion into local life, many reform efforts were attempted, although most were unsuccessful.

Established around a series of posting stations, the empire's postal service was based on the system of well-engineered Roman roads. Military personnel maintained the system, since it was vital to the state. The Roman postal service was highly efficient, with messages traveling as quickly as 50 miles per day. If necessary, the system moved much faster, such as in A.D. 69, when news of a revolt by the Roman army on the Rhine River traveled to the emperor Galba at a rate of 150 miles per day. (*See also* **Appian Way; Roads, Roman; Transportation and Travel.**)

153

## POTTERY, GREEK

See color plate 6, vol. 1.

The Greeks used pottery containers for several different purposes: storage, drinking, and rituals. This krater was used for drinking wine. Because the Greeks diluted their wine with water, they needed a wide-mouthed vessel for mixing.

The craft of pottery developed in Greece sometime before 1000 B.C., and the basic techniques of making pottery were well established by the 700s B.C. By this time, potters were producing a wide variety of items, such as vases, flasks for oil, bowls for mixing wine and water, storage jars for food and drink, drinking cups, and jugs. During the next 200 years, the Greeks refined their methods of painting and decorating pottery and produced increasingly elaborate and refined works of art. These advanced techniques enabled pottery painters to show more detailed scenes and to depict the human form in more realistic ways.

GEOMETRIC AND ORIENTALIZING STYLES OF POTTERY. The earliest existing Greek pottery dates from about the late 800s and early 700s B.C. This pottery was typically decorated with regularly repeated, abstract geometric shapes, such as zigzag patterns, circles, and lines that were painted in dark colors over the natural red clay of the pots. It is called the Geometric style. The few images of humans that appear were usually simple silhouettes that reflected little concern for lifelike accuracy.

From the late 700s B.C. to the early 600s B.C., pottery painting reflected the growing contact that the Greeks were having with Eastern cultures. The orderly geometric patterns gave way to a freer and more casual style that featured curved lines and a looser arrangement of figures. Another characteristic of this Eastern style was the portrayal of real and imaginary animals. Greek artists developed an interest in showing scenes from Greek myths and poetry, which led to more realistic representation of the human form and greater depiction of everyday activities.

BLACK-FIGURE AND RED-FIGURE POTTERY. About 700 B.C., potters in CORINTH developed the black-figure technique of painting pottery. In addition to using the natural mineral pigment (iron oxide) found in the clay, painters used a fine clay glaze to paint the outline of figures. Details, such as hair, muscles, or clothing, were then etched into the glaze to reveal the clay underneath, and the pot was then heated three times in an oven, or kiln. The glaze figures on the finished pot appeared shiny black against the red clay background, and the fine details were highlighted in red. The technique gave the artist more control over the work, and the result was both more refined and more realistic.

About 525 B.C., Athenian artists developed a new technique, called red-figure painting. Artists applied a black glaze over the entire pot, except for the figures, which were left as silhouettes in the original red clay. Details were then painted into the red figures. Pots decorated using this technique had a highly polished black finish, with red-clay figures that seemed to float on top of the black background. The effect was elegant, and the technique enabled artists to render fine details with remarkable precision. Pottery from this period shows just how much Greek artists knew about the human body and how it moved.

By the late 300s B.C., the red-figure style was replaced by less expensive methods and less elaborate decoration. Athens, which had been the most important center for the production of pottery, lost its celebrated position to locations in Italy, and the Romans gradually replaced the Greeks as the main producers and exporters of pottery in the Mediterranean region. (*See also* Art, Greek; Crafts and Craftsmanship; Pottery, Roman.)

# POTTERY, ROMAN

* **ceramics** pottery, earthenware, or porcelain objects; the manufacture of such objects

Roman pottery had its roots in both local and Greek traditions, and many characteristics of late Greek pottery can be seen in early Roman pottery. The Etruscans, the Romans' neighbors to the north, had a well-established tradition in ceramics*, one of the many artistic areas in which they strongly influenced Rome. The Greek pottery that the Etruscans imported had a further influence on local styles. Etruscan pottery was often decorated with designs borrowed from Greek artworks, as well as scenes from Greek mythology. Through their trade with other civilizations in ITALY, the Romans acquired Greek and Etruscan pottery that inspired much of the pottery they produced.

The best known type of Roman pottery was Samian ware, a bright red pottery originally produced on the Greek island of Samos. Also known as *terra sigillata,* Samian ware had a smooth, glossy surface and featured molded ornaments and reliefs* that often covered the entire surface of the vessel. Some Samian bowls were decorated with lead or bronze rivets—metal pins or bolts with a head on both ends. (A rivet is formed by passing it through an object, such as a piece of pottery, and hammering the end to form a head on the opposite side.) The finest examples of Samian ware were produced in Italy and Spain, although some may have been made in BRITAIN as well. The Romans also produced a pottery that was black, a result of its contact with the smoke of the kiln* in which it was fired.

* **relief** method of sculpture in which the design is raised from the surface from which it is shaped

While Samian ware was the finest Roman pottery, it was not typical of the ceramic ware used by the average Roman. Most Roman pottery was not as finely made or as elaborately decorated as Samian ware or the Greek pottery that had inspired it. Roman pots were typically plain, unglazed earthenware vessels used for everyday purposes, such as cooking or storing foods. Compared to the Greeks, Roman potters produced few specialized types of pots. Amphorae were used for carrying wine and other liquids, *dolia* were used on farms for storage and fermentation, and *mortaria* were large bowls for mixing and grinding.

* **kiln** oven for baking bricks, pottery, or other materials

Roman pottery included stamped impressions that revealed much about the pieces and the potters. Marks often indicated the name of the potter or the owner of the workshop in which the pottery was produced. Roman military units included potters who often stamped the name of their unit or legion* onto the bricks and roof tiles they produced. Such marks revealed that some manufacturers moved their operations to newly conquered provinces* or set up new workshops there to avoid the expense of transporting their wares to distant markets.

* **legion** main unit of the Roman army, consisting of about 6,000 soldiers

* **province** overseas area controlled by Rome

As the Romans established political and social control over Italy, they conquered communities that had already been producing high-quality pottery and ceramics, such as the Etruscans, the CELTS in northern Italy, and the Greek colonies in southern Italy. Pottery styles from these areas were adopted by the Romans and carried with them to places as far away as Germany and Britain. The reverse is also true, and the pottery from these distant lands often found its way into the selection of wares sold by Roman potters. As the Roman empire expanded, Roman pottery spread throughout the Mediterranean region. As in so many other areas of life, Roman styles came to dominate the pottery of Europe, North Africa, and the Near East, and these styles remained the major influence on the art of ceramics as late as the A.D. 600s. (*See also* **Art, Roman; Crafts and Craftsmanship; Etruscans; Pottery, Greek.**)

## PRAETOR

* **consul** one of two chief governmental officials of Rome, chosen annually and serving for a year

* **Roman Republic** Rome during the period from 509 B.C. to 31 B.C., when popular assemblies annually elected their governmental officials

* **province** overseas area controlled by Rome

In the government of Rome, praetors ranked just below consuls* in administrative authority. Like the consuls, praetors held official power, called IMPERIUM, for a term of one year. A praetor performed all the functions of a consul, but his power was less, and he could be overruled by a consul in a dispute. The praetor's main duties included administering the courts, presiding over the Roman Senate and assemblies, and commanding armies. Eventually, being a praetor became a prerequisite for becoming a consul.

The title of praetor was given to the two MAGISTRATES elected each year to serve as heads of government during the Roman Republic*. In 367 B.C., these two officials were renamed consuls, and the title of praetor was given to a third magistrate, who assisted in governing the state. Another praetor was added about 244 B.C., and four more praetors were added during the next 50 years to govern the territories conquered by the Romans. Although Rome continued to add new provinces* during the 100s B.C., the number of praetors remained at six. To ease the increasing burden of governing the provinces, the praetors' terms of office were extended. The extension enabled them to attend to their duties in Rome during the first year in office, before leaving the city to govern the provinces. The Roman dictator SULLA later increased the number of praetors to eight and fixed the minimum age for the office at 39.

Praetors continued to command armies during the Roman CIVIL WARS, but this practice ended under AUGUSTUS, the first emperor. During the Roman Empire, the number of praetors changed again, ranging from 10 to 16. They retained their traditional roles of presiding over the Senate and the criminal courts as well as organizing and financing major public games. Although somewhat reduced in power from the days of the republic, the praetorship still retained much of its importance, since it was a stepping-stone to more powerful posts. (*See also* **Armies, Roman; Consuls; Dictatorship, Roman; Government, Roman; Quaestor.**)

## PRAXITELES

FLOURISHED 375–330 B.C.
GREEK SCULPTOR

Praxiteles, the son of an Athenian sculptor, was one of the greatest sculptors in the ancient world. His style greatly influenced the work of future generations of artists. Although Praxiteles worked in bronze, he preferred to work in MARBLE. As was the style at the time, his marble statues were painted after they were sculpted. Praxiteles paid great attention to the finish on his works, preferring to employ the painter Nicias over other painters. Praxiteles specialized in religious statues, especially those that portrayed gods and goddesses, such as APOLLO and DIONYSUS, at a younger age than was usual for other artists.

Among the features of his work that influenced later sculptors was Praxiteles' use of the female nude. His ideal of the female body—wide hips, small breasts, oval face, and hair parted in the middle—characterized his masterpiece, the *Aphrodite at Cnidus.* While Aphrodite, the Greek goddess of love, had long been a popular subject for Greek sculptors, earlier statues showed her fully or partially clothed. Praxiteles was the first sculptor to show her completely nude.

Praxiteles was believed to have completed more than 75 sculptures during his career, although few, if any, of his original works still exist. The *Aphrodite of Cnidus* is known only from Roman copies. Many other statues that were once considered to be his originals have been shown to be copies as well. Although the famous statue of the god HERMES holding the infant Dionysus is considered by some experts to be the original work as described by the Greek writer PAUSANIAS, others doubt its authenticity. (*See also* **Art, Greek; Sculpture, Greek.**)

# PRIESTHOOD, GREEK

* **philosopher** scholar or thinker concerned with the study of ideas, including science

* **cult** group bound together by devotion to a particular person, belief, or god

* **oracle** priest or priestess through whom a god is believed to speak; also the location (such as a shrine) where such utterances are made

* **deity** god or goddess

* **celibate** unmarried and abstaining from sexual intercourse

In ancient Greece, religion was central to every aspect of daily life. Priests and priestesses played a crucial role in ensuring the peace, health, and prosperity of the state by intervening with the powerful—and often capricious—gods on behalf of human beings. The responsibilities of priesthood were taken very seriously, and priests and priestesses were important and highly respected individuals in Greece.

**QUALIFICATIONS FOR PRIESTHOOD.** Greek priests and priestesses needed little or no special training. According to the Greek philosopher* PLATO, the primary qualification was "good birth"—that is, being a member of a respected priestly or political family. Many in the priesthood were therefore restricted to the elite of Greek society.

Age also determined eligibility for many in the priesthood. For example, some cults* of the goddess ATHENA required that the priests be boys, not men. In contrast, only elderly Athenian women were eligible to become *gerairai,* who served the god Dionysus in the Anthesteria festival. The oracle* of the god APOLLO at DELPHI was originally a young girl, but later elderly women filled the post. Cults devoted to virgin deities*, such as the goddess ARTEMIS, usually required that their priests and priestesses remain celibate*, sometimes for life. Similarly, married priests and priestesses served the cults of the goddess HERA and other married deities.

The oldest and most common method of becoming a priest was by inheritance. Families and clans controlled such priesthoods, which were passed down from one generation to the next. For example, the two important Athenian priesthoods of Athena Polias and POSEIDON Erechtheus were held by two separate branches of the same clan, the Eteoboutads.

In democratic Athens, some priesthoods were filled by drawing lots. Some people understood this as a way of allowing the deity to make the choice of who would serve. Even priesthoods that required expertise in

See
color plate 6,
vol. 4.

* **sacrifice** sacred offering made to a god or goddess, usually of an animal such as a sheep or goat

* **ritual** regularly followed routine, especially religious

* **pagan** referring to a belief in more than one god; non-Christian

---

### ONLY SKIN DEEP?

Like the virgin priestesses of Artemis, Greek priests and priestesses often shared similar characteristics with the deities they served. Some scholars argue that this was the result of an ancient belief that the priest actually embodied the spirit of the deity during rituals. Descriptions of some prehistoric rites support this theory. For example, priests of Heracles wore lionskin robes, and the "bear-girls" of Artemis in the city of Brauron wore bearskins while performing ritual dances.

---

religious procedures were occasionally chosen by lot. Priests and priestesses were sometimes elected or appointed to their position, although election was less common than other methods. Outside the Greek mainland, wealthy individuals often purchased priesthoods, especially those in mystery cults and organizations known as "worshiper associations."

THE ROLE OF PRIESTS. Sacrifices* were the most important rituals* in most Greek religious festivals. While either a public official or the head of a family presided at a sacrifice, priests assisted in the ceremony and made sure that it was carried out correctly. The priest was responsible for dedicating the sacrifice to the god or goddess, killing the animal in accordance with proper procedure, and preparing the meat for eating. Because the priest or priestess was believed to have a special relationship with the god, he or she offered prayers on behalf of the congregation.

Priests and priestesses also handled other duties and responsibilities. They administered the affairs of the cult, fined members for improper behavior, made loans and maintained finances, prepared for festivals, maintained TEMPLES and shrines, and provided housing for priests and visitors. Priests also handled religious duties for individuals, such as purifying homes following a birth or death, officiating at weddings, and administering oaths.

If the priesthood in ancient Greece carried with it large responsibilities, it also provided many economic benefits and social rewards. All priests received an income from their religious activities. They were entitled to a share of the offerings placed on the altar of the deity, as well as a portion of the dues required of cult members. Regardless of the financial benefits of the priesthood, most priests were motivated by the religious and social importance of their position. Priests wielded great authority long after Greece had been conquered by the Roman Empire, and the cults they served flourished until pagan* faiths were banned by the Roman emperor THEODOSIUS I in A.D. 391. (*See also* **Death and Burial; Divinities; Festivals and Feasts, Greek; Omens; Oracles; Priesthood, Roman; Religion, Greek; Ritual and Sacrifice; Votive Offerings.**)

---

## PRIESTHOOD, ROMAN

* **deity** god or goddess

* **sacrifice** sacred offering made to a god or goddess, usually of an animal such as a sheep or goat

* **Roman Republic** Rome during the period from 509 B.C. to 31 B.C., when popular assemblies annually elected their governmental officials

The Roman priesthood was not a separate class of individuals who had special training or a spiritual calling to religious duty. Most priests were members of noble families whose dress and daily activities were no different from those of other Romans. Priests did not decide religious issues; this was the responsibility of the Senate. The duties of most priests focused on only a single deity*, on a few rituals and festivals, or on acting as advisers on religious matters to individuals or governmental officials. Although priests did not perform the actual physical act of sacrifice*, no sacrifice could take place without them.

Four different colleges, or official groups, of priests existed during the Roman Republic*. The most prestigious college was that of the pontiffs, who held a wide range of duties. The chief pontiff and head of the state religion was the *pontifex maximus,* or high priest. Pontiffs participated in many state festivals, administered religious law concerning such matters as adoptions

* **omen** sign, good or bad, of future events

* **oracle** priest or priestess through whom a god is believed to speak; also the location (such as a shrine) where such utterances are made

* **hearth** fireplace in the center of a house

* **chastity** purity in conduct and intention; abstention from sexual intercourse

* **cult** group bound together by devotion to a particular person, belief, or god

* **deify** to make or treat as a god

* **pagan** referring to a belief in more than one god; non-Christian

and burials, and advised the Roman Senate on religious matters. The augurs, members of another prominent college, were responsible for interpreting omens* and determining whether or not the gods approved of actions planned by the state. A third college was in charge of the care of the Sibylline Books, a collection of written oracles* that the augurs consulted upon instruction of the Senate in times of crisis. A fourth college, that of the feasters, was responsible for putting on an annual feast in honor of Jupiter.

Two special groups in the Roman priesthood were the Vestal Virgins and the *flamines*. The Vestal Virgins kept lit the flame of the sacred hearth* of Rome in the temple of VESTA. The Romans believed that if the fire were ever extinguished, dire consequences would befall the city. Chosen for their duties when they were young girls, the Vestal Virgins swore an oath of chastity* during their 30-year term of office. If a Vestal Virgin broke her vow, she was punished by being buried alive. The *flamines* were 15 priests, each of whom served one of the major Roman gods. The *flamines* were restricted in their activities. Some were prohibited from wearing rings or from taking oaths. Unlike other priests, the Vestal Virgins and *flamines* wore traditional costumes that marked their priestly status, and their religious duties were a full-time activity.

During the Roman Empire, the emperor controlled the priesthood. The emperor always took the title *pontifex maximus,* the title that had once belonged to the chairman of the college of pontiffs. Religious activities increasingly involved sacrifices and ceremonies on behalf of the emperor and his family, and new priesthoods devoted to the cult* of the deified* emperors arose. Although THEODOSIUS I banned pagan* worship in A.D. 391, the pagan priesthoods probably remained active in Rome into the A.D. 400s. (*See also* **Augur; Cults; Divinities; Festivals and Feasts, Roman; Omens; Priesthood, Greek; Religion, Roman; Ritual and Sacrifice.**)

**PRINCIPATE, ROMAN**

See *Rome, History of.*

**PROMETHEUS**

* **immortal** living forever

* **Titan** one of a family of giants who ruled the earth before the Olympian gods

* **underworld** kingdom of the dead; also called Hades

According to Greek mythology, Prometheus was an immortal* being who defended humans against the gods. In a famous story, Prometheus stole fire from the gods and gave it to humans, a crime for which he was sentenced to never-ending torture by ZEUS, the king of the gods. The poet HESIOD related many of the stories associated with Prometheus in his poems *Theogony* and *Works and Days*. The playwright AESCHYLUS adapted the myths for a trilogy of dramas, including his play *Prometheus Bound*.

Prometheus was the son of the Titan* Iapetus and Clymene, the daughter of Oceanus. His name means "forethought" in Greek. When Zeus and his fellow gods rebelled against the Titans for control of the universe, Prometheus foresaw the outcome. He advised the Titans to use cleverness to defeat Zeus, but they ignored his advice. Prometheus joined the side of Zeus and the gods, who ultimately defeated the Titans and imprisoned them in Tartarus, the deepest part of the underworld*.

# PROMETHEUS

As a defender of mortals against the gods, the hero Prometheus often angered Zeus with his rebelliousness and trickery. As a punishment for stealing fire from Mt. Olympus, Prometheus was tied to a rock, and every day an eagle ate part of his liver.

* **sacrifice** sacred offering made to a god or goddess, usually of an animal such as a sheep or goat

* **nymph** in classical mythology, one of the lesser goddesses of nature

* **hero** in mythology, a person of great strength or ability, often descended from a god

Prometheus soon found himself in disagreement with Zeus over human beings. In his poem *Theogony,* Hesiod relates how Prometheus created human forms out of clay, and ATHENA, the goddess of wisdom, breathed life into the clay figures. Although Prometheus taught humans many arts and crafts, they remained imperfect beings. When Zeus discovered Prometheus's creation, he decided to destroy humankind and make more perfect creatures instead. Zeus attempted to starve humans by demanding the best food in sacrifices*. Prometheus divided an ox into two portions. One portion contained the edible meat but was covered with the unappetizing stomach. The other portion contained bones that Prometheus covered with a thin layer of appealing fat. Zeus chose the portion with the inedible bones.

In revenge, Zeus withheld fire from humans, knowing that this would certainly lead to their deaths. To protect his creation, Prometheus stole a spark from Mt. OLYMPUS, the home of the gods, which he hid in the stem of a plant. He then gave the spark to humans. When Zeus saw the fires that people had set from the spark, he was enraged and ordered the capture of Prometheus. Prometheus was taken to a remote mountain peak at the edge of the ocean and chained to a rock. Every day an eagle landed on the rock and ate part of Prometheus's liver. Each night, his liver grew back. According to some versions of the myth, Prometheus taunted Zeus, who angrily threw a thunderbolt at the rock, forcing Prometheus into Tartarus.

Zeus eventually freed Prometheus in exchange for information. Zeus was in love with the nymph* Thetis, but he had heard a rumor that the son of Thetis would be greater than his father. Because Prometheus saw the future, he knew that the son of Zeus and Thetis would overthrow Zeus as king of the gods, just as Zeus had overthrown his own father, Cronos. After Prometheus gave this information to Zeus, he was then freed by the hero* HERACLES, who killed the eagle and broke the chains that bound Prometheus to the rock.

According to Hesiod, because Zeus was angry about the theft of fire, he punished humans by giving them Pandora. Created by the god Hephaestus, Pandora was taught household skills by Athena, and given charm by

APHRODITE, the goddess of love. She also carried with her a jar that contained all the evils in the world. Zeus presented Pandora to Prometheus, who saw through the ploy and refused the gift. Although Prometheus also warned his brother, Epimetheus, against accepting the gift, Epimetheus (whose name means "afterthought") gladly married Pandora. When Pandora unwittingly opened the jar, she released pain, disease, and all the other evils into the world. Only hope was left inside the jar. (*See also* **Divinities; Myths, Greek.**)

## PROPERTIUS

ca. 50–ca. 16 B.C.
ROMAN POET

* **elegiac** sad and mournful poem

* **Roman Republic** Rome during the period from 509 B.C. to 31 B.C., when popular assemblies annually elected their governmental officials

* **rhetoric** art of using words effectively in speaking or writing

* **patron** special guardian, protector, or supporter

Sextus Propertius was a Roman poet during the reign of the emperor AUGUSTUS. His fame rests on the elegiacs* that he addressed to his mistress, Cynthia. Propertius was probably the first poet to liken love to slavery and also to compare a person in love to a soldier at war.

Propertius was born in Assisi, a small city about 90 miles north of Rome. His upper-class parents had their property seized by Octavian (later known as Augustus) during the civil wars that ended the Roman Republic*. In preparation for a career of public service, Propertius was educated in rhetoric*. Disgusted by war and political strife, however, the young man chose to write poetry instead. He moved to Rome and published his first book of poems around 28 B.C. His fourth and final book of poems, published around 16 B.C., contained few love poems and instead addressed politics and the great events of Roman history. Although his patron* was a close friend of the emperor, Propertius was sometimes critical of Augustus's government and its policies.

Propertius's most famous poems recount his stormy love affair with an older woman he called Cynthia. She was probably a married woman named Hostia. Propertius portrayed his love for Cynthia as tormented, hopeless, and all-consuming. Although the faithless Cynthia rejected the young poet, his love for her never lessened, and he continued to be obsessed with her even after her death. Literary critics and several poets, including the American poet Ezra Pound, have praised Propertius for his political independence and his passionate depiction of love. (*See also* **Callimachus; Catullus; Poetry, Greek and Hellenistic; Poetry, Roman; Tibullus.**)

## PROSERPINA

See *Persephone.*

## PROSTITUTION

* **dowry** money or property that a woman brings to the man she marries

* **ritual** regularly followed routine, especially religious

Prostitution—the selling of sex in exchange for money—was legal and common in both Greece and Rome. A group that included women, children, and slaves, prostitutes were generally among the least protected members of ancient society. Both men and women worked as prostitutes for a variety of reasons. Although some slaves were forced into prostitution, others chose to sell their bodies to earn the money to buy their freedom, and some women turned to prostitution to earn a dowry*.

Prostitution was sometimes practiced in the TEMPLES. Temple prostitutes were regarded as sacred. In some regions, such as Babylonia, women were required to give themselves to a stranger as part of a religious ritual*. Prostitutes also worked in inns, taverns, public baths, and other places where there might be many potential clients. Some prostitutes had managers, to whom they gave their earnings. Some male and female prostitutes attached themselves to rich or powerful clients, who supported them financially. Aspasia, the mistress of the Athenian statesman PERICLES, was well known for her power and influence.

Although most Greeks and Romans considered prostitution necessary to society, some regarded it a threat to family life. PLATO and other philosophers* condemned the practice. The Roman educator SENECA THE ELDER called prostitution "unhappy and sterile submission." Despite these criticisms, the governments of Athens and Rome recognized prostitution as a source of income and taxed it. Brothels (houses of prostitution) were common. In fact, the ruins of several brothels were found in Pompeii, a city of about 20,000 people that was destroyed during the eruption of Mt. VESUVIUS in A.D. 79. (*See also* Homosexuality; Women, Greek; Women, Roman.)

* **philosopher** scholar or thinker concerned with the study of ideas, including science

# PROVINCES, ROMAN

* **magistrate** government official in ancient Greece and Rome

* **Roman Republic** Rome during the period from 509 B.C. to 31 B.C., when popular assemblies annually elected their governmental officials

* **tribute** payment made to a dominant power or local government

* **annex** to add a territory to an existing state

* **edict** proclamation or order that has the force of law

* **imperial** pertaining to an emperor or empire

Provinces were overseas territories controlled by Rome. Early in Roman history, the word *province* meant the sphere or type of activity of a magistrate*, whether in Rome or abroad. Later it became identified with the geographical region over which a magistrate held executive power. Beginning in the later Roman Republic*, the term referred to a territory outside Italy that owed tribute* to Rome. During the peak of the Roman Empire, during the late A.D. 100s, almost all the lands that bordered the Mediterranean Sea were Roman provinces.

The Romans began acquiring provinces after the first PUNIC WAR against CARTHAGE ended in 241 B.C. By 227 B.C. the Romans gave SICILY and the islands of Sardinia and Corsica provincial status so they would not fall again under Carthaginian control. The acquisition of provinces began to accelerate in 146 B.C., when AFRICA and MACEDONIA were annexed*. During the last decades of the Roman Republic, the Roman general POMPEY annexed SYRIA, and Julius CAESAR conquered all of GAUL. Many other provinces were acquired during the Roman Empire, starting with EGYPT in 30 B.C. JUDAEA became a province in A.D. 6, and the emperor CLAUDIUS added BRITAIN to the empire between A.D. 43 and A.D. 47.

At first, Rome ruled its provinces through elected magistrates. As the number of provinces increased, this system proved impractical. During the late republic, the Roman Senate, at the expiration of the magistrates' terms of office, would continue them as governors of the provinces with the title of proconsuls—those acting in the place of the regular consuls. The first governor of a province was usually the man who had conquered the territory. He was given complete military, judicial, and administrative authority over his province. Upon taking power, the governor issued an edict* in which he announced the laws he would enforce during his rule. Within his province, a governor was an absolute ruler. Because there were no checks on their power, some governors were inclined to be corrupt.

In 27 B.C. the emperor AUGUSTUS reorganized the provinces into two classes. The more settled and wealthier provinces were administered by the Roman Senate acting through proconsuls, who were appointed each year. Imperial* provinces, which were usually the lands on the frontiers of

* **legion** main unit of the Roman army, consisting of about 6,000 soldiers

* **aristocratic** referring to people of the highest social class

Provinces were valuable assets to the Roman Empire. They provided defense, paid tribute, and supplied important agricultural products to Rome. They were also home to some talented and influential individuals who served the empire.

the empire where Roman legions* were headquartered, were administered directly by the emperor. This system remained in place until the emperor DIOCLETIAN restructured the Roman Empire during the early A.D. 300s.

Provinces were administered for the benefit of Rome. The provinces supplied Rome with valuable commodities, such as corn, wheat, olive oil, and WINE. After 167 B.C., Rome stopped taxing its citizens, which placed the entire tax burden on the provinces. They were required to pay tribute to Rome and to support the soldiers who were stationed in their towns and cities, which at times caused friction between Rome and the peoples of the provinces. But provinces also benefited by their attachment to Rome. The Romans built TEMPLES, AQUEDUCTS, ROADS, HARBORS, and other public works projects that improved the lives of the people living in these outlying areas. There were also many colonies of Roman veterans who after discharge from the army settled in the provinces in which they had been stationed, thus helping along the process of Romanization. The name of the German city of Cologne (Köln) comes from the Latin word *castra,* meaning "camp," and the city of Merida in Spain comes from the Latin word *emerita,* meaning "discharged."

Roman provinces were governed in a variety of ways. In some provinces, local aristocratic* families, given the authority by the governor, administered the provincial government. Local town councils supervised the collection of taxes, public works projects, and the local police. In return for their work on behalf of the governor, these local rulers were granted

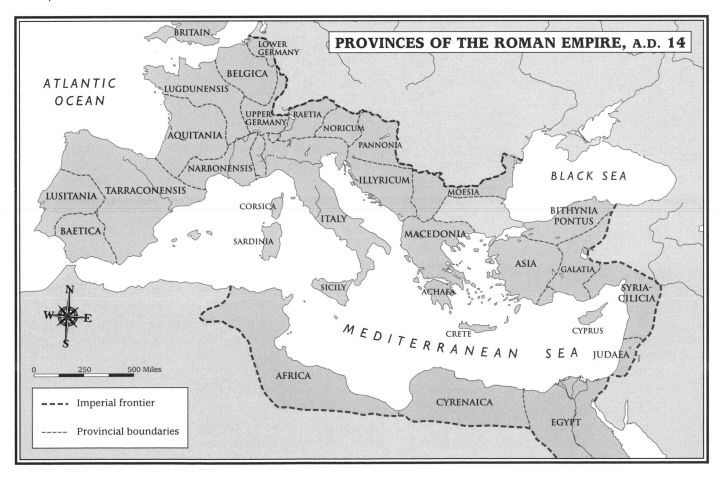

PROVINCES OF THE ROMAN EMPIRE, A.D. 14

ATLANTIC OCEAN

BRITAIN
LOWER GERMANY
BELGICA
LUGDUNENSIS
UPPER GERMANY
RAETIA
NORICUM
PANNONIA
AQUITANIA
NARBONENSIS
TARRACONENSIS
LUSITANIA
BAETICA
CORSICA
SARDINIA
ITALY
ILLYRICUM
MOESIA
BLACK SEA
BITHYNIA PONTUS
MACEDONIA
ASIA
GALATIA
SICILY
ACHAEA
CRETE
CYPRUS
SYRIA-CILICIA
JUDAEA
MEDITERRANEAN SEA
AFRICA
CYRENAICA
EGYPT

N W E S

0    250    500 Miles

- - - - Imperial frontier

- - - - - Provincial boundaries

Roman citizenship. Some provincial cities were given special status. In Sicily, cities that joined Rome were declared free and granted independence. Certain tribes within the provinces were self-governing.

Many talented people came from the provinces, including notable orators* and writers, as well as military and political leaders. The emperors TRAJAN and HADRIAN both came from the Roman province of Spain. (*See also* **Citizenship; Rome, History of; Taxation.**)

* **orator** public speaker of great skill

---

# PTOLEMAIC DYNASTY

* **dynasty** succession of rulers from the same family or group
* **satrap** provincial governor in ancient Persia

* **papyrus** writing material made by pressing together thin strips of the inner stem of the papyrus plant
* **Hellenistic** referring to the Greek-influenced culture of the Mediterranean world during the three centuries after Alexander the Great, who died in 323 B.C.

The Ptolemaic dynasty* was composed of members of the Macedonian Greek family that ruled EGYPT from shortly after the death of ALEXANDER THE GREAT in 323 B.C. until its defeat by the Romans in 31 B.C. The dynasty is named after its 15 kings, all of whom were named Ptolemy. The last ruler in the dynasty, the brilliant queen CLEOPATRA, became famous for her relationships with the Roman statesmen Julius CAESAR and Marcus ANTONIUS (Mark Antony).

After the death of Alexander, the generals of the Macedonian army divided Alexander's empire among themselves. Ptolemy I Soter, a childhood friend and wartime companion of Alexander, established himself as satrap* of Egypt. He named himself king in 305 B.C., the first monarch of the Ptolemaic dynasty. During the 200s B.C., the Ptolemies had numerous conflicts with the SELEUCID DYNASTY of SYRIA in an attempt to extend their rule into ASIA MINOR and Syria. Until around 200 B.C, the Ptolemies controlled JUDAEA and southern Syria as well as Egypt. Domestic strife and civil war disrupted the reigns of the later Ptolemies. With the death of Cleopatra in 30 B.C., the dynasty ended, and Egypt became a part of the Roman empire.

Because the Ptolemies were not Egyptian themselves, they often exploited the people for their own personal gain. The dynasty held monopolies on linen, papyrus*, beer production, and other industries. They claimed all Egyptian land as their own and then had it farmed by peasants. But the dynasty also supported the arts and scholarship, founding the famous Library and Museum of ALEXANDRIA, making the city a center of Hellenistic* culture. (*See also* **Hellenistic Culture; Rome, History of.**)

---

# PTOLEMY

ca. A.D. 100–ca. 170
ASTRONOMER, MATHEMATICIAN, AND GEOGRAPHER

Claudius Ptolemaeus, or Ptolemy, was a Greek astronomer, mathematician, and geographer. Between A.D. 146 and A.D. 170, Ptolemy wrote several major works, including a 13-volume textbook of astronomy that remained the standard work in the field until the end of the Middle Ages. An equally influential work was his 8-volume *Geography,* in which Ptolemy attempted to map the known world.

Little is known about Ptolemy's life. Born in Upper Egypt, he lived most of his life in ALEXANDRIA, where he served as superintendent of the Museum. Around A.D. 150, Ptolemy completed his major astronomical work, called the *Syntaxis.* (This work is now known as the *Almagest,* from the Arabic for "the greatest.") In the *Syntaxis,* Ptolemy recorded the information needed to determine the positions in the sky of the sun, the moon,

## THE CENTER OF THE UNIVERSE

Not all ancient astronomers believed in the geocentric theory—that the earth is the center of the universe. The astronomer Aristarchus of Samos suggested that the movements of the heavenly bodies could be explained if the sun were at the center and the earth and the other planets revolved around it. But Ptolemy and most other ancient astronomers rejected this argument for rational physical reasons. According to the scientific theory of the time, if the earth moved, an object thrown straight up into the air would not fall down in the same spot. It was not until after the work of Nicolaus Copernicus in the 1500s that astronomers adopted the sun-centered system.

* **projection** representation of the earth's surface upon a flat surface, such as a grid

the stars, and the five planets that were known at the time. He incorporated the work of the great Greek astronomer Hipparchus, who lived in the 100s B.C. Using observations of the stars made by the ancient Babylonians, Hipparchus had compiled a catalog that contained the positions in the sky of more than 850 stars. Ptolemy made his own observations of the stars between A.D. 127 and A.D. 147, which enabled him to create a star catalog that plotted the positions of more than 1,000 stars.

Along with most other ancient astronomers, Ptolemy believed that the earth was the center of the universe. According to Ptolemy, the earth is surrounded by hollow, transparent spheres that support and move the other planets, the moon, the sun, and the stars around the earth. However, because heavenly bodies move in irregular patterns across the sky, Ptolemy devised a complicated theory of interlocking movements of the planetary spheres. His theory explained the movement of heavenly bodies so well that it was not until the 1400s that scientists challenged the geocentric theory.

In his *Geography,* Ptolemy attempted to locate the known regions of the world by listing places by their latitude and longitude. In addition to this list of about 8,000 places, Ptolemy described important physical features of the land, such as rivers and mountain ranges. Book 1 of the *Geography* includes instructions on how to draw a map of the world using two different projections*.

The *Geography* also contains an atlas of maps. Although the maps accurately depict the outline of the Roman empire, areas beyond the boundaries of the empire are frequently distorted. Ptolemy made a number of mistakes in creating his maps. For example, he calculated that the Mediterranean Sea was much longer than it is in reality, and he connected the continent of Africa to China, making the Indian Ocean a large inland lake. Despite these mistakes, the *Geography* was the most accurate depiction of the known world until the 1500s.

Ptolemy wrote many other books on astronomy, astrology, optics, and music. In his *Planetary Hypotheses,* for example, he described the physical models that explain the movements of the planets he detailed in the *Syntaxis.* In the *Astrological Influences,* a companion work to the *Syntaxis,* Ptolemy attempted to show how the movements of the planets affect life on earth. These works had an important influence on astronomy and astrology throughout the Middle Ages. (*See also* **Astronomy and Astrology; Eratosthenes; Maps, Ancient.**)

# PUNIC WARS

* **province** overseas area controlled by Rome

* **orator** public speaker of great skill

* **blockade** military means used to prevent the passage of enemy ships or troops into or out of a place

The Punic Wars were three wars fought between Carthage and Rome for control of the western Mediterranean Sea. The name *Punic* comes from the Roman word for the race and the language of the Carthaginians. Before the wars began in 264 B.C., the two cities had a peaceful and cooperative relationship. Rome controlled most of the Italian peninsula; Carthage, located in northern Africa, controlled trade in the western Mediterranean. At the conclusion of the third war in 146 B.C., Carthage was completely destroyed, and Rome was the greatest power in the region.

The First Punic War (264–241 B.C.) arose from a quarrel between Messana and Syracuse, two cities on the island of Sicily. When Syracuse attacked Messana, the rulers of Messana called on both Carthage and

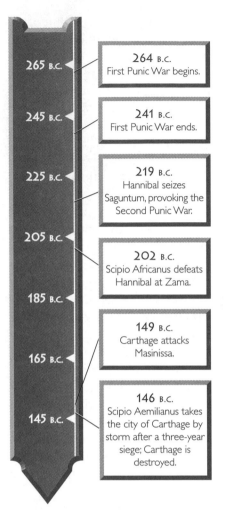

265 B.C.

**264 B.C.**
First Punic War begins.

245 B.C.

**241 B.C.**
First Punic War ends.

225 B.C.

**219 B.C.**
Hannibal seizes
Saguntum, provoking the
Second Punic War.

205 B.C.

**202 B.C.**
Scipio Africanus defeats
Hannibal at Zama.

185 B.C.

**149 B.C.**
Carthage attacks
Masinissa.

165 B.C.

**146 B.C.**
Scipio Aemilianus takes
the city of Carthage by
storm after a three-year
siege; Carthage is
destroyed.

145 B.C.

\* **siege** long and persistent effort to force a
surrender by surrounding a fortress with armed
troops, cutting it off from aid

## CARTHAGE MUST BE DESTROYED!

The Roman orator and statesman
Marcus Porcius Cato feared and
hated Carthage. In 153 B.C. Cato
served on a diplomatic mission to
Carthage. He observed that the
city had revived after the Second
Punic War and had once again become a prosperous and powerful
place. Cato believed that a revital-
ized Carthage was a serious threat
to the security of Rome. From then
until his death in 149 B.C., Cato
concluded each of his speeches in
the Roman Senate with the words
"Carthage must be destroyed!"

Rome for help. Although the Carthaginians arrived first and arranged a
peace treaty between the two cities, they were eventually forced out by
the Romans, who were fearful of Carthaginian control of the island.
Rome and Carthage became involved in a full-scale war against each
other. A Roman fleet, led by the general Marcus Atilius Regulus, landed
an invasion force in North Africa in 256 B.C. The next year, the Carthaginian general Xanthippus defeated the Romans and took Regulus captive.
Neither the Romans nor the Carthaginians, led by the general Hamilcar
Barca, were able to control Sicily. After a long period in which neither
side gained an advantage, a Roman fleet of 200 ships defeated the
Carthaginians at sea in 241 B.C., and the Carthaginians asked for peace.
They paid Rome a large fine and abandoned Sicily, which then became
Rome's first province\*.

The Second Punic War (218–201 B.C.) broke out when Hamilcar
Barca's son HANNIBAL seized the Spanish city of Saguntum, which was an
ally of Rome. Although Rome had immense economic resources and a
superb military organization, the Carthaginians had Hannibal, one of the
greatest generals in history. In the winter of 218 B.C., Hannibal crossed
the ALPS into Italy with 40,000 troops and dozens of war elephants to attack Rome. During a 16-year presence in Italy, Hannibal and his army
had several important victories, the most famous being the Battle of Can-
nae in 216 B.C., when Hannibal destroyed an entire Roman army. However, Rome and its Italian allies refused to surrender. The Romans had
great reserves of manpower and were able to fight Hannibal in Italy
while simultaneously conducting campaigns in other regions. In the late
200s B.C., Roman armies under SCIPIO AFRICANUS drove the Carthaginians
out of SPAIN. Cut off from their Spanish troops and resources, the
Carthaginians were unable to defend North Africa from a Roman invasion. Hannibal returned to Africa to protect the city of Carthage, but Scipio defeated him at the Battle of Zama in 202 B.C. When the war ended
the next year, Rome forced Carthage to surrender Spain and most of its
North African possessions. After the defeat of Carthage in the Second
Punic War, no other power was able to seriously threaten Rome's power
for centuries.

The Third Punic War (149–146 B.C.) broke out when Carthage attacked Masinissa, the king of Numidia, who was a Roman ally. Although
Carthage was defeated, the Romans declared war on the Carthaginians,
largely at the urging of the Roman orator\* and statesman Marcus Porcius CATO (the Elder). When Rome demanded that Carthage be abandoned, the Carthaginians decided to fight. Carthage was cut off from its
supply routes by a Roman blockade\*. After a three-year siege\*, the Roman general Scipio Aemilianus eventually conquered the city in 146 B.C.
Only 10 percent of the population of Carthage survived, and the victorious Romans sold them into SLAVERY. The Romans destroyed the city, and
Carthage's territory became the Roman province of Africa. But in the
later years of prosperity under the Roman Empire, a new, Roman
Carthage grew to become one of the greatest cities of the empire, second only to Rome itself. (*See also* **Rome, History of; Spain; Wars an
Warfare, Roman.**)

## PYRRHIC WAR

**B**etween 280 and 275 B.C., Rome fought the Pyrrhic War against Pyrrhus, the king of Epirus, a land northwest of Greece. The victory over Pyrrhus was a turning point in Rome's history. In addition to gaining control of the Greek cities of southern Italy, Rome transformed itself into an international power that dominated the Mediterranean region on both land and sea.

In 282 B.C. Rome defended Thurii, a Greek city in southern Italy, against a marauding Italian tribe called the Lucanians. Rome's intervention angered Tarentum, another Greek city in Italy. Tarentum sank Roman ships in the Gulf of Tarentum and ousted the Roman troops from Thurii. The leaders of Tarentum then turned to Pyrrhus for support.

Pyrrhus, a talented Greek general and second cousin of ALEXANDER THE GREAT, led a force of 25,000 men and 20 Indian war elephants across the sea into Italy, where he defeated the Romans at the Battles of Heraclea (280 B.C.) and Asculum (279 B.C.). The Battle of Asculum cost so many lives that Pyrrhus was reported to have said, "Another such victory and I am lost." The stubborn Roman resistance forced Pyrrhus to move his forces to the island of SICILY. He fought for the Greek colonies in Sicily against the North African city of CARTHAGE, which was attempting to extend its control over the western Mediterranean. Pyrrhus returned to mainland Italy in 275 B.C., and the Romans finally defeated him at the Battle of Beneventum. Returning to Epirus, Pyrrhus conquered MACEDONIA before he died in a street fight in 272 B.C. Pyrrhus is remembered in the expression "Pyrrhic victory," which describes a victory that is gained at too great a cost. (*See also* **Colonies, Greek; Punic Wars; Wars and Warfare, Roman.**)

## PYTHAGORAS

BORN ca. 580
GREEK PHILOSOPHER AND
MATHEMATICIAN

* **philosopher** scholar or thinker concerned with the study of ideas, including science
* **sect** religious group separated from an established church, usually due to its more extreme beliefs
* **tyrant** absolute ruler
* **abstinence** avoidance of certain foods, pleasures, or activities
* **sacrifice** sacred offering made to a god or goddess, usually of an animal such as a sheep or goat
* **ritual** regularly followed routine, especially religious
* **immortality** eternal life

**P**ythagoras was a Greek philosopher* who founded a philosophical and religious movement in the 500s B.C. His followers were known as Pythagoreans. Although no written records of his work survive, his teachings influenced several ancient thinkers, especially PLATO. Because later Pythagoreans attributed their own discoveries to the founder of their sect* as a mark of respect, it is uncertain how many of their beliefs originated with Pythagoras.

Pythagoras was born on the Greek island of SAMOS around 580 B.C. To escape the tyrant* of Samos, Pythagoras migrated to Croton, a Greek colony in southern Italy. It was in Croton that he founded his sect, which attracted both men and women. The Pythagoreans followed a distinctive way of life. They practiced abstinence* and were strict vegetarians. They refused to participate in sacrifices*, which were among the most important Greek religious rituals*. Followers of Pythagoras used secret passwords and carried out special burial rites. Pythagoras's organization angered local inhabitants, who forced him into exile. The Pythagoreans enjoyed a certain amount of influence in southern Italy until the middle of the 400s B.C., when they were violently suppressed. Although their school no longer existed, the philosophical and religious beliefs of the Pythagoreans greatly affected later philosophers.

Some historians believe that Pythagoras introduced the idea of the immortality* of the soul into Greek religious thought. The concept probably did not originate with Pythagoras but may have come from central Asia or India. The Pythagoreans believed that the immortal soul was confined within a mortal body. Trapped in an endlessly repeating cycle, the soul was reincarnated* into plant, animal, and human forms. This cycle was broken by acts of purification. Once the soul had been purged of pollutants, the cycle of rebirth was broken, and immortality was achieved.

* reincarnate to be reborn in a new body or life form

The Pythagorean philosophy focused on mathematical questions and the theories of numbers and music. Pythagoras and his followers believed that all of reality could be explained by mathematical relationships. According to the Greek philosopher ARISTOTLE, even abstract concepts, such as opportunity or injustice, were numbers within the Pythagorean system. Perhaps the most enduring result of the Pythagorean interest in mathematics is the theorem in geometry that bears his name. According to the Pythagorean theorem, the square of the length of the hypotenuse* of a right triangle is equal to the sum of the squares of the lengths of the other two sides.

* hypotenuse in a right triangle, the side opposite the right angle

The Pythagoreans' work in mathematics was accompanied by advancements in music and astronomy. Pythagoras himself is credited with determining the principal intervals of the musical scale. He discovered that the main musical intervals produced by a vibrating string could be expressed as ratios between the first four whole numbers. For example, the ratio of an octave is 2:1; a fifth is 3:2; and a fourth is 4:3. It was this discovery that may have led the Pythagoreans to explain the universe in terms of numbers and their proportions. They taught that distances between heavenly bodies were divided by regular intervals according to the laws of musical harmony. Some Pythagoreans believed that Pythagoras could actually hear this "music of the spheres." (*See also* **Cults; Mathematics, Greek; Religion, Greek.**)

# QUAESTOR

* **Roman Republic** Rome during the period from 509 B.C. to 31 B.C., when popular assemblies annually elected their governmental officials

* **consul** one of two chief governmental officials of Rome, chosen annually and serving for a year

* **province** overseas area controlled by Rome

A quaestor was the lowest political rank in the government of Rome. Quaestors mainly handled financial matters. During the early Roman Republic*, there were only two quaestors each year, but as the Roman empire grew, so did the number of quaestors required to manage financial responsibilities.

Before the founding of the Roman Republic, the Roman kings appointed quaestors to prosecute capital crimes—that is, crimes punishable by death. During the first years of the republic, the consuls* chose two quaestors to act as their deputies in administering finances. After 447 B.C. quaestors were elected each year by an assembly of the people. In 421 B.C. the number of quaestors was increased to four. Four more were added in 267 B.C., and as the Roman empire expanded and more financial officers were needed, additional quaestors were added. Two quaestors administered the *aerarium*—the Roman state treasury. Others served as the financial officers for the governors of Roman provinces*.

The Roman general SULLA reformed the Roman administration in the late republic, increasing the number of quaestors to 20 and setting the minimum age requirement at 30. He also required that candidates for higher political office must first hold the position of quaestor. After Sulla, a quaestor automatically became a member of the Roman Senate after his year of service. Julius

CAESAR doubled the number of quaestors to 40, but AUGUSTUS, the first emperor, reduced the number back to 20. He also lowered the minimum age to 25 but took away from the quaestors the responsibility for the Roman treasury.

During the Roman Empire, the emperor chose two quaestors himself from among the upper-class young men of Rome. Because the emperor's quaestors served as imperial* spokesmen and often drafted laws, prominent lawyers and men of literary talent often held the position. (*See also* **Aedile; Consuls; Government, Roman; Law, Roman; Magistrates; Praetor.**)

* imperial   pertaining to an emperor or empire

## QUARRIES

* excavate   to uncover by digging

See
color plate 13,
vol. 2.

The Mediterranean region had abundant supplies of stones, such as MARBLE and limestone, which the ancient Greeks and Romans used for sculpture and the construction of buildings. The Greeks began excavating* these sites in the 700s B.C. as a way to extract the stones. Greek quarrying techniques changed very little over the centuries, and the Romans later adopted these methods to extract stones on a much wider scale.

The Greeks and Romans built quarries wherever there was a valuable source of stone. The Greek colony of SYRACUSE (on the island of SICILY) had an abundant source of limestone that produced more than 100 million tons of limestone during the ancient period. Marble extracted from quarries on the islands of Paros and Naxos in the AEGEAN SEA was prized for its special characteristics. Parian marble had a glistening white sheen, and the marble quarried in Naxos was stone gray. Quarries in Spain yielded selenite, a variety of gypsum that was used to make plaster.

Although most quarries consisted of rock formations on the surface of the ground, some stones, such as a special variety of marble at Paros, were extracted by tunneling through the mountains. Quarry workers used hammers and picks to carve deep grooves into the rock. Soft stones were forced out of the rockbed with wooden wedges that had been saturated with water. When the wedges swelled, soft stones, such as tufa, split away from the rock face. Harder stones, such as basalt, required iron wedges that were heated by fire to extract the stone.

Once the stone was extracted from the rockbed, various methods were used to cut the stone. Some stones were cut with a conventional saw, but a more common method involved sand and a strong wire. The pressure of the wire moving back and forth on the sand was enough to cut the stone without leaving any roughness. By the A.D. 300s, waterpower was used to drive large marble-cutting saws. (*See also* **Construction Materials and Techniques.**)

## QUINTILIAN

ca. A.D. 40–ca. 96
ROMAN EDUCATOR AND WRITER

Marcus Fabius Quintilianus, or Quintilian, was a Roman educator and writer. The first professor in any subject to hold an official appointment in Rome, he taught rhetoric* to potential leaders of the Roman Empire. His most famous work is the *Institutio Oratoria (The Education of an Orator),* in which he described the training and career of an orator* from infancy to old age. It remained an important work in education until the 1800s.

RACES

* **rhetoric**  art of using words effectively in speaking or writing

* **orator**  public speaker of great skill

Born in Spain, Quintilian was educated in Rome. He returned to Spain but accompanied Galba, the governor of Spain, in a march against Rome to overthrow the emperor NERO in A.D. 68. In A.D. 71 the emperor VESPASIAN appointed Quintilian the first professional teacher of rhetoric employed by the state. Among his many students were the historian TACITUS, the senator and writer PLINY THE YOUNGER, and the heirs of the emperor DOMITIAN. Quintilian retired around A.D. 91 to write his great work on the theory and practice of education.

For Quintilian, the goal of education was to produce a civilized man of high principles. An admirer of the great Roman orator and statesman CICERO, Quintilian adapted Cicero's teachings to the needs of his own time. To excel at oratory, according to Quintilian, a speaker must be a good person and his objective a morally justifiable one. In the *Institutio Oratoria,* Quintilian discussed all aspects of education, including moral, literary, and rhetorical principles. He urged that education for young children be amusing and encouraging. After learning the Greek and Latin languages, he believed students ought to analyze the writings of great writers of the past. Only then was a student ready to learn rhetoric. Quintilian urged his students to write and speak in a natural style, as well as to exercise good judgment. (*See also* **Education and Rhetoric, Roman.**)

## RACES

See *Games, Greek; Games, Roman.*

## RACIAL AND ETHNIC GROUPS

See *Peoples of Ancient Greece and Rome.*

## RELIGION, GREEK

* **deity**  god or goddess

* **philosopher**  scholar or thinker concerned with the study of ideas, including science

* **ritual**  regularly followed routine, especially religious

Religious practices were central to every aspect of life in ancient Greece. The Greeks consulted their gods and goddesses before almost every activity, whether public or private, and they gave their deities* thanks for every success. The importance of the gods in ancient Greece is illustrated by the case of SOCRATES, one of the greatest Greek philosophers*, who was sentenced to death because he was thought not to respect the traditional gods.

The Greeks believed that the gods were everywhere and that they oversaw all human activities—from planting crops to waging war. By showing their respect for the gods, the Greeks hoped to receive the gods' support. Ritual*, the basic method of communicating with the gods, was the core of Greek religion.

### RELIGIOUS BELIEFS

The religious beliefs of the ancient Greeks were not based on religious texts but on myths. Myths informed the Greeks where their deities came from, how the gods and goddesses were related, and how they interacted.

170

**\* hero** in mythology, a person of great strength or ability, often descended from a god

**\* sacrifice** sacred offering made to a god or goddess, usually of an animal such as a sheep or goat

Myths related the deeds of heroes\*, many of whom were worshiped. Some myths revealed the existence of an AFTERLIFE and an underworld, where the souls of the dead lived.

The ancient Greeks believed that each of their many gods played a different role in human activities. For example, there was Ares, the god of war, as well as Demeter, the goddess of grain. Together, the gods and goddesses provided for human needs and protected human efforts. The Greeks believed that to receive benefits from the gods, they had to offer prayers, sacrifices\*, and gifts. They also had to respect the sacred places where the gods lived.

Twelve gods were the most important. First was ZEUS, the king of the gods, who was believed to live on Mt. OLYMPUS. The Greeks held a huge festival every four years at the great temple of Zeus at OLYMPIA. HERA, Zeus's wife, was the guardian of marriage and childbirth. The remaining gods of the 12 were POSEIDON, HADES, DEMETER, ARTEMIS, Ares, APHRODITE, ATHENA, HEPHAESTUS, HERMES, and Hestia. The Greeks worshiped many other gods as well, such as DIONYSUS, the god of wine, and the nymphs, who were lesser goddesses of nature.

The Greeks also revered their heroes. HERACLES is probably the best known of these. Hero worship set the stage for the worship of rulers, although only those rulers who accomplished great things were worshiped as gods. The Spartan general Lysander, who won a great victory against Athens in the PELOPONNESIAN WAR, was the first Greek to be worshiped as a god. After the reign of ALEXANDER THE GREAT, who was proclaimed a descendant of the gods, ruler worship became widespread throughout the Greek world.

## PRIVATE AND PUBLIC RELIGION

**\* hearth** fireplace in the center of a house

**\* patron** special guardian, protector, or supporter

The ancient Greeks held both private and public religious ceremonies. At the private level, the head of the family performed rituals around the family hearth\*, which was considered sacred, on behalf of the members of his household. Small images of household gods and family ancestors, which were kept in cupboards shaped like temples, were respected, cared for, and honored in ritual.

At the public level, each city had its own patron\* god or goddess, who was believed to support and protect the city and its inhabitants. The patron deity was usually honored with a temple at the center of the city. Each city had TEMPLES and altars for many other gods and heroes. The year was organized around festivals in honor of these gods, and each city had its own calendar of festivals. In Athens, 150 days of the year were devoted to religious festivals. Common features of the festivals included processions, dancing, and hymn singing, as well as athletic and dramatic competitions. These activities provided recreation for the Greeks, and animal sacrifices that were part of the festivals provided meat for the participants. Religious festivals were an important part of the social life of ancient Greek cities.

The Greeks participated in many CULTS, which were groups bound together by the worship of a particular god or hero or by a shared belief. One of the most widespread was the cult of ASCLEPIUS, the god of healing. Sick people, or people who simply wanted to maintain their good health, worshiped the god at his temple and attended festivals in his honor.

## RELIGIOUS PEOPLE AND PRACTICES

The Greek system of priesthoods and religious practices developed over a long period. Specific rituals were performed to ensure the well-being of the people and the state.

PRIESTS.   Greek priests ensured that religious rituals were performed perfectly and that they followed the customs of their ancestors exactly. A priest performed rituals for a particular god at a temple or other sacred place. A priest's other duties included managing temple finances and preparing for festivals. Some priests also performed wedding and funeral rituals, purified homes after births and deaths, and administered oaths.

Although both men and women were priests, the Greeks believed that goddesses must be served by female priests, and gods by male priests. Regardless of their sex, priests had high social status. They were greatly respected and very powerful. For their services, priests were rewarded with housing, a salary, and parts of sacrificial animals. Other rewards included free meals for life and front-row seats at the theater.

Most priests inherited their position, but priests were also appointed, elected, and chosen by lottery. Some priests even purchased their positions. Nonetheless, a priest generally had to have come from a good family. Priests who inherited or purchased their positions remained priests for life, while others served as briefly as a year.

DIVINATION AND ORACLES.   The ancient Greeks used many different methods of divination, or the art of foretelling the future. One of the most important was the reading of OMENS, which were messages from the gods about the future. Almost any chance event might be considered an omen. A sneeze, for example, was regarded as an omen of good luck. Because DREAMS were believed to contain messages from the gods, their interpretation was an important method of divination. Another method was staring into a basin of water, the ancient Greek equivalent of gazing into a crystal ball.

For important matters, such as whether to wage war, the Greeks consulted one of the ORACLES that were located throughout the Greek world. Oracles were places where specific gods were consulted regarding public or private matters. The person requesting guidance asked a question, and a special priest (also known as an oracle) gave an answer that was supposed to have come from the god. The most commonly consulted god was Apollo, and the most famous oracle was at DELPHI. Its authority was rarely questioned.

RITUAL.   The purpose of all ritual was to communicate with the gods and gain their goodwill. Rituals were performed at all major life changes—birth, puberty, marriage, death—and at all important public events. Animal sacrifice was central to most rituals. The Greeks sacrificed animals for three reasons: to honor the gods, to thank them, and to ask them for favors. They made several other types of offerings to the gods, including libation, which was the pouring of a liquid (usually wine) on the ground. Before each meal, a small amount of food was offered to the gods. The Greeks offered gifts of flowers or objects made of precious metals as well. The gods received so many gifts that special buildings were constructed to store them.

See color plate 1, vol. 2.

## RELIGION AND THE STATUS OF WOMEN

Men dominated ancient Greek society, and women were forbidden by law to act on their own behalf. Women had to be represented by a male guardian—usually their father before marriage and their husband afterward. The requirement that goddesses had to be served by female priests provided a few Greek women with an opportunity to improve their status. A female priest could rise to a high administrative position. Once she reached her high position, she was no longer required to have a male guardian act on her behalf.

Rituals were conducted in sacred places where the gods were believed to live. A sacred place could be a building, a grove of trees, a spring, or a cave. In many sacred places, the Greeks built temples dedicated to the deities who lived there. Because a temple was considered the dwelling place of a deity, it was not used as a place of worship. Instead, worshipers gathered outside the temple at a nearby altar. The main room of the temple, which was open to the public only during festivals, usually contained a statue of the god or goddess. In addition to temples, some sacred places had theaters and stadiums where dramatic and athletic competitions were held.

Prayers requesting favors or giving thanks always accompanied rituals. Hymns were prayers set to music and sung to the deities. Hymn singing by trained choruses was a regular feature of public worship. Greek armies also sang hymns as they marched into battle.

Secret rituals, called mysteries, were attended only by people who had been initiated into the cult. The mystery cults promised special rewards after death to those who participated in the rituals. This concern with death set mysteries apart from most other ancient Greek rituals, which generally focused on the concerns of life. The most famous mysteries were the ELEUSINIAN MYSTERIES. People initiated into the Eleusinian Mysteries believed that they were protected by the goddess Demeter in the afterlife. (*See also* **Death and Burial; Divinities; Festivals and Feasts, Greek; Furies; Heroes, Greek; Myths, Greek; Priesthood, Greek; Ritual and Sacrifice; Rulers, Worship of.**)

## RELIGION, ROMAN

* **ritual** regularly followed routine, especially religious

* **deity** god or goddess

* **guild** association of professionals that set standards and represented the interests of its members

* **patron** special guardian, protector, or supporter

Ancient Roman religion was a matter more of performing prescribed rituals* to win the favor of the gods than of faith or personal devotion to a deity*. The main purpose of ritual was to communicate with the gods. Receiving the approval of the gods was believed to be essential for any undertaking to be successful.

Religion and politics were closely related in ancient Rome because the chief priests were generally political figures as well. As the Roman empire expanded, Roman religion spread. The religion of the Romans was enriched, in turn, by the religions of the people Rome conquered.

SPIRITS AND GODS. Roman religion was animistic—that is, it included the belief that spirits (called *numina*) dwelled within natural objects, such as trees or rocks, creating a sort of "force field" around them. It was believed that these forces had to be reckoned with and that human beings should try to pacify the spirits. Gradually, under the influence of Etruscan and Greek religion, these spirits were conceived more and more as having human shape—an interpretation known as anthromorphism.

The early Romans believed in many different spirits and gods, most of whom had specific functions. Each river and grove of trees had its own spirit, and each trade guild* and town had its own patron* god or goddess. Spirits and gods were believed to control all aspects of human existence.

From the great number of spirits and gods, three emerged as most important—JUPITER, the god of the sky and the supreme god; MARS, the god of war; and Quirinus, the god of the Roman people in assembly. Later Mars and Quirinus lost their supremacy to two goddesses—Juno, the goddess of female fertility, and Minerva, the goddess of crafts.

### NEW ROMAN GODS.

As the Romans encountered neighboring peoples, especially the Greeks, they adopted some of their gods. For example, in the 200s B.C., the Roman Senate introduced ASCLEPIUS, the Greek god of healing. Over time, most of the original Roman deities became identified with major Greek gods. For example, Jupiter became identified with the Greek god ZEUS, and Juno with the Greek goddess HERA. Each of the 12 most important Greek gods had its Roman counterpart. Because the Romans had few myths about their own gods, they also adopted Greek myths.

After about 200 B.C., the Romans were not as tolerant of foreign religions. Roman worship of the cults* of Bacchus (adopted from the Greek god DIONYSUS) and of Isis (adopted from the Egyptian goddess of the same name) was severely restricted. The Romans were inclined to persecute the Christians and to barely tolerate Judaism. The Roman government continued to adopt new gods from other cultures but in a carefully controlled way. In the late A.D. 200s, the emperor Aurelian installed the Persian sun god Mithra as the supreme god of the Romans. Years later, the emperor THEODOSIUS made the Christian god the supreme god of the empire.

### RITUAL.

Because rituals were believed to be the means of gaining the favor of the gods, the ancient Romans were extremely concerned that religious rituals be carried out with the greatest care. They believed that even the smallest mistake ruined the entire ritual. If a priest missed a word in a prayer, the whole ritual, not just the prayer, had to be repeated from beginning to end, even if it lasted several days.

The central feature of most rituals was animal sacrifice*. Each sacrifice was bound by rules and traditions at every step. After the animal was sacrificed, the meat was cooked, the skin and entrails (internal organs) offered to the gods, and the rest of the meat divided among worshipers and priests for a feast.

### DIVINATION AND ORACLES.

For the Romans to receive the approval of the gods, they first needed to find out what the gods wanted. This was usually done through divination—the interpretation of signs believed to be messages from the gods. The Romans relied on many different methods of divination, such as observing the flight of birds and inspecting the intestines of sacrificial animals. The Romans also interpreted DREAMS and unusual events, such as comets or lightning strikes, as foretelling the future.

The Romans further relied on ORACLES, which were messages from the gods or special places where such messages were received. When consulting an oracle, they asked the god a question and received the answer through a priest.

### PRIESTS AND OTHER RELIGIOUS OFFICIALS.

When Rome was ruled by kings, the kings served as the chief priests. After Rome became a republic, the top political officials of the state took over the king's religious duties. These officials did not have any special training, and they worked only

* **cult** group bound together by devotion to a particular person, belief, or god

* **sacrifice** sacred offering made to a god or goddess, usually of an animal such as a sheep or goat

part-time as priests. Their main religious duties were to conduct important rituals on behalf of the state.

There were many other types of priests, all with different titles, functions, qualifications, and methods of being chosen for the priesthood. Priests were assigned to tend the temples of each of the major Roman gods. Priests called AUGURS watched for and interpreted signs from the gods. Still other priests were in charge of annual Roman religious festivals. Although some priests had only a few rituals to conduct, others had many time-consuming administrative and ritual duties. Most priests were male, but a few were female. Most priests held office for life, although some served for a fixed period. Some priests were chosen by existing priests, others by popular election.

During the Roman Empire, priests came to be dominated by the emperor. Many of the ritual duties of a priest were concerned with the emperor and his family rather than with the state as a whole. With the rise of CHRISTIANITY in the A.D. 300s, the priests of traditional Roman religion became less important. During the following century, they gradually disappeared.

FAMILY AND STATE RELIGION.  Roman religion was practiced both privately within the family and publicly on behalf of the entire state. Family religion centered on the home and members of the household. The main gods worshiped within the family were VESTA, the LARES AND PENATES, and Genius. Vesta was the goddess of the hearth*. The Lares were gods of the family farm and of the family ancestors who were buried there. The Penates were gods of the inside of the household. Genius was the god of male fertility and was believed to live within the male head of the family. All important life events, such as births and marriages, were accompanied by family rituals to ensure that the events would turn out well. The family also regularly performed rituals to honor their dead ancestors.

The religion of the state was closely connected with the religion of the family. Many of the same gods were worshiped, but instead of seeking their protection just for a family, their protection was sought for the entire state. Instead of the head of the family performing the rituals, priests or high-ranking political officials performed them. Vesta was not only worshiped at each family's hearth but also at her temple in Rome. Special female priests called the Vestal Virgins attended these rituals.

The state ensured that all religious rituals were carried out according to tradition. The Roman state decided whether new religious practices and new gods were to be adopted or outlawed. In addition, the state priests drew up the schedule of religious festivals that were celebrated each year.

RULER WORSHIP.  Although popular in Greece during the Hellenistic* period, the worship of rulers was alien to traditional Roman religion. As long as Rome was a republic, ruler worship did not take hold. Starting with the reign of AUGUSTUS, the first emperor of Rome, ruler worship became part of Roman religion. Although Augustus did not permit himself to be worshiped during his lifetime, after his death the Roman Senate gave him a place among the gods of the Roman state and provided him with a temple and priests. The Roman people worshiped Augustus for the peace, prosperity, and security he had restored to the Roman world.

## ROMAN PRIESTS

Given the Roman obsession with the details of ritual, it is not surprising that Roman priests had to follow strict rules regarding their own behavior. This was true of the *flamines*—the priests who served the major Roman gods. The priest who served Jupiter, the supreme Roman god, could not ride a horse, watch the army assemble for war, take an oath, wear a ring, have a knot in his clothing, touch or name a female goat, go outside without a hat, touch bread containing yeast, pass under an arbor of vines, or touch a dead body. Unfortunately, the reasons for this interesting set of restrictions are unknown.

* **hearth**   fireplace in the center of a house

* **Hellenistic**   referring to the Greek-influenced culture of the Mediterranean world during the three centuries after Alexander the Great, who died in 323 B.C.

After Augustus, the Roman Senate declared other emperors gods after their deaths, including CLAUDIUS, TRAJAN, and HADRIAN. Because other emperors failed to achieve greatness for the Roman state or its people, they were denied the status of a god. During the A.D. 200s, the importance of ruler worship declined. With the rise of Christianity, ruler worship died out completely.

CHRISTIANITY.    Exactly when Christianity first came to Rome is not known, but the religion was well established by A.D. 100. At first, Christians were persecuted by the state for refusing to worship the traditional gods. The persecution ended when the emperor Constantine came to power in the early A.D. 300s. Constantine promoted tolerance and religious harmony. Among other reforms, he made Christian clergy the equals of the priests of the traditional state religion. Later, under Theodosius's rule, Rome became a Christian state.

In the A.D. 360s, the emperor JULIAN returned Rome to its traditional religion. He also began persecuting Christians again. However, Julian's reign was too short and Christianity too firmly rooted for his efforts to have a lasting effect. (*See also* **Death and Burial; Divinities; Festivals and Feasts, Roman; Priests, Roman; Religion, Greek; Ritual and Sacrifice; Temples.**)

## REPUBLIC

* **dialogue**  text presenting an exchange of ideas between people

See color plate 11, vol. 3.

* **allegory**  literary device in which characters represent an idea or a religious or moral principle

The *Republic* is among the greatest philosophical works of all time. One of the longer works of PLATO, the *Republic* made an important contribution to political philosophy, and it is considered by many to be a masterpiece of world literature. Written around 375 B.C., the *Republic* describes Plato's vision of justice and an ideal state. Like most of Plato's writings, it is in the form of a dialogue* and portrays SOCRATES as the leader of the discussion among a group of pupils.

Underlying the philosopher's vision of the ideal state is the concept of the philosopher-king. In the *Republic,* Plato argues that states cannot be governed well unless either philosophers become kings or kings become philosophers. Philosophers study ideas and science, and kings have the power to lead the state. Only people who have both knowledge and power, Plato wrote, have the wisdom to understand what is in the common interest and the power to guide the state along a course that will benefit all citizens equally.

Plato's idea of the philosopher-king arose from even more basic ideas about the state. Plato believed that the state and the individual are similar in structure. Each is divided into three parts, and both the state and the individual function best when the parts of each work in harmony. According to Plato, the individual's three parts are reason, emotion, and desire, and there is harmony in the individual when emotion and desire are ruled by reason. Similarly, the state's three parts are its rulers, the rulers' assistants, and the rest of the citizens (the producers). A state is just when the ruler uses his expert knowledge to guide the others.

In the *Republic,* Plato uses an allegory* to underscore the importance of education. He describes a cave in which prisoners have been chained since childhood. The prisoners can only see the shadows cast upon the cave wall by a fire behind them—they know nothing about the real world. They are not even aware of the existence of the objects whose shadows they see on the wall. For them, only the shadows are real. One day a prisoner escapes from the cave and emerges into the world of real people and things. For a while, he continues to think that the shadows are more real than the new environment in which he finds himself. Eventually, however, he becomes aware of his misconception.

For Plato, education is similar to what the prisoner experienced after he left the cave. Without education, people lack the wisdom to understand their true situation. They need wise and knowledgeable rulers who can see things as they really are and who can guide them.

Some modern philosophers criticize the ideal state Plato describes in the *Republic* as too authoritarian, that is, having too much power concentrated in the hands of a select few. In Plato's ideal state, philosopher-kings not only make decisions for everyone else, they are even encouraged to tell "noble lies" if necessary to further the interests of the people. The *Republic* has also been criticized for its treatment of poetry and literature. Plato wrote that literature should be censored if it portrays the gods or mythical heroes* in a negative light. Gods who lie or heroes who cry, Plato believed, set a poor moral example for society. (*See also* **Education and Rhetoric, Greek; Philosophy, Greek and Hellenistic.**)

* **hero** in mythology, a person of great strength or ability, often descended from a god

## RHETORIC

See *Education and Rhetoric.*

## RHODES

* **maritime** referring to the sea

Rhodes is an island in the AEGEAN SEA near the southwest coast of ASIA MINOR (present-day Turkey). According to Greek myth, Rhodes was named after Rhodos, the daughter of the goddess APHRODITE, and the island arose out of the sea as the special possession of Helios, the god of the sun. Because of its location and excellent harbors, Rhodes remained a prominent maritime* and trading power throughout the ancient period.

Around 1200 B.C., Rhodes was settled by DORIANS, a people from mainland Greece who established towns and developed trade in the region. Because Rhodes was well situated on the sea route between Asia Minor, the lands of the eastern Mediterranean Sea, and EGYPT, Rhodian ships carried goods to and from these places. During the 500s B.C., settlers from Rhodes established colonies on the island of SICILY, in northeastern Spain, and in southern Asia Minor. After the PERSIAN WARS between Greece and Persia in the early 400s B.C., Rhodes became a member of the Athenian-led Delian League, which was an alliance of Greek states against the Persians. Rhodes ended its alliance with Athens during the PELOPONNESIAN WAR between Athens and Sparta in the late 400s B.C. The three main cities of the island— Lindus, Ialysus, and Camirus—united as a single state around 408 B.C. The capital of this new state was also called Rhodes.

* **Hellenistic** referring to the Greek-influenced culture of the Mediterranean during the three centuries after Alexander the Great, who died in 323 B.C.

* **Stoicism** philosophy that emphasized control over one's thoughts and emotions

Rhodes prospered during the Hellenistic* period. The islanders took advantage of their harbors to become leaders of commerce, especially in the grain trade. In the eastern Mediterranean, Rhodes's fleet protected merchant vessels from marauding pirates. Rhodes was also a major center for HELLENISTIC CULTURE. An important school of Stoicism*, which the

Roman statesman Cicero and other prominent Romans attended, was located on Rhodes.

In the early 300s B.C., the island successfully defended itself during a siege* by the Macedonian general and ruler Demetrius I Poliorcetes. To celebrate their victory, the people of Rhodes erected a 110-foot-high statue of Helios at the entrance of the harbor. Called the Colossus of Rhodes, this immense statue became one of the Seven Wonders of the Ancient World. An earthquake destroyed the statue in 227 B.C.

During the early 100s B.C., Rhodes supported the Roman Empire in its wars against Philip V of Macedonia and Antiochus III, the ruler of Syria. To reward Rhodes for its loyalty, Rome gave the Rhodians lands in Asia Minor. Eventually, relations between the two states soured, and Rome took back those territories. As Rome shifted its support to the island of Delos, a rival port, trade suffered and Rhodes ceased to be a power in the Mediterranean. The Roman general Julius Caesar sacked* the city of Rhodes in the middle of the first century B.C., and one of his assassins, Cassius, captured the island and destroyed its fleet in 42 B.C. (*See also* **Naval Power, Greek; Naval Power, Roman; Pergamum; Trade, Greek; Trade, Roman.**)

* **siege** long and persistent effort to force a surrender by surrounding a fortress with armed troops, cutting it off from aid

* **sack** to rob a captured city

# RITUAL AND SACRIFICE

See
color plate 6,
vol. 4.

A ritual (or religious ceremony) consists of a sequence of actions and words (or rites) that are performed or spoken as part of religious worship. The ancient Greeks and Romans performed many rituals in the observance of their religion. Some rituals, such as the recitation of prayers, were simple. Others, such as animal sacrifices, were very elaborate. Sacrifices, the most important of the ancient religious rituals, were offerings to the gods. Although offerings were usually animals, other typical sacrificial gifts included cooked food, plants, pottery, or even a stone or flower.

RITUALS. In ancient Greek and Roman religion, performing a ritual according to specific tradition and custom was crucial. Failure to do so rendered the act meaningless. Thus, preserving rituals and passing them from one generation to the next became an important social function. Some of the earliest accounts of rituals and sacrifices are found in the epic* poems of Homer, in the historical writings of Herodotus, and in the plays of Aeschylus. Priests were the main keepers of ritual knowledge. They maintained written records of specific rituals, such as those involving magic. Mystery cults*, such as the Eleusinian Mysteries, had rituals of an exceptional and secret nature, and little is known about them.

The elements of ritual often included prayer, washing, and libations (the pouring of liquids), as well as incense or flowers, food, and objects of value. An individual might pray on his or her own to a household god. If the person wished to address the god of a particular shrine*, he or she would enlist the help of a priest.

Cleansing oneself with water to remove the dirt of daily life or specific impurities was almost always done. Purification was an important part of Greek and Roman religious practices. The aim of purification, or cleansing, was to rid the person or the community of pollution. Pollution could

* **epic** long poem about legendary or historical heroes, written in a grand style

* **cult** group bound together by devotion to a particular person, belief, or god

* **shrine** place that is considered sacred because of its history or the relics it contains

In the ancient world, ritual and sacrifice played a significant role in religious worship. Animals were sacrificed to the gods as a way of honoring, thanking, or requesting favors from them.

* **impiety**  lack of respect for the gods

* **immortal**  living forever

* **underworld**  kingdom of the dead; also called Hades

* **philosopher**  scholar or thinker concerned with the study of ideas, including science

* **sanctuary**  place for worship

## PURIFYING THE TOWN FOR APOLLO

The Thargelia was the main festival of the god Apollo. It was held in Athens during the months of May and June. Prior to the festival, the city was purified by the expulsion of human scapegoats (*pharmakoi* in Greek). A man was chosen to represent the city's inhabitants. After being led around the city to "absorb" its pollution, he was stoned with rocks, beaten with tree branches, and then driven from the city. The Athenians believed that the scapegoat took all the sins of the city and of its inhabitants with him.

be caused by an act of impiety* or failure to carry out a religious obligation properly. For example, performing a sacrifice without first washing one's hands caused pollution. Committing murder caused serious pollution, and a murderer had to perform special acts to rid himself of the victim's blood. (Blood shed in battle was more easily washed away.) One common Greek purification ritual involved associating the pollution with an object (such as an animal or a human scapegoat) and then burning the animal or banishing the human beyond the walls of the city.

Ritual actions were set apart from usual behavior in several ways: the wearing of special clothing and adornments, the avoidance of certain behaviors or foods, the burning of incense, or the offering of flowers and branches. Food was also used in many rituals. Cakes, fruit, or GRAIN was offered to the gods as a gift. Sometimes special ingredients were cooked together to prepare a ritual dish. Libation of WINE, milk, water, oil, or honey was another type of offering.

SACRIFICES.   One of the main rituals of both Greek and Roman religion was animal sacrifice. Sacrifices established the appropriate relationships among gods, humans, and animals. The gods were superior and immortal*, whereas humans were mortal and ought to be pious and submissive to the deities. Animals existed to be used by humans in their worship of their gods. Sheep and goats were the most common sacrificial animals, although some special sacrifices involved bulls. Certain animals were associated with certain gods. For example, dogs were sacrificed to Hecate, a goddess of the underworld*. The Greeks believed that she traveled at night accompanied by ghosts and howling dogs.

A sacrifice (*thusia* in Greek) to the gods was the most important activity in Greek religion. According to the Greek philosopher* Theophrastus, the Greeks sacrificed to the gods for three reasons: to honor them, to thank them, or to request a favor from them. Sheep, goats, pigs, and cattle, as well as fish and birds, were offered to the gods. The sacrifice of an animal was carried out according to strict guidelines. First, the animal was decorated with flowers and garlands and led in a procession to the sanctuary* of the god. At the sanctuary, participants washed their hands in water and sprinkled a few drops on the victim. The priest or leader recited a prayer declaring the reason for the sacrifice. The sacrificial victim was killed quickly by having its neck cut with a knife. Large animals were first stunned with a blow from an ax and then similarly killed with the knife. The victim's blood was spattered over the altar in the sanctuary. Then assistants butchered the animal and divided the parts. The thighbones were wrapped in fat and, along with small portions of meat cut from the limbs, were placed on the altar and burned as a gift to the gods. Wine was poured on the burnt offerings. Occasionally, these gifts were placed on the knees of a statue of the god. Next, the liver, lungs, heart, and other internal organs were roasted and shared by all the participants. The rest of the meat was boiled and either eaten at the altar or taken home. OMENS were often taken from the burnt offerings to the god.

A typical Roman sacrifice consisted of four phases. The first involved the purification of the participants and the victim. Purification was followed by a procession to an altar. At the altar, participants honored the gods with the pouring of wine and the burning of incense, marking the beginning of the sacrifice. The leader of the sacrifice then poured wine on the victim's brow, sprinkled its back with salted flour, and then passed a knife over the animal's spine. These actions symbolized the transfer of the victim from mortal ownership to that of the god. In the next phase, the animal was killed and then butchered. Its heart and other internal organs were examined. If the entrails* looked suspicious or unhealthy, the sacrifice was deemed unacceptable to the gods, and another animal had to be sacrificed. The final phase of the Roman sacrifice was the banquet. The sacrificial meat and entrails were cooked and offered to the god. Then the rest of the animal was cooked and eaten by the participants or distributed for sale in butchers' shops. Sometimes the banquet was attended only by the aristocracy*. At other times, the banquet was financed by a wealthy benefactor for the public at large. (*See also* **Cults; Divinities; Festivals and Feasts, Greek; Festivals and Feasts, Roman; Religion, Greek; Religion, Roman.**)

* **entrails** internal organs, including the intestines

* **aristocracy** privileged upper class

## ROADS, ROMAN

The Romans built a vast network of roads to connect the various parts of their extensive empire. Symbols of Roman conquest, the roads eased the movement of armies, military supplies, and governmental couriers. The roads also offered a means for moving goods from one part of the empire to another, as well as a convenient way for merchants, peddlers, and peasants to travel to the MARKETS. Sections of some ancient Roman roads can still be seen today and are still in use.

The oldest and longest Roman road was the APPIAN WAY, which was begun in the late 300s B.C. The Appian Way started in Rome and ran 360 miles southeast to the city of Brundisium on the coast of the Adriatic Sea. By the A.D. 100s, the Roman empire had more than 50,000 miles of paved highway and about 200,000 miles of secondary roads. This extensive Roman road network was extremely well constructed. Several former Roman provinces* did not have such fine roads again until the late 1800s.

Although the Etruscans, who developed an advanced culture in Italy prior to the rise of Rome, also built roads, only short stretches of their roads survived. Portions of Roman roads still exist because of the careful surveying and building techniques used by Roman engineers. The most durable roads—and the most expensive to build and maintain—were called deep roads. A deep road was set on a foundation about 3 to 4½ feet in depth, which prevented the pavement from sinking and forming depressions. A trench was carefully smoothed and leveled out, and large, rounded stones were set in place. Over this foundation, road builders placed a layer of smaller stones that were sometimes held in place by cement. Gravel, cobbles (small, slightly rounded pieces of stone), or massive square paving stones formed the road surface (*pavimentum* in Latin). The road surface was slightly arched to help drain the roadway, and ditches were constructed beside the road. Major roads were at least 8 feet wide, while important intersections might be 14 or 18 feet wide.

* **province** overseas area controlled by Rome

Roads that led into Rome expanded to a width of 30 feet as they neared the city gates.

Construction methods varied from one region of the empire to another. In some areas of Asia Minor, for example, paving stones were placed directly on the ground. Minor roads often consisted solely of a layer of gravel. Roman engineers constructed BRIDGES that were as well built as their roads. If a bridge was not really needed (because the river was low in the dry season), the engineers paved the river bottom with flat stones.

Wherever possible, Roman roads were straight. Surveyors laid out a course by taking sightings from one high point of land to the next. In level areas, surveyors used smoke from fires to take sightings. Milestones, which were placed every 95 yards, marked the distance from the starting place of the road. In the provinces, milestones were used to mark the distance between one town and the next. Often the name of the builder of the road and the date of completion were inscribed on the marker.

The cost of building and maintaining roads was enormous. Latin inscriptions indicate that the cost of repairing a Roman road on the Italian peninsula in the A.D. 100s was the staggering sum of 30,000 denarii per mile. Major road repairs, regularly done, may have cost Rome a quarter as much as supplying her vast army. During the Roman Republic*, censors* were responsible for roads. They gave contracts to bidders, who in turn hired workers for road construction and repair. Roads required large numbers of workers, from engineers and skilled stonemasons to unskilled peasants and stone breakers. Many worked involuntarily for little or no pay. During the Roman Empire, convicts and slaves were widely used as road construction crews. (*See also* **Architecture, Roman; Construction Materials and Techniques; Transportation and Travel.**)

* **Roman Republic** Rome during the period from 509 B.C. to 31 B.C., when popular assemblies annually elected their governmental officials

* **censor** Roman official who conducted the census, assigned state contracts for public projects (such as building roads), and supervised public morality

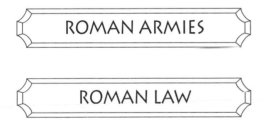

**ROMAN ARMIES**

See *Armies, Roman.*

**ROMAN LAW**

See *Law, Roman.*

## ROMAN NUMERALS

* **numeral** symbol used to represent a number

The Romans formed their numerals* from seven symbols: I = 1, V = 5, X = 10, L = 50, C = 100, D = 500, and M (and alternate forms ∞ and Ɪ) = 1,000. All numerals were made by adding these symbols together or by subtracting one from another. When two symbols were next to each other, their values were added if the smaller numeral was on the right and subtracted if the smaller numeral was on the left. For example, the Romans made the numeral *4* by adding basic signs together (IIII = 4) or by subtracting the value of the numeral on the left from that on the right (IV = 4).

The Romans also had a system for expressing fractions. One horizontal stroke (—) represented ¹/₁₂. The fraction ³/₁₂ was written " = —." The letter *S* (for the Latin word *semis*) was used to represent ½. It could stand alone or precede other numbers to form new fractions, such as the fraction $^7/_{12}$, which was written as "S —" (½ + ¹⁄₁₂).

The basic Roman numbering system worked well for small numbers, but it proved awkward for larger numbers. The inventive Romans solved this problem. They modified the basic signs to indicate numbers above 1,000. A horizontal bar above a numeral indicated that the number was to be multiplied by 1,000—for example, $\overline{X}$ = 10,000. Bars above and on both sides of the symbol—such as $\overline{|X|}$—meant that the value was to be multiplied by 100,000. A *D* that enclosed a small semicircle (Ð) stood for 5,000. Beginning in the 100s B.C., the Romans used these symbols to represent words that referred to numbers. For example, X stood for the Roman coin called a denarius, which was worth ten of the smallest Roman coins.

Like the Greeks, the Romans used the abacus for counting. The abacus is a device consisting of a frame and columns of beads, which represent numbers. The beads are manipulated along wire or wooden rods to perform calculations. (*See also* **Alphabets and Writing; Calendars; Mathematics, Greek.**)